Foundations of International

Foundations of International Political Economy

Matthew Watson

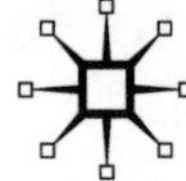

First published 2005 by
PALGRAVE MACMILLAN
Houndmills, Basingstoke, Hampshire RG21 6XS and
175 Fifth Avenue, New York, N.Y. 10010
Companies and representatives throughout the world

PALGRAVE MACMILLAN is the global academic imprint of the Palgrave Macmillan division of St. Martin's Press, LLC and of Palgrave Macmillan Ltd. Macmillan® is a registered trademark in the United States, United Kingdom and other countries. Palgrave is a registered trademark in the European Union and other countries.

ISBN-13: 978–1–4039–1350–0 hardback
ISBN-10: 1–4039–1350–1 hardback
ISBN-13: 978–1–4039–1351–7 paperback
ISBN-10: 1–4039–1351–X paperback

This book is printed on paper suitable for recycling and made from fully managed and sustained forest sources.

A catalogue record for this book is available from the British Library.

A catalog record for this book is available from the Library of Congress.

10 9 8 7 6 5 4 3 2 1
14 13 12 11 10 09 08 07 06 05

Printed in China

To Katie, with love

Contents

Acknowledgements

This book is dedicated to Katie, in return for the many personal debts of thanks that I owe her.

In addition, there are a number of other people who must be acknowledged for the influence they have brought to bear on the academic content of what follows. First, there are my students who have taken my third-year course, 'Contemporary International Political Economy', over the six years that I have been responsible for teaching it. My thoughts on the subject field have developed considerably over the years, and one of the reasons for this is the interaction I have had with students who have continually forced me to re-think my position.

Second, there are the people within the profession who have helped to shape my ideas. The conversations we have had may not be lodged in their memories as anything particularly important, but they have certainly been influential in the way that I now think. At Birmingham, I think in particular of Daniel Wincott, Magnus Ryner, Julie Gilson, Steve Buckler, Ingrid van Biezen, Paul Williams, Simon Caney and Peter Preston. Beyond Birmingham, I think of Ben Rosamond, David Coates, Andrew Gamble, James Mittelman, Jan Aart Scholte, Tony Payne, Randall Germain, Mark Blyth, Matthew Paterson, David Richards, Paul Furlong and Mark Wickham-Jones.

Third, there are the three Heads of Department that I have worked under at Birmingham: David Marsh, Jeremy Jennings and Colin Hay. As well as all proving to be good friends, confidants and advisers, their sheer enthusiasm for both the Department and the research culture within it has been responsible for creating the stimulating environment in which the book was written. Of these three, I owe my biggest intellectual debt to Colin, with whom I have worked closely over the years. He has been a constant source of help, advice, support, encouragement and banter – all of which I have benefited from greatly.

Finally, there is my publisher at Palgrave Macmillan, Steven Kennedy, who has overseen the development of this project from its most formative moments. He has been unwavering in his enthusiasm for the contents of the book and unflagging in his optimism that I would be able to deliver it to him.

MATTHEW WATSON

Introduction

The subject field of International Political Economy

The number of people consciously identifying themselves as students of International Political Economy (IPE) has grown appreciably in recent years. There is now a well established and well developed body of IPE literature, which contributes to both academic and public debates on international economic affairs. Despite such developments, however, little progress has been made in terms of specifying exactly what is meant when referring to oneself as a student of International Political Economy. The eclectic nature of IPE suggests that no necessary intellectual commitment is entailed by such an appeal, whether conceptual, methodological or ontological. IPE certainly does not have what Imre Lakatos dubbed a disciplinary hard core, which deliberately and explicitly structures academic analysis around a strictly limited number of issues, questions and techniques (see Lakatos 1978). The ensuing flexibility of thought is admirable. It also provides for a subject field in which it is possible to shape academic debates by proposing a set of standards against which individual contributions to the literature can be judged. It is one attempt to establish such standards that defines the undertaking in this book.

My preference is for an IPE that is distinct from the techniques of orthodox economic analysis but, at the same time, that is released from comparisons with an overly caricatured understanding of economics. Existing scholarship within the field tends to be positioned at one of these two extremes when reflecting upon the relationship between IPE and economics. It either accepts (usually unquestioningly) neoclassical economic enquiry as the definitive account of the economy, or it rejects (similarly unquestioningly) the whole canon of economic thought. However, these two positions are equally unhelpful. What is needed is an IPE that moves beyond an instinctive dismissal of all economic theories, but that stops short of the reification of economic laws that operate behind the backs of human agents. There would be much to gain were IPE scholars to learn more about the subject matter of economics, especially if they were to do so from economists who are sceptical of the desirability of the market-based relationships that neoclassical theory treats as a natural condition of social existence.

The view from the economics profession is much more diverse and much more richly textured than tends to be acknowledged within the IPE literature. This is particularly so when we delve into the history of economic thought. Here we can discover alternative intellectual traditions that understand the way in which people act in their everyday economic lives in a manner that is greatly at odds with the neoclassical assumption of simple, unthinking and unreflexive utility-maximizing economic agents. It is true that the vast majority of models that structure contemporary economic thought are based on an unquestioned and undefended assumption of the existence of such agents, yet it remains necessary to avoid mistaking current economic orthodoxy for the full range of potential forms of economic analysis. Neoclassical economics is not economics in its entirety; much less is it the only way to think about the social relationships that constitute the economy.

Despite this, it would be disingenuous to say that models of constrained optimization problems, which are the staple fare of neoclassical theory, are anything other than dominant within economics. Such dominance is evident in the extent to which the core of neoclassical theory tends to be treated as a definition of the economics discipline per se. It centres on the openly paradoxical appeal to a choice-theoretic framework within which the image of active agential choices is subordinate to the assumption of instinctive utility-maximizing behaviour. As IPE scholars are well versed in reminding us, this is not a suitable ontological foundation for their subject field, if IPE is to do anything other than replicate the findings of neoclassical economics. However, there is a vibrant – albeit minority – research community within economics that positions itself knowingly and intentionally beyond the neoclassical core. My aim is not to promote a wholesale appropriation of any particular heterodox variant of economics as an alternative foundation for IPE; it is only to encourage an enhanced awareness of economic heterodoxy as a means of animating a critically grounded IPE.

This becomes ever more important insofar as IPE scholars have incorporated neoclassical economic assumptions about instinctive utility-maximizing behaviour into their own explanations of the social world. To my mind, such assumptions have been internalized to a greater degree than is commonly identified. For fear that this position may elicit a less than sympathetic response from many within the IPE community, let me offer some necessary qualifications to it. Three points in particular require attention.

First, this is not to say that there is an absence of a critical tradition within contemporary IPE. Indeed, it would be more to the point to suggest the existence of a critical consensus amongst the community of IPE scholars. Few texts in IPE tell the reader that the status quo should merely be reproduced because the world is fine as it is. However, the nature of the dominant critique is somewhat limited. It tends to focus on the *outcomes* of utility-maximizing behaviour in practice. What follows, typically, are important and sophisticated normative assessments of the world thus created. Yet, when it comes to analysing the actions that produce such a world, the *assumption* of utility-maximizing behaviour receives less by way of concerted challenge. As a consequence, there is something of a disparity within the IPE literature. There is clear evidence of a deep-seated desire amongst IPE scholars to question the moral and political propriety of socio-economic institutions that are designed specifically to encourage instinctive utility-maximizing behaviour. By contrast, much less work has been undertaken on the assumption that precedes the design of such institutions: namely, that it is appropriate to model human behaviour on the basis of a simple instrumental rationality in the first place.

Second, I make no claim that the incorporation into IPE of orthodox economic assumptions about utility-maximizing behaviour is in any way intentional. In almost no instance does it represent a conscious commitment to a social ontology that understands a crude instrumental rationality as the essential motivation for human agency. Instrumental rationality implies act-evaluation using self-interest. In this way, we are presented with a standard – yet only one standard – against which to judge the appropriateness of alternative courses of action. Explanations founded on this standard abound within the IPE literature, in relation to all actors within the international economy, be they individually or collectively constituted. However, such explanations tend not to reflect a belief that instinctive utility-maximizing behaviour is the essence of human nature, so much as a means of highlighting the inequities that result from creating socio-economic institutions that serve to embed such patterns of behaviour. *Homo economicus*, the instinctively super-rational 'economic man', is not a person whom the vast majority of IPE scholars expect us to meet in everyday life; but he is someone whose actions IPE theory is set up to critique.

Third, it is not even to suggest that it is usual within IPE to focus the enquiry at the level of individual behaviour. One obvious commonality across the competing perspectives within IPE is the tendency to understand the subject field in the context of the relationship between states and markets. Each theoretical perspective operationalizes this relationship in its own way, as the following chapter will explain, but they share a similar starting point, namely that IPE can proceed on the basis of a 'states and markets' approach. It is within this underlying 'states and markets' approach that the assumption of instinctive utility-maximizing behaviour feeds into the analysis. Within IPE, both states and markets tend to be treated as actors in their own right, rather than as social arenas in which action takes place. As a consequence, they are imbued with human attributes, such that it can be argued that they display particular patterns of behaviour. That behaviour tends to be modelled on a utility-maximizing understanding of self-interest; hence, it is simplistic *homo economicus* assumptions applied either to the level of the state or the market. Few attempts are made instead to theorize the way in which the individual, as a conscious human agent acting within the realm of the international economy, experiences socio-economic relations that are bounded by 'state' and 'market' norms, which are themselves contextually specific to a particular time and place. This once again blurs the distinction between, on the one hand, the assumption that utility-maximizing behaviour is the essence of human nature and, on the other hand, highlighting the inequities that result from creating socio-economic institutions which serve to embed such patterns of behaviour.

The limits of the subject field

My argument here is that debate within IPE would benefit from a more explicit recognition of this distinction. It is surely ironic that much of the literature at the critical edge of IPE includes detailed empirical accounts of the adverse social consequences that can be attributed to attempts to socialize people into acting in an instinctive utility-maximizing manner, yet it says little about the tendency of IPE scholars to accept the tradition of economic thought that depicts such traits as a necessary condition for understanding the economy. The critical consensus that prevails in IPE provides an effective platform from which to expose the pattern of interests that underpins the process of international economic management. However, if behaviour is assumed to respond simply to instrumentally rational stimuli, all action must by definition be oriented towards the satisfaction of interests. Most arguments in IPE are stronger politically than they are analytically. On the whole, they are able to sustain the political case for dissolving the status quo by embedding a different pattern of interests as a basis for an alternative form of economic life, but they are unable to conceptualize behaviour as anything other than a means to the end of satisfying interests. There is little debate about whether everyday economic practices fulfil criteria other than serving interests; it tends to be taken as given that they do not. Instead, debate is concentrated at the normative level, on which pattern of interests provides the most appropriate grounding for everyday life.

Once again we are faced with a curious disparity within the IPE literature. Some actions are to be encouraged over others (because they enhance a preferred set of interests), but all action is generically the same (because it all aims to satisfy interests). In order to explain this disparity, we must look to IPE's peculiar subject history, whereby it has developed in the general absence of a foundational debate about its own essential features.

IPE should be the study of individual action within the context of institutionalized economic norms. Some individuals may internalize those norms to the point at which they are subject to routine reproduction within their conduct, while others will attempt to operate outside them having first accepted the legitimacy of alternative bases of behaviour. However, the founding assumption of instrumentally rational action, on which so much of IPE operates, impedes an analysis of the complex and contingent relationship between conduct and context. The rationality postulate simply overrides such an analysis. Those working within IPE have tended to import assumptions about fundamentally rational economic behaviour from the neoclassical tradition that they would otherwise align themselves against. The danger of this, to my mind, is that IPE becomes a study of the economic effects of the rationality postulate, rather than a study of economic relations per se.

Without a more in-depth recognition of its own foundational assumptions, IPE is likely to become increasingly restricted in relation to the questions that its practitioners can ask, the issues that they can tackle and the techniques that they can employ. Definite limits are being imposed on the field of IPE, although not because of a shared sense of purpose amongst the community of IPE scholars aimed at establishing a homogeneous and internally consistent body of theory across the whole of the subject field. Rather, those limits are in place because of the general lack of concern shown by IPE scholars to debate the foundational essence of their own subject. IPE has typically been thought of as something you *do* rather than as something that you reflect on *how to do*. This has led to a general failure to situate the subject field within the context of a broader disciplinary history of political economy. As a consequence, alternative theories of action that are an integral feature of political economy debates tend to be overlooked in IPE, in favour of the neoclassical conception of rational action. The 'E' in IPE is overwhelmingly neoclassical in orientation, despite attempts by IPE scholars to invoke neoclassical economics as the conscious 'other' of their subject field.

My aim in this book is to begin to think through the foundations of IPE from first principles, with a view to proposing an alternative starting point for the subject. That starting point must be one in which the 'E' in IPE refers not to logical propositions about the economy that can be derived from the rationality postulate, but to the study of economic relations as they are constituted and experienced in everyday life. My hope is to be able to outline the type of IPE that becomes possible by situating the study of the subject field within the style of analysis of classical political economy.

One of the key insights from the classical political economists, which has been lost in the turn towards neoclassical economics, is that all experiences of the social relations that constitute the economy are contextual. Neoclassical economics accepts a conception of human agency that reduces to instinctive utility-maximizing behaviour and, as a consequence, it has a restricted scope for understanding the social implications of individual economic action. Indeed, the very concept of society is dissolved within such a framework. The human bonds that unite individuals in a distinctively social existence cannot be discussed at anything other than a highly superficial level. Such a focus has largely been imported into IPE. Society tends to disappear from the analysis in IPE, amid a focus on purely formal political settings and the impact of decisions taken in such settings on the relationship between states and markets. The existing body of IPE literature contains many important critical evaluations of the social consequences of contemporary decision-making processes within the international economy. However, this is not the same as being able to theorize the economy from first principles as a fundamentally human condition, involving life set within the context of a number of institutionalized social norms.

Moreover, we have reached a time in the history of economic thought when more and more economists are thinking through the implications of abandoning a conception of human nature based on the assumption of atomistic, pure pleasure-seeking automatons (for a review of such developments, see Lawson 1997; Colander 2001; Oakley 2002). The agents of neoclassical theory are individuals who, by their very nature, are devoid of social reflexivity, an awareness of the situation of others and the ability to comprehend the moral consequences of their own choices. It would surely be ironic if, at the very moment at which a greater number of economists than ever before are dispensing with assumptions about an unthinking *homo economicus*, such assumptions continue to permeate IPE. This would be particularly ironic given the fact that the process through which such assumptions are incorporated into IPE, via its underlying 'states and markets' approach, does not represent a conscious commitment to a social ontology of simple utility-maximizing self-interest. In short, there is virtually no IPE scholar who, to my knowledge, takes the assumption of *homo economicus* seriously as anything other than an 'as if' assumption on which to base subsequent analyses.

Indeed, even as an 'as if' assumption it is necessary to be cautious about the applicability of the behaviour of *homo economicus* to explanations of everyday life. The particular form of rationality displayed by the instinctively super-rational 'economic man' is not a universal feature of social existence. Instead, it must be viewed as a specific feature of life within particular economic structures. The assumption of utility-maximizing conduct applies only to particular groups of people, who have experienced particular patterns of socialization through their exposure to a particular set of institutionalized social norms. Certain people may well experience a combination of pressures and incentives to act in a manner that is at least partially consistent with the character traits of *homo economicus*; yet this is by no means a universal experience which applies irrespective of time, place and the ideological construction of 'common-sense' in which individuals find themselves. It is shared only by those whose everyday lives are bounded by a particular type of economic system at the particular stage of capitalist development that is reified in the explanatory models of neoclassical economics. The assumption of *homo economicus* becomes more valid the more that social life is structured by intense processes of commodification, and the more that the very logic of commodification finds justification in the widespread acceptance of individualistic ideologies of acquisitiveness and personal gain. In short, the personal attributes that are required in order to be able to engage in instinctive utility-maximizing behaviour are themselves an effect of being thoroughly and completely socialized into a system of market norms (Cole, Cameron and Edwards 1983: 17; Gill and Law 1988: 7; Tooze and Murphy 1996: 681).

For most people within the world, the experience of such a system has been only a fleeting and temporary phenomenon, or else they have no experience of it whatsoever. There are thus no valid grounds on which to suggest that either this form of economic life, or the structure of rationality on which it is predicated, is a generic aspect of the economy. To imply as much is to engage, however inadvertently, in methodologically ethnocentric analysis. Insofar as IPE scholars adopt general models of rationally-based economic behaviour, it is clear that their work privileges certain experiences of the world over others. More specifically, IPE scholarship tends to be organized within a conceptual framework that allows us to learn about the economic experiences of the world's rich minority. Within such a framework, utility-oriented consumption, activated through the process of market exchange, is elevated to the status of normal economic relations. Alternative forms of everyday economic life are consequently placed outside the boundaries of normality. However, this construction of normal economic relations downplays the significance of the everyday lives of the great majority of the world's population. It is a minority experience to live within an advanced capitalist society, let alone to live within an advanced capitalist society shaped by a system of free market norms. Neoclassical economics tends to be ruthlessly ethnocentric in the extent to which it disregards all potential forms of rationality that are inconsistent with the continued reification of the exchange structures of a modern market economy. It is the task of IPE to be positioned not to replicate such a tendency, but to critique it.

Chapter outline

In order to develop a theoretical framework capable of providing such a position for IPE, the book is split into eleven chapters. In turn, these chapters fit into four distinct groupings.

In Chapters 1–3, I provide an overview of existing theoretical perspectives within IPE, while situating the general features of the IPE literature in relation to both a brief history of the rationality postulate and an appreciation of decisive disciplinary developments in the history of economic thought. This allows me to locate IPE with respect to the tradition of economic thought, that of neoclassical economics, which is so often invoked by practitioners of IPE as that to which their subject field is a response. In particular, by focusing on the 'states and markets' approach to IPE, I show that IPE and neoclassical economics share a similar theory of action, which is rooted in the assumption of innate instrumental rationality. I argue for the classical tradition of political economy to be used as an alternative foundation for theories of action within IPE, and I provide the rationale for my preferred synthesis of approaches within the classical tradition.

In Chapters 4–6, I review in more depth the economic theories of three prominent scholars from the classical tradition: Adam Smith, Thorstein Veblen and Karl Polanyi. This enables me to specify the contributions that their work can make to the way in which action is understood in IPE. In general, the classical tradition focuses analysis less on 'the economy' per se, and more on the economic relations that constitute functioning systems of production and distribution. Action is theorized in the context of such relations and, as a consequence, at all times possesses an irreducibly social character. To understand action requires first that we understand the socially situated character of human nature, which in turn requires that we reject the fundamentally asocial rationality postulate as the basis for behaviour. I concentrate on the work of Smith, Veblen and Polanyi, because each of them explains action in relation to the social environment in which agential intentions are formed.

In Chapters 7 and 8, I tackle the issue of IPE's 'states and markets' approach directly. I work to the assumption that the task of IPE is to study the way in which individuals are integrated into habituated patterns of behaviour that have implications for inter-personal relations that span borders. As such, I depart from all those in IPE who study the actions of 'states' and 'markets'. Neither states nor markets are actors in their own right; to impute agential characteristics to them is to issue them with a will of their own. At most, 'the state' and 'the market' can be understood as contexts in which individuals act. The aim of IPE must be to specify how behavioural norms that structure the individual's experience of those contexts in turn shape the process through which individuals first contemplate, and then undertake, action.

In Chapters 9–11, I attempt to demonstrate the utility of an approach to IPE that is rooted within the classical tradition of political economy. The concerns I express throughout the book are not with what IPE scholars study, but with the way in which they study it and, in particular, with the theory of action which underpins that study. In this concluding group of chapters, I take three of the standard debates within the existing IPE literature – those relating to globalization, trade and development respectively – and I reformulate the terms of those debates in line with the classical political economy approach outlined earlier. By locating the foundations of IPE within the classical tradition of political economy, it is possible to have an IPE that allows for greater analytical depth to its theory of action, while sacrificing none of its political relevance.

Chapter 1

Approaches to International Political Economy: Beyond 'States and Markets'

Introduction

Most books on International Political Economy begin in much the same way. They point to a flourishing field, a newcomer to the social scientific family, whose origins are not to be traced to intellectual developments within the social sciences themselves, but rather to political developments that required a response from the academic community. At the time of its inception, IPE was very much an events-led field of study (such a claim features prominently in reviews of the field from Gill and Law 1988; Murphy and Tooze 1991a; Denemark and O'Brien 1997; Onuf 1997; Pearson and Rochester 1998; Strange 1998a; Murphy and Nelson 2001; Woods 2001; Dash, Cronin and Goddard 2003; O'Brien and Williams 2004). The particular event that did so much to concentrate the minds of the early IPE scholars was the breakdown of the Bretton Woods system of international economic management in the early 1970s. These authors were writing at a time of widespread economic instability, as the dissolution of the system of fixed exchange rates added a new degree of uncertainty, made manifest in exchange rate risk, into international trading relations.

A conventional narrative of IPE developed from privileging the collapse of the Bretton Woods system as the defining moment in the formative history of the field. Looking back from a time at which international trading relations were becoming increasingly fractious, as they were buffeted by the effects on floating exchange rates of attempts to pursue increasingly strict counter-inflationary policies, it must surely have been tempting to operate with an idealized image of the recently departed 'golden age' of postwar capitalism. Indeed, it was a temptation that the early IPE scholars found impossible to resist. Observed instability in the present is often the most important stimulus for looking back fondly at the past, and so it proved in this instance. Moreover, superficial evidence abounds to support the claims of the early IPE scholars. Postwar reconstruction had occurred at an impressive pace, leading to what appeared to be the routine reproduction of historically high levels of economic growth across the advanced industrial world.

A series of binary distinctions was therefore drawn between the world that preceded the collapse of the Bretton Woods system and that which followed. Within the interpretive framework constructed by these binary distinctions, the Bretton Woods system was synonymous with the orderly integration of an increasing number of countries into the international economy and, as a consequence, systemic stability ensued. The contrast was duly made with the post-Bretton Woods era and its apparent disorderliness and systemic instability.

Reading again today the early contributions to the field of International Political Economy, it is impossible not to be struck by the invocation of a systematic shift in world economic affairs of near instantaneous effect. It is sometimes implicit, sometimes explicit, but always there. The undoubted benefit of over thirty years of hindsight suggests that there is much to question in this interpretation of events. Contemporary historians have asked just how golden the 'golden age' of postwar capitalism really was (Marglin and Schor 1990), while those whose concern is to understand the full complexity of the richly textured prehistory of particular events have dismissed the idea that the world can suddenly change as if a historical trip-switch had been triggered (Braudel 1980). For current purposes, however, both these objections to the conventional narrative of IPE are largely beside the point. More important is the way in which that narrative frames the dominant issue areas of the subject field. Certain issues are privileged a priori, simply due to the way in which the origins of the subject field were first specified. By extension, other issues, which might otherwise be considered crucial to political economy, remain largely unexplored.

In this chapter, I review the range of competing approaches to the study of International Political Economy. However, my aim is not that of standard textbook fare. I do not review the theoretical basis of these competing approaches in their own terms. Instead,

I point to the way in which theoretical debates take place against the backdrop of common concerns for studying certain issues at the expense of others. Of particular significance to conventional narratives of IPE is the question of order (see, for instance, Krasner 1976; Gilpin 1987; Frieden and Lake 1995; Grieco and Ikenberry 2003). A number of different actors are appealed to, and mechanisms invoked, in individual contributions to theoretical debates about what 'order' means, how it is created, and its overall significance to the subject field (Woods 2001: 286). However, issues of order, and attempts to derive conditions for maintaining order from particular manifestations of the relationship between 'states and markets', represent what it means to be doing IPE to so many of its practitioners.

The chapter proceeds in four stages. In the first section, I provide a brief disciplinary history of IPE. For most people working within the subject field, IPE is little more than the application of the theories and methods of International Relations (IR) to issues of an economic nature. Within such a framework, the broad concern for theorizing the constitution of economic relations is lost amidst attempts to suggest how the economy might be structured in the interests of orderly system management. In the second section, I outline the most important effects of IPE following the theories and methods of International Relations. I argue that the legacy of IPE's disciplinary heritage is to be found in a series of undefended dualisms that structure debate within the subject field. Particularly important in this respect is the separation of 'politics' and 'economics'. From this, a similar opposition is drawn between those activities that are conducted under the remit of 'the state' and those activities that are conducted under the remit of 'the market'. While order tends to be the substantive issue that brings together those whose IPE originates in International Relations, their chosen analytical framework tends to revolve around the relationship between states and markets. In the third section, I argue that the distinction between 'the state' and 'the market' is a false one and, as such, an IPE that is based on theorizing the relationship between the two must necessarily be limited. I offer political economy and, in particular, the tradition of classical political economy as an alternative starting point for IPE. The potential for classical political economy to act in this way takes us into what, as yet, is relatively uncharted territory (although see Gamble 1995). However, it has much to commend it as a possible foundation for IPE. In the fourth section, I highlight some of the advances that can be made by reformulating the foundations of IPE in this way. In particular, I demonstrate how a suitably reworked IPE can answer the most important criticisms that can be levelled against those who work within the subject field.

International Political Economy as a sub-field of International Relations

It is frequently remarked that IPE, especially for such a young subject field, displays a notable breadth. Opinions diverge, however, as to whether this breadth is real or superficial. It may be the case that a variety of theoretical perspectives co-exist comfortably within IPE, but these perspectives tend to be called upon to provide insight into a strictly limited number of issue areas. Openness to theoretical debate may be a distinguishing feature of IPE, but this does not necessarily lead to a broad subject field if debates are trained upon a narrow range of questions. Different ways of studying the same thing leads only to a superficially broad discipline. By contrast, accepting that there should be different ways of studying different things adds real breadth, but it also invites an 'anything goes' approach which undermines IPE's ability to be portrayed as a discipline.

Yet perhaps this is no bad thing. Disciplinary status provides an identity for a subject field and a sense of belonging for its practitioners. At the same time, though, disciplinary knowledge tends to be disciplined knowledge. As outlined in the Introduction, the core of a discipline – certainly in its Lakatosian form – involves the absence of debate about its underlying principles and methods of explanation. The day-to-day task of knowledge production is taken as given, with the role of the practitioner becoming increasingly perfunctory. Within such a framework, there is no scope to ask novel questions that will lead to potentially innovative research.

While it would be overstating the point to suggest that IPE has a Lakatosian disciplinary core, most appraisals of the subject field point to the narrow range of questions that drive research output in the field. Robert O'Brien and Marc Williams suggest that IPE is dominated by only three questions: the economic interdependence of nations; the role of hegemonic states within the international system; and the nature and causes of the contemporary experience of globalization (O'Brien and Williams 2004: 32; for a similar argument see Grieco and Ikenberry 2003: 3). The sociological assumptions and the social scientific methodology used to provide an answer to those questions might differ (Gilpin 1987: 42), but the questions themselves remain the same (Woods 2001: 278). The subject field of IPE can be delineated as a discrete entity as much by the sets of questions its practitioners ask as anything else. Yet it may be that a settled hierarchy of issues has developed, which limits the scope of IPE as a question-asking field. Craig Murphy and Roger Tooze certainly think so, arguing that IPE is 'defined more by agreement among scholars about what to study than by agreement about how to study it' (Murphy and Tooze 1991a: 1).

The result has certainly been increasing theoretical sophistication within IPE, but doubts must be raised about the overall contribution embedded in these developments. The process of knowledge production may be of strictly limited value in IPE, if all that has been produced is more rigorous answers to questions whose political relevance has long since faded.

The restrictions that are placed on IPE as a question-asking approach arise from its origins as a minor sub-field of International Relations. These are disciplinary shackles from which IPE has not even started to break free, as the imprints of IR are evident wherever one looks in IPE. But this does not necessarily mean that IR is an adequate starting point for IPE, whereby the theories and methods of the former can simply be transposed onto the latter. As Stephen Krasner suggests, 'Analysts of international relations have an almost pro forma set of variables designed to show the distribution of potential power' within the international system (Krasner 1976: 28). Krasner himself is content to work within the limits of these standard explanatory variables, as were many of the early IPE scholars (see, for instance, Blake and Walters 1976; Spero 1977). However, others have challenged what they see as the false attribution of autonomous disciplinary status to International Relations (Strange 1997: 236–7), in particular because of the consequent opportunity cost of crowding out political economy concerns from IPE. Any attempt to consciously fashion IPE as a sub-field of IR imposes self-induced constraints on the subsequent analysis. As Jeffrey Harrod argues, such constraints arise from treating international relations as 'a separate, specialised, compartmentalised and professionalised segment of human activity', which is capable of sustaining a theory of its own (Harrod 1997: 105).

The focus of such theory is typically to reify the 'international' as a discrete sphere of political activity, and hence to emphasize the significance of those actors – in particular, states – who are assumed to be central to the dynamics of the international system (Editors 1994: 1–2). On the basis of such observations, Robert Denemark and Robert O'Brien suggest that two broad traditions of IPE co-exist (Denemark and O'Brien 1997: 214–16). They label the first 'traditional IPE', in which IPE is seen to be a natural outgrowth of International Relations, and attempts only to explain the political dynamics of the inter-state system on matters of an economic nature. Susan Strange has identified a similar trend and, bemoaning the fact that this reduces IPE to the economic branch of foreign policy studies, she calls this the 'Politics of International Economic Relations' approach to IPE (Strange 1998a: 14). For those who seek to distance themselves from the disciplinary heritage of IR, there is the approach of 'inclusive IPE'. This tradition accepts Robert Cox's plea to place social forces at the heart of the subject field, and to study their mode of incorporation into the international economy without resorting to an ontology of social action that accords explanatory primacy to the role of the state (Cox 1981).

Either/or distinctions, such as that between Denemark and O'Brien's 'traditional' and 'inclusive' IPE, are common in appraisals of the subject field. Craig Murphy and Douglas Nelson, for instance, distinguish between an '*IO* school' (which is mainly US-based and associated with the leading US journal, *International Organization*), and a 'British school' (which is self-consciously critical of the theories and methods that dominate the output of the *IO* school). The minority British school is associated with a plurality of voices, as scholars are drawn to study the subject matter of IPE from a range of disciplinary homes. The more populous *IO* school, on the other hand, tends to operate within the disciplinary framework of International Relations (Murphy and Nelson 2001). At a methodological level, the point of departure between the two schools is most evident in their very different attitudes to the encroachment of rational choice approaches into IPE (on which see Woods 2001: 287–9). The *IO* school, with its roots in US political science, is typically much more tolerant of the incursion of rational choice theory. For the British school, by contrast, rational choice theory is that which must be argued against. In particular, its presence in IPE evokes fears of the colonization of all social scientific enquiry by the crudest variant of neoclassical economics. Such fears appear justified when set within the context of calls from within US political science for the abandonment of disciplinary specialisms and the move to a trans-disciplinary social science constructed on the basis of rational choice theory (on this point, see Blyth and Varghese 1999).

The idea of trans-disciplinary enquiry finds favour with many whose work is emblematic of the British school of IPE, yet it is not a trans-disciplinary rational choice theory that they have in mind when forwarding such a position. For most such authors, trans-disciplinarity simply means transcending the disciplinary rigidities of IR and exorcising the focus on inter-state dynamics from the analysis. Much work has been undertaken from this perspective by feminist and green political economists, whose substantive areas of concern fall beyond an explanatory framework that privileges the activities of states (see, for instance, Whitworth 1994; Helleiner 1996). Neo-Gramscian attempts to understand the economic ideologies of everyday life are also consistent with this notion of trans-disciplinarity (see, for instance, Gill 1991).

Taking the argument one stage further, Bob Jessop and Ngai-Ling Sum have called upon all political economists, whether practitioners of IPE or otherwise, to embrace a flexible synthesis of predisciplinary and postdisciplinary perspectives (Jessop and Sum 2001). Where the early IPE scholars accepted as a template for study what Krasner calls IR's 'pro forma explanations', to Jessop and Sum such templates appear overly mechanistic. Indeed, for them, it is even necessary to challenge the fact that IPE exists as a discrete subject field, let alone as a subject field constructed specifically in the image of IR. The usual rationale for IPE is that there are objective material and social conditions, associated with international economic affairs, which are sufficiently distinctive and coherent to warrant independent investigation. Yet, this is by no means an uncontentious claim. As Nicholas Onuf observes, IPE is a 'self-defining world of scholarship' (Onuf 1997: 91). In other words, it exists only to the extent that its practitioners adopt such a label for their work. The same research could be undertaken without the appeal to IPE to render it meaningful. Such work is necessary to the continued presence of IPE, but the continued presence of IPE is not necessary to such work. However, for the label 'IPE' to apply, some resemblance – whether theoretical or methodological – must be apparent to similar work within the subject field. Yet this in turn is the process through which disciplinary boundaries are established, and it is through the establishment of disciplinary boundaries that subsequent restrictions on research output are imposed.

The most important features of disciplinary boundaries are that they are essentially arbitrary and inherently artificial. This is evident in the imposition of the disciplinary boundaries of IR to act as the framework within which research is undertaken in IPE. Writing in the very first issue of their journal in 1994, the editors of the *Review of International Political Economy* concluded that 'the social sciences are experiencing their own glasnost... But to achieve that, IPE has to break away from the confines of IR and its restricting assumptions' (Editors 1994: 12). More than ten years on and the appeal has to be made again, for the liberation of IPE from its disciplinary heritage has not been achieved, despite the fact that many within the social sciences are now actively distancing themselves from the demands of disciplinarity.

Jessop and Sum note that postdisciplinary work is growing in importance across many different subject fields. Such work emphasizes the social construction of both knowledge of everyday life and the broader truth regimes in which that knowledge takes on meaning and informs action. As such, it recognizes the inevitably contextual nature of all social knowledge, and it attempts to historicize our understanding of how the social world takes shape in our experience of it. Disciplinary truths tend to be based on meta-narratives of social existence. Therefore, by prioritizing contextual knowledge it is necessary to transcend disciplinarity. This is possible in relation to the subject matter of IPE by turning to insights from the classical tradition of political economy. Classical political economy predates the division of social enquiry into academic disciplines and, in this sense, is predisciplinary. Yet it shares much with more recent work that is self-consciously postdisciplinary. The classical political economists were polymaths who wrote on a variety of subjects; they did not study 'the economy' as an enclosed and self-contained entity. Instead, they studied the historical development of economic *relations*. Moreover, they did so from a perspective that emphasized, amongst other things, the significance of politics, jurisprudence, philosophy, ethics, rhetoric and the liberal arts in the contextual constitution of economic relations.

What I am proposing here is that a new starting point can be fashioned for IPE from the style of analysis bequeathed by the classical political economists. However, such an alternative is currently frustrated by continued attempts to construct IPE as a sub-field of International Relations. I investigate the substantive effects of such attempts in the following section.

The 'states and markets' approach in International Political Economy

There is no more conventional an opening to appraisals of the subject field of IPE than the observation that the distinction between 'politics' and 'economics', as if each was an autonomous aspect of a broader social reality, is a false dichotomy. However, it is not always clear from those appraisals exactly where IPE is being positioned in relation to that dichotomy. For some, the task of IPE in the future is to transcend the boundaries of the distinction between 'politics' and 'economics'. The identification of the continued existence of those boundaries is an open acknowledgement of the weaknesses and the immaturity of IPE as a theoretical mode of study. For others, though, the present success of IPE is that its practitioners have already overcome the tendency of other disciplinary specialists to think in terms of isolated categories of 'politics' and 'economics'. The call for IPE to transcend the dichotomy between the two is a plea for its practitioners to continue what they are already doing, not an exhortation for change.

My position on this point is to reiterate the claims of those who suggest that most IPE scholars still have some way to go before their mode of enquiry breaks down the false dichotomy between 'politics' and 'economics'. Indeed, I will go further to say that, while most IPE scholars pay lip-service to the artificial nature of that dichotomy, in practice their studies serve merely to reinforce it. In all likelihood, this is not deliberate; rather, it arises from the fact that IPE has conventionally been seen as a sub-field of International Relations, and the dichotomy between 'politics' and 'economics' to be found in IR has simply been imported into IPE.

This is not to say that IPE scholars whose disciplinary home is IR do not recognize a complex reciprocal causation between 'politics' and 'economics'. Most clearly do. They ask how states shape markets in the interests of international order or, perhaps more precisely, how a structure of governance norms institutionalized through the inter-state system provides a standard for market exchange as well as the basis for a stable economy. They also seek to highlight the constraints on autonomous policy-making that arise from the actions of a self-interested private sector or, much more simply, how markets shape states in an attempt to impose an order of their own.

Yet, as Stephen Gill and David Law argue, in general few attempts have been made to specify 'the way in which ideas about what constitutes the *political* and the *economic* have emerged historically' (Gill and Law 1988: xviii). Within IPE, 'the state' continues to be understood by many of its practitioners as acceptable shorthand for the site of activities that encompass the political sphere. Likewise, 'the market' continues to be understood as acceptable shorthand for the site of activities that encompass the economic sphere. 'The state' and 'the market' are the two most important taken-for-granted reifications through which IPE in its IR form constructs explanatory devices for us to make sense of the world (on which see Inayatullah and Blaney 1997). But, as with 'politics' and 'economics', it tends to be assumed that 'states' and 'markets' are linked in a purely causal manner.

There is a façade of trans-disciplinarity in the IR variant of IPE, given that the vast majority of its practitioners dismiss a 'states *versus* markets' approach to the subject field (on which see Woods 2001). However, it does not follow that a truly trans-disciplinary mode of study ensues simply by advocating a 'states *and* markets' approach rather than a 'states versus markets' approach. Within IPE's IR framework, attention turns to what Joseph Grieco and John Ikenberry call the 'dual logics of state and market' (Grieco and Ikenberry 2003: 3). Two objections may be raised against characterizing the subject field in this way. First, the assumption that both 'the state' and 'the market' bear an internal *logic* of their own leads to an overly homogenized conception of both political and economic activities. To talk of 'logics' is also to suggest that such activities are simply reflections of a determining structure (this is the focus of Chapters 7 and 8). Second and, for the purposes of the current argument, more importantly, the assumption of a *dual* logic of state and market appears to confirm their autonomy from one another at the point of their constitution.

This sense of dualism is perhaps most vividly illustrated in Robert Gilpin's assertion that, 'Debate has raged for several centuries over the nature and consequence of the clash of the *fundamentally opposed logic* of the market and that of the state' (Gilpin 1987: 12, emphasis added). Gilpin enlists such standard bearers of the tradition of social theorizing as David Hume, Adam Smith, David Ricardo, John Stuart Mill and Karl Marx, in order to suggest the intellectual pedigree of conceptualizing 'politics' and 'economics' as discrete elements of the wider social world. Although this is a reading of these authors' work that I would dispute, Gilpin's position provides much sustenance for contemporary IPE scholars. It is usual for those scholars to write about the *interaction* of 'states and markets', thus emphasizing their autonomy at the point of constitution. Such a framework then tends to be used to specify the constraints that the logic emanating from one sphere imposes upon those who seek to act in the other – once again emphasizing their autonomy at the point of constitution. The 'states and markets' approach thus does nothing to address the possibility that political and economic activities are co-constituted within a single social reality. While that reality has been artificially divided by the institutional separation of the rule of law and systems of exchange (on which see Jessop and Sum 2001), it is nonetheless experienced as a totality within everyday life.

The notion of a single social reality cannot be captured fully within an analytical framework that focuses on the interaction of 'states and markets', rather than the co-constitution of activities that might be characterized as either predominantly political or predominantly economic in nature. However, most contributions to the IPE literature have been couched in terms of the causal relationship between one entity called 'states' and another called 'markets'. IPE, of course, does not operate on the basis of a unified theory. Disagreement abounds amongst its practitioners as to which of IPE's different theoretical perspectives offers the most useful insights into the nature of the world. Such disagreements, though, tend to take place against the shared backdrop of a common 'states and markets' approach.

The subject field of International Political Economy is perhaps best characterized, then, as the aggregation of a range of potentially incommensurable theoretical claims, made in relation to a number of basic substantive issues, all of which tend to be framed in terms of the relationship between 'states and markets'. The key difference between competing theoretical claims in IPE relates to the normative position that individual authors adopt on the preferred mix of values to be embedded within the state–market nexus (Murphy and Tooze 1991a: 2). For Susan Strange, such values are fourfold: security, prosperity, freedom and justice (Strange 1988: 18). The preferred combination of these values differs according to the theoretical orientation of the individual author. However, the fact that this combination is understood within the framework of an underlying 'states and markets' approach tends to remain the same.

1. For liberals, the basic question of IPE is how best can the regulatory authority of the state be harnessed to ensure that individuals are sufficiently uninhibited by political demands to establish systems of exchange that operate on the basis of free will alone. Individuals are assumed to have the propensity for organizing both the demand-side and the supply-side of commodity markets, enabling a coherent economic structure to be created as a result. This may well involve the development of institutions designed to act as an automatic pilot for market relations. Such institutions have a directive capacity and, as a consequence, enforce particular patterns of behaviour that might be seen to contradict the exercise of free will. However, within liberal thought, such constraints on the exercise of free will are associated with a positive payback for society as a whole, which is predicted to be higher levels of prosperity via the effective operation of the market economy. A Panglossian future is portrayed, in which a just order based on free will is also a prosperous order based on market exchange.

2. Marxists challenge such a conclusion. They argue that, so long as wealth is generated within the context of a capitalist economy, it reflects not so much the freedom as the subordination of the individual. The state is an epiphenomenon of the capitalist economy and, as such, is an integral feature of the process through which this subordination occurs. Wealth is linked to surplus value extraction, which in turn requires that public authority be marshalled to ensure the continued reproduction of an exploitative system of production that operates in the interests of the few. Distributive justice is impossible within a market economy in which order is maintained in direct opposition to the material interests of the many. The process of surplus value extraction divides society into two classes. First, there are those who own the means of production, the capitalists,

who enjoy the wealth that is generated by the labour power of others. Second, there are those whose labour power drives the production process, the proletariat, but whose labour is less than fully remunerated in order to sustain the extraction of surplus value.

3. Feminists also focus on the exploitative nature of capitalist production. Unlike Marxists, however, they do not prioritize class as the axis along which exploitation takes place. Instead, they chart the way in which systems of ostensibly free exchange have been established within the context of social norms that reflect deeply gendered assumptions about family role specialization. The ability of women to participate fully in the economy – whether as producer or consumer – is constrained by the reproductive tasks that they are required to undertake in an attempt to maintain the existing economic structure. The economy is not distinct from broader social trends so much as constituted by them. Insofar as public authority is summoned to secure the maintenance of the economic structure, the state is part of the process through which a particular set of life roles for women are both created and rendered normal. Feminists tend to search for a conception of the state as a site where gendered economic relations are both constructed and also contested. The market economy may well require gendered economic relations in order to function effectively, but this is not the only form of economic life that the state could seek to maintain.

4. The mercantilist tradition in IPE stands at odds with the above three perspectives. Whereas liberals, Marxists and feminists all focus on how social systems are established in order to facilitate the process of wealth creation, within the mercantilist tradition wealth creation is a means, not an end. Taking their cue from realist International Relations, mercantilists focus on strategies to strengthen the capacity of the state through a dynamic and successful economy. Only strong states are able to provide security for their citizens and, in turn, only a secure society can be confident of introducing a framework of law that allows for justice claims to be satisfied in an impartial and objective manner. From such a perspective, economic management is clearly subordinate to the preservation of existing state structures. The state is the archetypal actor within the international economy, and every state will approach the process of negotiating international economic treaties from a perspective of defending its economic sovereignty. Mercantilists emphasize how economic management occurs in line with the national interest; any

state that voluntarily cedes economic sovereignty operates against its national interest by jeopardizing the security of the nation.

5. Ecologists share with mercantilists a concern for security issues, but they do so in a very different way. They highlight the environment as a security issue, albeit one that transcends the typical spatial demarcations of the inter-state system. As such, the process of international economic management should take place not in line with the national interest, but in line with a global interest in protecting the earth's shared ecosystem. Justice is an inter-generational concern, and the ability of future generations to experience an ecosystem that can sustain everyday life is impeded by prior generations' search for ways to enrich themselves. For ecologists, then, the economy is at the heart of environmental problems. Current levels of prosperity are rooted in production systems that treat nature as a commodity, for which exchange relations develop so that it can be freely bought and sold. To the extent that public discourses of politics promote market ideology, in which the development of exchange relations is assumed to be a routine aspect of everyday life, states are implicated in the process through which environmental problems arise.

6. Neo-Gramscians also focus on the impact of market ideology in the structuring of everyday life. With its origins in Marxist political economy, neo-Gramscian theory highlights both the exploitative nature of capitalist production and the strategic use of the state apparatus in order to place capitalist production beyond claims for justice made on behalf of the exploited. Market ideology is crucial in this respect. The economy provides the material basis of identity and of the individual's sense of their role within society. Market ideology, in turn, provides the context within which economic relations are both activated and understood. The capitalist economy becomes progressively more difficult to challenge in circumstances in which market ideology is the systemic 'common-sense' of society. This occurs through the development of institutions designed specifically to integrate individuals into the capitalist economy, while at the same time providing constraints that impede sustained political mobilization for alternative forms of economic life. 'Common-sense' ensues when the ideological roots of the status quo are masked by assumptions that the prevailing order is simply 'the way things are'.

7. The poststructuralist turn in IPE also emphasizes the ideological constructions of everyday life. However, poststructuralists

deny that the economy provides a material basis for those constructions. Whereas neo-Gramscians focus on the institutional coherence that capitalist production lends to society and that market ideology lends to capitalist production, poststructuralists start from the assumption that no such institutional unity exists. The task instead is to analyse how identities form through the normalization of economic ideologies which, in and of themselves, provide no material basis for the maintenance of order. From this perspective, the state is unable to sustain conditions that lead necessarily to either a prosperous or a just society, because no such conditions exist a priori. Yet still the state can be seen to act. The aim of IPE is therefore to understand the way in which state strategies come to reflect certain economic ideologies, as well as the reasons that state officials give for dismissing alternative economic ideologies as either an unfeasible or an undesirable grounding for everyday life.

The 'states and markets' approach can therefore be seen to provide a common analytical framework for theoretical debate within IPE. Consistent with the IR roots of much IPE, this approach is used to provide a commentary on the question of international order. As is clear from the skeletal overview presented above of competing theoretical perspectives within IPE, the substantive character of the prevailing order is a topic of much dispute. The different theoretical perspectives clash on four separate issues: how is order produced; which type of order best befits a modern society; what is the nature of the prevailing order; and whose order is this. Yet the contribution to the subject field of each perspective is framed by the broader contextual assumption of order. To the extent that IPE coheres as a subject field, it does so because a genuine theoretically-informed debate is possible across its separate perspectives. But this in turn is only possible because that debate takes place against the backdrop of common concerns for the question of international order. In effect, the question of international order is the meta-debate within which more in-depth theoretical debates occur in IPE. From this perspective, however, IPE is reduced to the problem of how economic agents negotiate systemic features of anarchy so that they are able to pursue their own chosen goals (Inayatullah and Blaney 1997: 65). Indeed, there can be few other issues on which IPE *can* focus, given that general agreement exists about the broader constitution of the international system.

The assumption that the international system necessarily takes what Stephen Gill calls a 'primordial anarchic form' is particularly important (Gill 1991: 60). According to Richard Ashley, the 'anarchy problematique' conditions all subsequent analyses of individual behaviour within International Relations (see Ashley 1988). Key here is the way in which behaviour is assumed to follow rationally from an assessment of the likely costs and benefits of alternative courses of action. Under conditions of anarchy it is rational to act self-interestedly, because the mere fact of anarchical relations will cause all others to act self-interestedly as well. The substantive content of much work within IPE highlights the adverse social consequences of purely self-interested actions within the economy. As such, the outcomes of self-interested behaviour are consistently challenged. However, few attempts are made to challenge the assumption that behaviour itself is predicated upon self-interested norms (Tooze and Murphy 1996: 682–5). As Ashley argues, the assumption of rationality 'reflects not at all on the truth content of values or ends, and never on the structures or boundaries of the agent, but only on the efficiency of means', and it is the contextual assumption of anarchy that renders such means efficient (Ashley 1983: 476).

It is on this point, perhaps more than any other, that I part company with the IR variant of IPE. The assumption of rational behaviour is treated by IR IPE scholars almost as if it were axiomatic. Agents are assumed to optimize subject to certain constraints. Disagreement ensues between the theoretical perspectives as to the substantive character of those constraints – indeed, as to whether they are given or constructed. However, within the IR variant of IPE, there is general agreement that behaviour proceeds from an instinct for optimization.

Let me be clear at this stage what I am arguing. This is not to say that IPE scholars offer an unconditional endorsement of rational choice theory as a suitable methodology for their subject field; far from it. In the previous section, I reviewed Craig Murphy and Douglas Nelson's argument that we can think of two schools of IPE, an *IO* school and a British school. One important distinction between the two is their respective position on rational choice methodology. Those in the *IO* school tend to be more comfortable than their British school counterparts in modelling economic relations on the premises of rational choice theory. However, my argument here is not about the adoption of rational choice theory per se, so much as working with generic assumptions about the innate rationality of behaviour. Even though the British school may reject rational choice theory as a formal methodology, the theoretical perspectives that dominate work in this tradition still conceptualize individual conduct on the basis of assumptions about rational behaviour. Despite the identification of two schools, then, they come together in underlying assumptions about rationality.

In the following section, I suggest the possibility of reworking IPE from a perspective that challenges the very core of the assumption of inherently rational behaviour. Rationality cannot be simply taken-as-given as a starting assumption on which to conduct analysis, for it is an outcome whose explanation is the *goal* of that analysis. Instead of operating within the IR variant of IPE, I argue for IPE to be reformulated in line with the tradition of classical political economy. Working to the standards of this latter tradition, there is no need to make a priori assertions about the nature of human rationality. By contrast, the focus of the analysis is the socialization process through which conduct is shaped at any particular moment of time and space.

Political economy as the basis for IPE

Discussions of the disciplinary routes into the subject field tend to divide into three, depending on whether what is being advocated for the field is more 'I' (International Relations), more 'P' (Political Science) or more 'E' (Economics). My concerns are somewhat different. The IPE that I envisage is much more sensitive to its position in relation to the established tradition of political economy. This is a tradition that can be traced back at least as far as Aristotle, but which became a recognizable field through the reflections of the classical political economists on the advent of the modern industrial world in the eighteenth century. There is an obvious irony that a subject field such as IPE, in which 'Political Economy' is two-thirds of its name, should have paid so little attention to the historical debate about the essence of political economy; nonetheless, this is the case. IPE lacks a generic debate about its own foundations, certainly if we understand those foundations in terms of the longer history of political economy. International Political Economy is a subject field that is notably thin on political economy.

This much has been acknowledged by scholars within the field. Susan Strange, for instance, argues that the development of IPE in the 1970s was entirely necessary, because the classical tradition of political economy had suffered wholesale eclipse at the hands of a purportedly scientific neoclassical economics (Strange 1998a: 4). Economics, then, had developed its own disciplinary profile in such a way as to all but eliminate genuine political economists from amongst its ranks. For Strange, the emergence of IPE presented an opportunity for political economy to be rescued from economics, but this is an opportunity which has almost certainly been missed.

Perhaps what is at issue here is the precise meaning that IPE scholars attribute to 'political economy'. For most IPE scholars, political economy simply appears to mean the management of the economic affairs of the state (Caporaso and Levine 1992: 1). From such a perspective, Strange's exhortation for IPE scholars to discover political economy is only ever likely to fall on deaf ears, because in studying the economic affairs of the state, most of them believe that they are *already doing* political economy. I disagree. Political economy cannot be reduced merely to policy studies, however tempting it may be to treat the analysis of economic policy in this way.

In order to make it clear exactly what I mean by adopting a genuine political economy approach, it is useful to return to a distinction that has an intellectual lineage which dates at least to Aristotle. Aristotle suggested that it was important not to conflate production and a singular process of wealth creation. While it is true that wealth cannot be created in the absence of production, production is a means to at least two different ends. On the one hand, production can be harnessed to create wealth that serves merely to enhance the short-term monetary position of those who own the factors of production. This is creating wealth primarily for the social gratification that follows from holding wealth. On the other hand, production can be harnessed to create wealth that serves to meet the provisioning needs of society. This is creating wealth in order to satisfy fundamental criteria of distributive justice. Following the Greek derivation, the former relates to the realm of 'chrematistics', in which wealth creation responds to the search for prestige via the dynamics of individual utility-maximization. The latter, by contrast, relates to the realm of 'oikonomia', in which wealth creation responds to the prevailing pattern of human needs (on which distinction, see Daly and Cobb 1990).

There is rich irony in the fact that the English language word, 'economics', has its origins in the Greek oikonomia, for modern economics pays almost no attention to activities that take place in the realm of oikonomia. Very few economists recognize the dynamics of social provisioning as an integral part of the subject matter of economics. Moreover, those that do so typically are not recognized as 'proper economists' by their peers. The test of a good economist tends to be whether they can apply the rigours of formal modelling to the issue of utility-maximizing behaviour (Niehans 1990; Colander 2001). As Mark Blaug notes, 'So strong and persuasive has been the hold of the rationality postulate on modern economics that some have seriously denied that it is possible to construct any economic theory not based on utility maximization' (Blaug 1992: 230). Economics in its modern form is all about testing the rationality postulate (see Chapter 2). However, this typically is not the *empirical* testing of the rationality postulate: that is, very few economists provide evidential data based on observations of actual behaviour in order to ascertain the conditions under which rational calculations influence human conduct (1992: 241–3). It is usual instead for them to test the logical coherence of the rationality postulate *as a matter of logic alone*. Either way, though, it is clear that the overwhelming majority of economic studies currently reside in the realm of chrematistics. Contemporary economic analysis has not only subordinated oikonomia to chrematistics, it has almost entirely excluded the former from its purview (Hutchinson, Mellor and Olsen 2002: 42).

The remainder of the book is written from a perspective that privileges the provisioning dynamics of oikonomia. This, for me, represents a true political economy approach. Merely by recognizing the distinction between chrematistics and oikonomia, we are drawn to specify the relationship between the money economy and the social institutions within which it is embedded. The money economy is made manifest in price dynamics and the derivation of market demand and supply as aggregates of the activities of individuals. This is the subject matter of modern economics. It may well be possible to construct models of behaviour within the money economy solely on the basis of utility-maximization. However, this works only to the extent that the money economy can be seen as an autonomous entity, independent of and abstracted from the social institutions in which it is embedded. All we need to do is to acknowledge the existence of these institutions and we are immediately required to reject models of utility-maximizing behaviour if we are to understand the essence of economic relations.

We are hereby confronted with a crucial distinction between '*the* economy' and economic *relations*. In focusing primarily on the economic affairs of the state, IPE tends to follow neoclassical economics in emphasizing the former while downgrading the significance of the latter. In this way, the whole sphere of economic activity is condensed into an enclosed and self-contained entity called 'the economy', enabling this entity to be studied as a whole. By contrast, recognition of the social institutions that provide the context for economic activity necessitates an alternative focus on economic *relations*. Such a focus is integral to the IPE that I advocate in this book. It emphasizes the fact that 'the economy' exists only insofar as it represents the complex and cumulative combination of innumerable instances of human interaction. 'The economy' is, therefore, at one and the same time, an arena of human action, a context for human action and the outcome of human action. In short, 'the economy' is a product of economic relations.

As such, any explanation of economic activity first requires that we understand the process through which human intentions, desires and emotions – what the classical political economists called the full range of the 'passions' – are shaped in order to allow economic relations to form. This cannot be achieved by following the explanatory methods of neoclassical economics, in which the passions are reduced to a simple instinct for utility-maximizing behaviour. Instead, we must return to a style of political economy that predates the advent of neoclassical economics, one that understands the true human significance of the way in which economic relations are constituted.

Modern economists' utility-based theories can be usefully juxtaposed with the classical political economists' value-based theories. The majority of IPE incorporates a utility-based tradition of political economy. This is often unknowing and, particularly at the critical edge of IPE, almost never deliberate, but it is nonetheless the case. The decision to engage in economic activity tends to be reduced to an implicit calculation of costs and benefits relative to market price. Of course, this is not to deny the analytical contribution of much critical IPE that allows us to see the way in which political power is exercised to influence the process through which prices form. However, the explanation of why individuals engage in economic activity in the first place tends to rely on utility-based theories of decision-making.

An IPE whose foundations are located in the value-based tradition of classical political economy would clearly add extra dimensions to existing debates. For a start, it opens up our study of economic relations to the possibility that economic activity reflects the character of the dominant provisioning institutions of society (Hodgson 2001: 346). As such, it provides us with a contextual explanation for why individuals engage in particular forms of economic activity at particular moments of time and, furthermore, it means that our theories of decision-making no longer have to rely on either assumptions of utility-maximization or the rationality postulate on which such assumptions are grounded. To be sure, the classical political economists experienced significant difficulties when attempting to identify a 'scientific' unit for measuring value (Robinson 1964: 29–47), but for current purposes this is largely irrelevant. My intention is not to construct the foundations for a 'scientific' IPE, so the lack of scientific explanation within the classical tradition of political economy is not an issue. I am much more interested in the abstract concern of the classical political economists, which was to demonstrate that value was generated in and through the process of production, and that this in itself is a *social* process. For the classical political economists, value is a relationship between people, which is activated only at the point at which people interact to engage in economic activity. From this perspective, political economy is the study of irreducibly human experiences.

By contrast, utility-based theories emphasize the moment of exchange, which is theorized in fundamentally asocial terms, as exchange takes place between atomized individuals whose only relationship with one another is mediated by the product that is being exchanged. In neoclassical economics, exchange relations tend to be modelled in the context of pure price economies that require textbook conditions of perfect competition (Keen 2001: 23–53). This, quite clearly, is not the sort of economy that anyone could hope to experience in reality. In comparison, value-based theories emphasize the process of production and analyse production relations as a sub-set of wider social relations. As a consequence, production is assumed to occur within the context of particular social structures of power and powerlessness, dependency and interdependency, and coercion and consent. By conceptualizing production in this way, it is necessary to focus on relations between people that link them not only through an economic process but also within a broader moral framework.

As should be clear, then, the classical tradition of political economy does not respect the distinction, made popular by John Stuart Mill but usually accredited to Nassau Senior, between positive and normative economics (on which, see Blaug 1992: 112–14). Economic process (traditionally the subject matter of positive economics) and moral framework (traditionally the subject matter of normative economics) do not exist in parallel universes which bear no relation to one another. Within the work of the classical political economists, there is no logical distinction that can be sustained between the realm of facts and the realm of values. All economic activities have a factual basis, in that they rely on declarative statements of cause and effect to render them meaningful to participants in the activity. At the same time, though, such meanings rely on broader truth regimes for their overall intelligibility, and these in turn reflect prescriptive evaluations of alternative states of the world. An IPE constructed in the image of the classical tradition of political economy therefore places moral questions at the heart of the analysis.

The absence of a constitutive role for moral theory is only one issue on which existing appraisals of IPE find fault with the dominant perspectives within the subject field. In the following section I outline a number of key criticisms that are raised against the 'states and markets' approach in IPE. I also show how such criticisms can be addressed through the adoption of an IPE that reflects the style of analysis of the classical political economists.

Beyond the 'states and markets' approach in International Political Economy

Most appraisals of the subject field of IPE include a checklist of potential pitfalls that await the unwary exponent of IPE. In this section, I emphasize why it is preferable to work with value-based, rather than utility-based, theories of political economy. I do so by focusing, in turn, on five meta-theoretical concerns, each of which I identify as weaknesses of the existing IPE literature. To my mind, these are the five seminal absences to be found in the IR variant of IPE, each of which can be overcome by undertaking the move from chrematistics to oikonomia.

The absence of moral theory as a constitutive feature of International Political Economy

Value-based theories analyse the process through which value is produced, and this is assumed to be a fundamentally social process. Abstract assumptions about equilibrium conditions of production are replaced by a focus on how people are integrated into the process through which value is produced. The classical political economists studied both the way in which individuals are socialized into particular patterns of work and the psychological effects that the routine and coercive nature of work has on them as individuals. Utility-based theories of the economy, residing in the realm of chrematistics, focus only on the exchange values that workers generate for themselves, via wage labour, from being involved in making products. By contrast, value-based theories reflect the worldview of oikonomia. They ask whether the provisioning needs of individuals are infringed by their incorporation into systems of work that affect who they are as individuals and that instil within them social characteristics they would not otherwise have. Karl Marx wrote famously about the link between the capitalist system of work and the alienation of the individual. This represented the culmination of almost a century of reflection after Adam Smith had first voiced his suspicions in *The Wealth of Nations* that the division of labour came complete with adverse social consequences for those whose labour power was utilized in such a system.

The process of production, therefore, is not simply an economic process that the individual enters temporarily whilst 'acting economically', only then to leave in order to act in other social realms. The economic relations in which we are embedded, and the economic activities that we undertake as a result of that embeddedness, are constitutive of our make-up *as* individuals. We bear the imprints of our economic relations in all aspects of our social life. The socializing effects of those relations shape who we are, how we act, how we think before we act, and the broader truth regime within which we locate ourselves as meaningful actors. As such, the economic relations in which we are embedded are imbued with a fundamentally moral character. In utility-based theories, actual people are largely absent, to be replaced by a concern for understanding abstract relations of monetary exchange. As a consequence, moral theory has no place at the heart of the analysis.

It would be to overstate the case to suggest that anything but a handful of IPE scholars follow the pure chrematistics of neoclassical economics. Nonetheless, the 'states and markets' approach to the subject field privileges an implicit utility-based theory of the economy. This results, in general, in the absence of moral theory as a constitutive feature of IPE. When adopting a 'states and markets' approach, it is still possible to analyse the human *impact* of policies that are constructed on utility-based theories of the economy. Moreover, much important critical work has been undertaken in IPE from such a perspective. The international debt problem, the incorporation of women into newly proletarianized workforces in the developing world, and the development agendas of international organizations more generally are three such issues where critical attention has turned to the impact on human lives of the increasing institutionalization of particular economic processes. However, we can say little, if anything, from a 'states and markets' perspective about the moral dimension of human experience at the point at which we engage in our theoretical development. Utility-based theories render us silent on the moral implications of using those theories. Moral judgement must be suspended until after the process of theoretical reflection is complete, because that reflection is an exercise in logic rather than moral theorizing. In placing IPE firmly in the tradition of classical political economy, we are able to do more than merely pass moral judgement on observed outcomes; we are also able to incorporate moral theory as a constitutive feature of IPE.

The absence of a historicized conception of economic relations

Both the economic relations in which individuals are embedded and the socializing effects of such relations are aspects of a particular historical juncture. Indeed, it is possible to go so far as to say that all economic relations are unique, because they are specific to a certain point in time and space, and their impacts are mediated by the coping strategies of the particular individuals that they affect. In arguing from this latter position, though, we are unable to make general statements about the nature of economic relations and, as a consequence, theoretical analyses are all but ruled out. However, it is not necessary to push the argument to such an extreme to see that the underlying point holds: that economic relations are formed historically, and arise as the result of individuals taking decisive context-shaping actions in the past. It is frequently asserted that every generation since the Industrial Revolution has viewed the past as a period of economic stability relative to the unprecedented change of the present. While it is much easier to identify as significant the changes that one is living through than the changes experienced indirectly through the accounts of one's predecessors, this only goes to prove that the economy is continually being made and re-made. In fact, there is no such thing as '*the* economy', if by that we mean a static set of institutions that always reproduce economic relations in their extant form. The task of political economists must be to specify the characteristic features of the prevailing social environment, which in turn serve both to condition the dominant form of economic relations and to provide the ideological basis for reducing such relations to the level of the routine.

Utility-based theories of the economy are inadequate to such a task. Chrematistics concentrates on the short run – indeed, on the immediacy of the moment of exchange – where short-run dynamics are determined by the impersonal relationship between consumer and product. From this perspective, the analytical space for theorizing the historical constitution of economic relations is simply not forthcoming. What is needed is a perspective that enables us to historicize the present, to show that it is the contingent outcome of decisions taken in the past. Oikonomia differs from chrematistics in that it concentrates on the long run (Daly and Cobb 1990: 139) and, as such, it provides a route to a historicized IPE.

As Stephen Gill argues, it is usual for IPE scholars to 'use transhistorical theorizations based upon sets of a priori categories that appear to take on an ontological autonomy' (Gill 1991: 52). By contrast, a historicized IPE denies the ontological autonomy of all analytical categories in International Political Economy, not least of which 'the economy' itself. To think in terms of 'the economy' per se is to run the dual risks of reifying a specific theory of economic relations, and of treating the activities demanded by the dominant form of economic relations as a natural reflection of an invariant economic structure; yet they are no such thing. Economic relations form at a particular moment of time within a dominant truth regime. Therefore, the activities that those relations are established to undertake are also specific to the way in which knowledge is constructed about 'the economy' at that moment of time. We experience 'the economy' in part as a process of production and in part as a series of ideological claims about the nature of the world. Such claims can momentarily appear to naturalize certain forms of economic relations, but this is all it ever is: an appearance of stasis. Despite seeming consistencies in everyday life, economic relations are always open to decisive political interventions, which could potentially change their underlying mode of constitution. A historicist perspective on IPE challenges its practitioners to understand the way in which economic relations can temporarily appear to be frozen in time, so that they can then specify strategies through which such relations can be reshaped (Amoore *et al.* 2000; Jessop and Sum 2001).

The absence of challenges to all manifestations of a rationalist ontology

It is necessary to operate with a historicized conception of economic relations in order to demonstrate the contextual nature of economic agency (Oakley 2002). Agents are conditioned by the structural elements of the economic relations in which they are situated, but they are also complicit in creating the character of those relations through the responses that their actions evoke in others. The economic context in which individual agents act presents itself to those agents in terms of the socially constructed characteristics that are imputed to them by others. Gendered agents, for instance, will confront a gendered context in which their subject positions are defined for them in those terms (Whitworth 1994: 122). Likewise, class-based institutions provide a different context for action depending on the class position of the actor who is attempting to effect agency (Spencer 2000: 547). However, utility-based theories offer no insight into the contextual nature of economic agency. The chrematistic concern for the *moment* of exchange renders superfluous any analysis of the socialization processes that both precede the instant of exchange and condition the form that the exchange relation will take at that instant. From this perspective, all parties to the exchange relation must be considered social equals. Chrematistic agents therefore operate in a virtual world that is, in some sense, beyond structure.

Within such a world, it is possible to model behaviour solely on the basis of the rationality postulate, yet outside such a world – in other words, within all possible worlds that we could conceivably experience – the rationality postulate is of strictly limited use. To be rational in a purely logical sense provides few clues as to how socially situated individuals will respond when called upon to act in circumstances in which the likely impact of their actions on other people is known to them. When faced with the decision of whether to act purely on the basis of rational instincts or whether to make a normatively informed choice that takes account of the conditions in which others find themselves, there is no reason to assume that the former option will be chosen. As a consequence, methodologically individualistic perspectives serve little purpose in IPE. We do not approach our economic relations as isolated individuals, but as part of a wider social grouping.

This argument is well rehearsed in existing appraisals of IPE (see, for instance, Gill 1991: 56–7). But still it bears repetition, because the challenge to methodological individualism has tended only to take the form of a challenge to neoclassical economics. It has not taken the form of a challenge to the rationality postulate in all its manifestations and, as such, those variations that have been incorporated into IPE are typically overlooked as being part of the methodological individualist family. This is particularly so in relation to the common 'states and markets' approach shared by the various theoretical perspectives in IPE. While those perspectives conceptualize the interaction between states and markets in different ways (see the second section of this chapter), each tends to understand the activities that take place in both the state and market environment in fundamentally rational terms. Different perspectives diverge on the nature and severity of the constraints on rational action that can be imposed by actors in one environment on actors in the other, but the assumption of rational action tends to form a common core across those perspectives. As Craig Murphy and Roger Tooze argue:

> Orthodox IPE scholarship displays a clear, if often unstated, commitment to explaining events in terms of the rational action of

> individuals or of state actors treated as individuals – a commitment to a relatively radical form of methodological individualism that denies ultimate validity to contextually bound explanations as well as explanations in terms of concrete social wholes. (Murphy and Tooze 1991b: 19)

The social provisioning approach of oikonomia necessitates explanations such as these, but they are precisely what is crowded out of IPE by the failure to challenge all manifestations of a rationalist ontology.

The absence of a theory of social action

Economic relations provide a context for human action. Political economy should therefore be a study of humans *in action*. Perhaps the most surprising omission from IPE is a theory of social action. Most research in IPE concludes without ever having captured the sense of humans in action. There is little concern for specifying the dynamics through which action actually occurs within the context of economic relations. This is maybe only to be expected, as the focus of the 'states and markets' approach tends to be on 'the economy' rather than economic relations. As such, there are few analyses of the motivations for action, whether such action aims to reproduce or reconfigure the extant form of economic relations, what impact consciousness has on action, or the circumstances in which conscionable action dominates self-serving behaviour. In general, there is a conflation of action and essence within IPE scholarship. 'To be' (which relates to essence) and 'to act' (which relates to action) are analytically distinct, as one refers to existential conditions and the other to choice between alternative forms of conduct. However, the difference between the two tends to be lost in IPE. On the one hand, what discussion of human nature there is typically is reduced to assumptions about the way in which individuals act; on the other hand, the discussion of human action typically is reduced to assumptions about the manner of individuals' being. This leads to an attenuated and somewhat perfunctory theory of social action, insofar as the conduct of human affairs is distanced from the act of conscious thought, instead being assumed to proceed on the basis of an instinctive response to prevailing circumstances.

Given the dominance of utility-based theories of political economy within IPE, the circumstances to which actors respond relate to a context of want satisfaction. In this way, much IPE scholarship is cast in the image of neoclassical economics, despite the frequent assertion that the latter establishes analytical standards that the former should consciously reject. However, while the formal modelling rigour of neoclassical economics remains very much on the periphery of IPE, the underlying mode of explanation within IPE is surprisingly similar to that of neoclassical economics. In particular, both attribute action directly to the pattern of interests in which the agent is embedded. Want satisfaction is achieved when the agent successfully acts upon those interests. In neoclassical economics, such interests reside simply in the derivation of utility. Action is therefore conducted in an attempt to maximize utility. The pattern of interests in which the agent is embedded tends to be more complex than this in theories of IPE, such that explanations of utility-maximization come complete with additional qualifications and commentary. Yet action still tends to correspond to interests, and those interests are largely assumed to be given, notwithstanding the recent constructivist turn in the social sciences.

It is typical of chrematistic approaches to the economy to model action solely on interests and to understand interests in methodologically individualistic terms. By contrast, the social provisioning approach of oikonomia stresses the social identity of the individual, and proceeds on that basis to study humans *in action*. This is not to say that, as a heuristic, we have nothing to learn from assuming that individuals have interests; however, it is to follow the classical political economists' concern to show that interests and identity are inter-related. 'What we do' and 'who we are' are not analytically separable questions. In general, the classical political economists assumed that individuals understand their interests to be materially based, at least in part, insofar as we act in line with the subject positions that we derive from the economy. Moreover, our incorporation into particular processes of production also helps to shape the identity we assume when attempting to understand our interests. However, our identity is never fully determined by the economy and cannot be simply read off from it. If we are to analyse humans in action, then, IPE must be sensitive both to the co-constitutive relationship between interests and identity and to the extra-economic influences on the process of identity construction.

The absence of the individual from explanatory accounts in International Political Economy

By reducing action to the response to interests, IPE tends to lack an integral analysis of individual subjectivities. Indeed, despite the incorporation of important elements of the explanatory framework of methodological individualism, it is unusual for practitioners of IPE to focus their enquiry at the level of individual behaviour at all. This is one obvious casualty of the dominance of the underlying 'states and markets' approach to IPE. The activities of state officials may well be modelled in terms of a rationalist ontology based on methodological individualism, and those of market actors likewise; but this on its own does not constitute a focus on the individual *as an actor*. However, the international economy would not exist for IPE scholars to study were it not for the actions of individuals consolidating existing patterns of economic relations across national borders and seeking to forge new ones. Such relations are the result of a myriad of interactions between conscious and reflexive human agents. The constituent unit of all economic relations is the individual and, as such, studies in political economy must begin with an analysis of human nature.

However, it is precisely these foundations that chrematistic approaches do not allow. This is an important reason why I advocate classical political economy as an alternative starting point for IPE. Classical political economy has a much more rounded conception of human nature than the chrematistic approaches that superseded it. As a consequence, it also has a much more sophisticated theory of the individual in action. The classical political economists were in general concerned to theorize 'the economy' as a social system that incorporates the human desire for both material and moral contentment within broader structural relations of production and distribution. While the utility-maximizing economic agent is able to find satisfaction purely through material contentment, this is not enough for the economic agent in classical political economy. The origins of the classical tradition are generally traced to Adam Smith's *Wealth of Nations*. But *The Wealth of Nations* was itself an extension of his earlier *Theory of Moral Sentiments*, in which Smith argued that material fulfilment was insufficient on its own to counteract feelings of moral unease arising from recognition of the conditions of others. *The Wealth of Nations* provides a benchmark against which the classical tradition developed and, as a result, Smith's attempt to theorize the human condition in general terms became a hallmark of that tradition. Chrematistic approaches fall down in comparison because they cannot show how we are answerable to our conscience as we attempt to satisfy material wants.

The classical tradition of political economy offers a more complex conception of the self than is generally to be found within IPE. As such, it also provides the basis for an integral account of individuals in action within the context of the economic relations in which they are embedded. The decision-making matrix of the economic agent of classical political economy is attuned to the social provisioning needs of oikonomia. Individuals are locked into a continual struggle between the competing priorities of satisfying their own concerns and meeting the needs of others with whom they share their social existence. The individual is also susceptible to the dominant ideological constructions of the day, which are likely to influence the way in which that struggle is mediated. This is especially so in circumstances in which those constructions do not present themselves as ideology, but merely as common-sense statements about the nature of the world. From this perspective, issues such as duty and justice become part of the theory of action, because they form part of the process of reflection that precedes the individual taking action. However, duty and justice are not universal categories. Their meaning is contextual and only takes shape within a particular ideological context. The theory of the individual within IPE must take account of the context within which agency is attempted, and it must not treat the individual in atomistic terms.

Conclusion

The five seminal absences of IPE have done nothing to prevent the development of a subject field that permits intensive discussion of the merits of alternative proposals for managing the international economy. My concern is not that IPE scholars work within a bounded political worldview, which limits the subject field to finding different ways to say that the world is fine as it is. However, it is possible to identify a bounded analytical worldview, in which disagreements over the correct procedure for international economic management are set within a common context for understanding action.

In Chapters 4–6, I develop an alternative conception of action to that which dominates IPE, on the basis of an alternative interpretation of human agency within economic relations. This interpretation is derived from three authors whose work is emblematic of the classical tradition of political economy: Adam Smith (1723–90), Thorstein Veblen (1857–1929), and Karl Polanyi (1886–1964). Their contributions span the best part of two centuries. The origins of the classical tradition arise from the work of Smith, who wrote in the latter part of the eighteenth century, at a time when industrial capitalism was beginning to shape the modern world. Veblen worked in the decades around the turn of the twentieth century. This was a time at which the process of industrialization was complete for the major powers, capitalist logic had encroached upon an increasing number of aspects of everyday life, and the conversion of the economics profession to neoclassical theory served merely to emphasize that logic. Polanyi's contribution dates to the immediate aftermath of the outbreak of the Second World War, a time at which the classical tradition of political economy had been entirely eclipsed by neoclassical economics, but the capitalist system which neoclassical theory reified had broken down amidst the developments that led to war.

Each of these three authors provides a distinctive view of the human agent which, when combined, creates the basis for an alternative conception of action within IPE. From Smith, I take his emphasis on cognitive structures of propriety as a guide for action. Economic agents in Smith's work are irreducibly moral agents, who reflect upon the appropriateness of their conduct in relation to the likely response it will receive from others. From Veblen, I take his emphasis on the habituating effects on action of life within a relatively well-ordered society. Economic agents in Veblen's work develop particular habits of thought, which locate them within their social environment and give meaning to their intended conduct. From Polanyi, I take his emphasis on the social embeddedness of the individual, and the threat to that embeddedness of purely self-serving behaviour. Economic agents in Polanyi's work are prey to the competing influences of socially regulated and purely individualistic behaviour, but in prioritizing the latter they run the risk of undermining the social conditions of their own existence.

The work of each author provides analytical space in which to liberate the conception of the human agent from assumptions of innate rationality. Before I move on to the individual contributions of Smith, Veblen and Polanyi, however, I turn more specifically in the intervening chapters to the rationality postulate itself. In particular, I situate the rationality postulate within the history of economic thought. In turn, this enables me to situate the 'states and markets' approach to IPE, which draws heavily upon the rationality postulate, within a specific tradition of economic theorizing.

Chapter 2

Historicizing Rationality Assumptions: International Political Economy in the History of Economic Thought

Introduction

The previous chapter arrived at a conclusion that, on first reading, might appear somewhat paradoxical. Most studies of IPE reflect upon the rich diversity of theoretical frameworks within the field. From such a perspective, it is all but impossible to identify a disciplinary core. However, I have argued that such a core exists.

To focus upon it, we must overlook disputes within the literature on the interpretation of the current trajectory of international economic management. In other words, IPE does not have a disciplinary core at the level of understanding economic outcomes. There is no sense from IPE that the economy works in a certain way. We must also overlook normative disagreements about the preferred nature of the world. There is no settled position within IPE about how economic relations should be organized.

Moreover, what core there is does not result from conscious efforts to develop one. It is through the process of *doing* IPE that a disciplinary core has emerged, rather than exponents of the field agreeing on what IPE *is*, before then embarking on their studies. It is not so much the questions IPE specialists ask that constitute its core, I argue, as the ontological perspective within which those questions are set.

This perspective has the habit of naturalizing optimizing behaviour, before focusing subsequent analysis on attempts to understand the effects of such behaviour on the world in which we live. The questions that shape the output of so much of the IPE literature are those that ask how optimizing behaviour conditions the structures of the economy and, as a consequence, how they impact upon the life chances of economic agents. By contrast, I ask on what grounds can the *assumption* of optimizing behaviour be taken as given. Perhaps more importantly, I also ask about alternative forms of enquiry that can be opened up in IPE if its foundations are thought through in a way that refuses to countenance the reification of utility-maximizing behaviour.

In order to set the context in which such questions can be answered, this chapter proceeds in three stages. In the first section, I show that the assumption of utility-maximizing behaviour has provided the *foundation* for economic analysis only relatively recently. I draw a distinction between classical and modern forms of political economy, with the dividing line between the two being the marginalist revolution of the last three decades of the nineteenth century. Assumptions of optimizing behaviour as the foundation of economic analysis very much reflect the minority view within classical political economy. This does not become the majority view until classical political economy is usurped by modern economics in its distinctively neo-classical form. While emphasizing the significance of the neoclassical turn in economics, in the second section I guard against treating the broad tradition of neoclassical economics in overly homogenized terms. The neoclassical tradition has simultaneous origins in the work of three authors: William Stanley Jevons (1835–82), Carl Menger (1840–1921) and Léon Walras (1834–1910). I offer a brief synopsis of each, focusing in particular on the status accorded to the assumption of utility maximization. It is from a synthesis of these three positions that contemporary concerns emerge for *homo economicus*, or rational economic man. In the final section I offer an ontological critique of *homo economicus* from a philosophy of social science perspective.

Classical political economy versus modern economics

As David Williams has shown to great effect, contemporary forms of international economic management, as embodied in World Bank development programmes, take the characteristics of *homo economicus* as given (Williams 1999). The World Bank concerns itself with educating individuals in the ways of utility-maximization, replacing traditional forms of cognition and social interaction with self-interested conduct based on rational calculus. *Homo economicus* therefore becomes a universal standard for institutionalizing economic relations between individuals. Moreover, the World Bank feels justified in acting in this way, because it assumes that utility-maximizing behaviour is a fundamental condition of human nature, which is denied to some only on account of the underdevelopment of the economies in which they live. It is therefore assumed to be a potentially time-invariant character trait that applies irrespective of the specific economic structures into which the individual is socialized.

The briefest history of the concept of instrumental rationality is sufficient to suggest otherwise. To act in an instrumentally rational manner, one must first be able to calculate the costs and benefits that will attend all available courses of action, before selecting the particular course of action that maximizes benefits relative to costs. This, in turn, requires a specific type of mathematical skill. It is necessary for one to be able to think in terms of both utility (arising from perceived benefits) and disutility (arising from perceived costs). Mathematically, this implies a form of cognition whereby one's instinctive grasp of negative numbers (–1, –2, –3, etc.) is as developed as one's grasp of positive numbers (1, 2, 3, etc.). In other words, it is necessary to be able to think symmetrically around the concept of zero, lining up numbers instinctively in the arithmetic progression –3, –2, –1, 0, 1, 2, 3, and so on. Otherwise, it is impossible to set up even the most basic cost/benefit analysis. However, the development of a concept of zero, from which our whole perception of negative numbers makes sense, is a relatively recent addition to mathematical cognition (Russell 1992 [1937]).

It is well known, for instance, that Roman numerals contain no zero (Barrow 2001). Irrespective, then, of the relatively advanced nature of certain sectors of the Roman economy, it could not provide the context for the activities of *homo economicus*, because the Roman mathematical system did not provide the means for utility-maximizing individuals to engage in the calculations that would enable them to act in a utility-maximizing manner. *Homo economicus*, therefore, is the product of more recent shifts in the underlying structure of human cognition.

The concept of zero is not an innate aspect of human thought; it is part of a counting procedure that has to be taught and learnt. As a concept, it literally had to be invented, and this took place over a long period of time. An important distinction must be drawn between what it *is* as a concept and what it *does* as a concept. Focusing on what it *is* as a concept, Bertrand Russell dates the introduction of zero into western life and western thought to the late tenth century (Russell 1992 [1937]: 185–7). Focusing by contrast on what it *does* as a concept, Robert Kaplan argues that zero only began to inform modern mathematical cognition in the early seventeenth century, following John Napier's prior discovery of logarithms and its subsequent impact on the development of differential calculus (Kaplan 2000: 129–36). The techniques of differential calculus allowed mathematical functions to be maximized; before their development there was no formal procedure through which optimization problems could be resolved. As a consequence, it was only after the early seventeenth century that humans could be taught the basic cost/benefit computations of *homo economicus* and, as such, that they could learn to embody the character traits associated with utility-maximizing behaviour.

Interestingly, the modern use of the concept of zero was developed as a response to the prior invention of double-entry bookkeeping in Italy in the fourteenth century (Kaplan 2000: 110). Here, all assets appear on one side of the accounts and were balanced against the liabilities that appear on the other side of the accounts. In other words, the modern use of the concept of zero, which is a fundamental element of the cognition of *homo economicus*, came *after* the institutionalization of forms of economic life that *homo economicus* is now said to create.

What do we learn from this brief digression into the historical development of modern mathematical structure? For a start, it should caution us against the assumption that utility-maximizing behaviour is a generic feature of human nature, which applies irrespective of social circumstance. Moreover, it suggests that we should take care to locate the assumption of *homo economicus* within particular traditions of thought. One key to this task is to draw the distinction between the classical and modern traditions of political economy.

As George Stigler notes, the dividing line 'between past [i.e., classical] and present [i.e., modern] economics is a matter of intention more than of time' (Stigler 1969: 217). For the sake of clarity, what I term the classical tradition originates with Smith, encompasses all those who made seminal contributions to the study of political economy prior to the 1870s, such as Ricardo, Malthus, Mill and Marx, and also includes those who have swum against the neoclassical tide since the marginalist revolution, such as Veblen, Myrdal, Polanyi and Keynes. The latter group is included because their analyses share so many of the intentions of their classical predecessors, even though they were writing at a time in which the modern tradition was dominant. What I term the modern tradition originates with the neoclassical turn, embodied in the work of Jevons, Menger and Walras, and includes later authors such as Marshall, Edgeworth, Pareto, Hicks, Samuelson, Friedman, Becker and Lucas.

The classical political economists were concerned with the human impact of increasingly complex production systems and, perhaps more importantly, how the rewards from such systems were distributed throughout society. Rather than treating the economy as a self-contained system, the classical political economists focused on economic *relations* as a sub-set of the broader social relations into which individuals were integrated as members of a society that was based on asymmetric distributions of power. At all times within the classical tradition the economy was conceptualized as a manifestation of the social relations of production and distribution. By contrast, modern economists have focused not on *relations* of production and distribution, but on *moments* of exchange. The sole concern within this latter tradition is the decision-making matrix with which the individual is faced when assessing the preferred course of action. Note, however, that this choice is condensed purely at the level of the individual. The individual is assumed to select the desired course of action solely on the merits as he or she sees them. No other consideration influences the decision. As a consequence, the conception of the economy as a socialized arena of action is somewhat lost.

To my mind, the analysis that is symptomatic of the core of IPE bears little resemblance to the style of analysis of the classical political economists. This is not to say that there has been no concern within IPE for changing relations of production internationally. Much important work has been undertaken on the international division of labour, both old and new, and the impact of multinational diversification on local labour (see, for instance, Wallerstein 1979; Lipietz 1997; van der Pijl 1997; Dumenil and Levy 2001). Neither is it to say that there has been no concern within IPE for uneven development and skewed distributions of economic rewards internationally. Much important work has been undertaken on the effects of inequalities resulting, inter alia, from the structure of international debt and the flawed development programmes of international institutions (see, for instance, Johnston 1991; Nitzan 1998; B. Cohen 2002; Wade 2002). However, I do argue that this results not from a concern to theorize the relations of production and distribution per se, but from a concern to study the effects of self-interested behaviour, whether they result from the utility-maximizing decisions of individuals, firms, states or international institutions (on a similar point, see Tooze and Murphy 1996). In this respect, I suggest that the core of IPE is cast in the image of the modern tradition of economic analysis.

The shift from classical to modern traditions of economic analysis encompasses a shift in substantive focus (see, for instance, Tabb 1999: 91–110). Those working within the classical tradition were concerned with the way in which ordinary people were incorporated, particularly as workers, into the prevailing regime of accumulation. They were therefore interested in the human dimension of economic growth. The underlying economic problem was to ascertain how economies grow and with what impact on the mass of the population. The individual appears in classical analysis in relation to the types of behavioural characteristics that he or she must display if the prevailing accumulation strategy is to be successful. Growth strategies impact upon the individual, recreating both the conduct and the cognitive capacities of the individual in line with ever more complex systems of production.

By contrast, those working within the modern tradition tend to take the individual as given. All individuals are assumed to have the same set of optimizing characteristics, which are evident in all economic systems, irrespective of their underlying structure. As a consequence, economic analysis can be reduced to the question of how individuals allocate the scarce resources in their possession between competing ends. The economy is therefore conceptualized as a given entity for satisfying individual wants, rather than as a dynamic set of social relations that are reshaped by changing patterns of human behaviour (Bernstein 2003). As William Tabb argues, modern political economy, especially in its neoclassical form, eschews a socialized theory of the economy in which value is added to the economy, and rewards taken from it, by individuals acting collectively in irreducibly social contexts. Instead, the economy is seen as a 'natural mechanism in which independent, freely acting agents interact to produce the best possible allocation of resources' (Tabb 1999: 110).

For the classical political economists, a concern for distribution supersedes the study of the pricing system because prices reflect current conventions on distribution and not vice versa (Hollander 1987: 6). For modern economists of a neoclassical persuasion, on the other hand, the hierarchy of concerns is reversed. It might not be too much of an exaggeration to say that the study of the pricing system *is* economic analysis for neoclassical economists (see, for instance, Stigler 1969: 221). At the very least, prices are seen as 'a social mapping of the means–end framework that defined the market to begin with' (Bernstein 2003: 141). This certainly facilitates the ease with which idealized economic circumstances can be modelled (Niehans 1990), but it also empties neoclassical economics of any concern for distributive justice (Colander 2001). This leaves us with a form of economic analysis that can only describe the economy, as well as the human relations of which it is constituted, in fundamentally amoral terms (see Grimmer-Solem and Romani 1999; Brockway 2001).

The person who did more than anyone else to institutionalize neoclassical theory as the pedagogy of economics, Alfred Marshall, remained agnostic throughout his career about the applicability of that theory (Marshall 1920; for a commentary, see Barber 1991). His worry was that neoclassical theory, as a set of analytical techniques, provides no means of understanding the habitually instituted behaviour of individual economic agents. It cannot tell us how those agents think, or how their thought processes subsequently inform their actions. Economic agents are denied the very reflexivity that allows them to conduct themselves within actual economic contexts (Worswick 1972: 85). All interaction between agent and context is considered to be exogenous to economic analysis, which means that most of the economic decisions that individuals undertake in order to conduct their everyday lives is excluded by assumption.

Indeed, the assumption that underpins the whole of neoclassical theory, that of utility-maximizing behaviour, is rarely rendered explicit *as an assumption* in contemporary applications of the theory. Instead, it is treated as a truism of modern life: an axiom which is so self-evident that it requires no further explication (Phelps-Brown 1972).

This must be contrasted with the focus of the classical political economists, who attempted to study not the idealized characteristics of economic models, but the structural characteristics of economic life – what Samuel Hollander refers to as 'the social, anthropological and demographic factors at play' (Hollander 1987: 12). The historically contingent outcomes resulting from these 'factors at play' differ markedly from the deterministic outcomes that follow from studying allocation decisions beyond the social context in which they are set (Tabb 1999: 91). As George Stigler notes, the shift to neoclassical forms of economic analysis 'replaced the individual economic agent as a sociological or historical datum' (Stigler 1969: 225). In the search for more scientific economic enquiry, the strict application of neoclassical theory presents an essential timelessness to individual behaviour. But note, once again, what this is at the expense of: any sense of the social relations in which individuals are situated, and any sense of the historical development of those relations. In superseding the classical tradition within economics so completely, Michael Bernstein argues that 'modern economists succeeded in bringing centuries of analysis (and debate) to ostensible closure'. In short, the shift to neoclassical economics involved developing 'a professional expertise that could put... a polemical ancestry to rest' (Bernstein 2003: 135, 136). It is to the roots of the neoclassical revolution that I turn in the following section.

The heterogeneous roots of neoclassical economics: Jevons, Menger and Walras

While the foregoing might be read to imply the existence of a homogeneous body of neoclassical theory, this would almost certainly be misleading (see, for instance, Blaug 1996: 277–310). The most that we can say is that neoclassical economics has a core. As with IPE, such a core represents broad agreement on the ontological framework within which subsequent analysis is to be set, rather than detailed agreement on the substantive answers which that analysis is expected to deliver. Exponents of neoclassical economics may agree that the basis for their analyses is utility-maximizing behaviour; but there remains divergent opinion on the extent to which utility-maximizing behaviour captures the essence of actual conduct, what the origins of such behaviour are, and whether and to what degree it requires the regularizing influence of social institutions that are designed specifically to elicit such conduct.

Neoclassical economics therefore does not have a linear history as an intellectual movement. Indeed, even the term 'neoclassical economics' has a much more chequered history than the ubiquity of its use today might suggest. It was popularized in the 1950s, mainly through the work of Joan Robinson (see Robinson 1964). However, it was first coined by Thorstein Veblen in 1900, in order to describe changes to the professionalized thought of economists during the previous three decades, to which he considered himself to be an outsider. The term was never used to describe their own work by those who, retrospectively, can be shown to be the founders of the tradition. It has always been a term used more readily by those who were seeking to construct a position *against* which their work was oriented, than by those who were seeking a description of their own work. As David Colander notes, we are consequently left with two very different ways in which the term 'neoclassical economics' is applied: '(1) to describe the economics from 1870 to the 1930s, and (2) to describe modern economics in reference to heterodox thinking today' (Colander 2001: 157).

Moreover, few practitioners of otherwise orthodox economics currently accept all the restrictions of early neoclassical writings. Whatever economics they are practising, it is not the mindless replication of the most extreme variants of neoclassicism.

Important as these caveats are, however, the term 'neoclassical economics' can still be used to capture the underlying essence of economic analysis, so long as it is used with due care. It is not a settled paradigm, from which individual accretions to the knowledge base of economic science can simply be read off. However, its development does still represent a significant point of departure in the history of economic thought, which continues to have a consequential impact upon other fields of study, such as IPE, that draw upon economics. First, neoclassical economics constitutes a reversion against the style of political economy originated by Adam Smith: that of a comprehensive normative social science (Boulding 1970; Grimmer-Solem and Romani 1999). It is the rejection of Smithian political economy to which the vast majority of the economics profession has subsequently been won over. Second, its assumptions of mechanically optimizing behaviour are often implicit even in the work of those who consciously position themselves in opposition to the neoclassical tradition. As William Tabb argues, across the social sciences, and often without the implications being explored, 'a neoclassical world is the background assumed for many rhetorical purposes' (Tabb 1999: 102). The language of optimizing behaviour provides the substance of so much social science discourse.

There is still much to be gained, then, from analysing the origins of neoclassical theory. There is a tendency amongst historians of economic thought to present contemporary economics as a unified field and, as a consequence, to retrace the roots of this singular discipline within an overly homogenized conception of its past (see Blaug 1996: 278). Despite this, it is clear that there are three separate founders of neoclassical economics: in Manchester, Stanley Jevons; in Vienna, Carl Menger; and, in Lausanne, Léon Walras. I now briefly review the key contributions of each in turn.

Jevons struck out at the dominant classical tradition for its lack of scientific pretensions (Jevons 1970 [1871]: 78) and, by implication, for being a mere branch of sociology (1970 [1871]: 89). For Jevons, the sociological basis of classical political economy was embodied in its concern for developing a labour theory of value. Under such a theory, the value of a good is related to the production system in which it is made and, in particular, to the way in which workers are incorporated into the production system (Heilbroner 1988: 104–33). Jevons's break with the past came with his attempt to invert the labour theory of value. The prevailing wisdom of his time was that value accrues from additional labour and, as such, wages are paid to reward those who create value through their labour. In other words, value results from the process of production.

Jevons dismissed this whole line of reasoning, saying that 'wages are clearly the effect not the causes of the value of the produce' (Jevons 1970 [1871]: 71); that is, goods have an intrinsic value that is unrelated both to the way in which they are made and to the amount of labour required for their production. The source of a good's value, according to Jevons, lay in the estimation of its worth in the minds of potential consumers. On the very first page of *The Theory of Political Economy*, Jevons identifies that source in the starkest terms imaginable. 'Repeated reflection and inquiry have led me to the somewhat novel opinion', he writes, 'that *value depends entirely upon utility*' (1970 [1871]: 77). In other words, value results from the moment of consumption.

For Jevons, the moment of consumption was amenable to study using scientific principles. According to Collison Black, Jevons was 'thorough-going' in his adoption of Benthamite utilitarianism (Black 1970: 30), and his analysis of the moment of consumption was no exception. Jevons states that the task of economic enquiry is that of 'tracing out the mechanics of self-interest and utility' (Jevons 1970 [1871]: 50), which allows economic theory to be 'entirely based on a calculus of pleasure and pain' (1970 [1871]: 91). For Jevons, pleasure and pain – or utility and disutility – are quantities. By adding our total pleasures together and then subtracting our total pains, we are left with a resultant that determines whether our overall experience will be pleasurable (net positive utility) or painful (net negative utility). He treats it simply as a matter of human nature that, 'Our object will always be to maximise the resulting sum in the direction of pleasure' (1970 [1871]: 97).

Moreover, the pleasure of which Jevons writes is purely economic, deriving solely from the consumption of goods. Jevons does not deny either that we are moral beings or that we experience feelings of self-worth from acting morally. He distinguishes moral acts, which relate to a 'higher motive', from purely self-interested and utility-maximizing acts, which relate to a 'lower motive'. In contrast to his classical forebears, however, Jevons believed it to be improper for economic analysis to be concerned with the 'higher motives' of life within society: 'It is the lowest rank of feelings which we here treat' (1970 [1871]: 93). He justifies this position in the casual remark that, 'when that higher calculus [i.e., ethics] gives no prohibition, we need the lower calculus [i.e., self-interest] to gain us the utmost good in matters of moral indifference' (1970 [1871]: 93). Yet the justification itself involves analytical sleight-of-hand. Jevons reduces economic enquiry to the study of utility-maximizing self-interest simply by treating the ethical dimension of life within society as a constant. Thus was *homo economicus* placed at the forefront of neoclassical theory.

Two related effects follow from Jevons's calculus of pleasure and pain. The first is that Jevons remodels political economy along the lines of a simple cost/benefit analysis. As he puts it, 'we may treat pleasure and pain as positive and negative quantities are treated in algebra' (1970 [1871]: 97). Hence, Jevons's theory relies on a type of mathematical cognition that would not have been possible before the invention of the modern use of the concept of zero some time in the seventeenth century (Kaplan 2000). Second, Jevons turns economic enquiry into a formal mathematical exploration of abstract economic relations. Benthamite utilitarianism offers an acceptable ontological basis for his theory of the economy, precisely because it is 'thoroughly mathematical in the character of the method' (Jevons 1970 [1871]: 82). For Jevons, economics could lay no claim to scientific status unless it adopted the mathematical techniques of the physical sciences (Backhouse 2002: 167–72).

However, Jevons's preference for treating economics as a mathematical science (Jevons 1970 [1871]: 79–81) was not shared by another of the founders of neoclassical economics, Carl Menger. Menger objected to the use of mathematics in economics for exactly the same reason that Jevons advocated it. For both, mathematical methods were appropriate only to understanding the relationship between quantities (Backhouse 2002: 177). Within Jevons's framework, the study of quantifiable relationships *was* economics. For Menger, by contrast, the purpose of economic enquiry was somewhat different. He believed that it should be directed towards understanding and establishing the essence of economic phenomena (Menger 1950 [1871]: 72). Political economy, then, as Menger made clear in a letter to Walras dismissing the mathematical approach, was a qualitative rather than a quantitative endeavour (Blaug 1996: 279).

Menger's opinions about the nature of political economy were informed by the philosophical context within which he framed his ideas. The influence of Bentham is unmistakable in Jevons's work, but Menger's is constructed on Aristotelian themes. The utilitarian consumer in Jevons is driven by wants, for it is through the satisfaction of individual wants that utility can be maximized. However, no such character appears in Menger's work. For Menger, the self-interested pursuit of wants is not the catalyst for economic activity, and the concept of utility plays no role in his theory.

First, Menger dismisses the notion of pure self-interest, suggesting that it can no more exist than can pure oxygen (Backhouse 2002: 177). It is an approximation of a human characteristic rather than one that any human could truly exhibit in actual social circumstances. Second, instead of Jevons's focus on utility, Menger writes of the 'importance of satisfactions' (Menger 1950 [1871]: 58). While for Jevons the utility of a good reflects purely the pleasure that could be received from consuming it, Menger's concept of 'satisfaction' is more broadly defined to include the wider social stimuli that condition action. Third, Menger rejected the proposition that economic activity was directed towards wants (1950 [1871]: 43). He believed that economic activity is initiated in order to prevent needs from remaining unattended. In this respect, while Jevons practised chrematistics, Menger's neoclassical economics, true to his Aristotelian roots, was oikonomic in inspiration (on the distinction between which see Chapter 1).

Taken together, these points are sufficient to confirm that neoclassical economics is anything other than a unified field of study. One issue on which, with hindsight, it is clear that the three founders agreed was the need to move beyond the labour theory of value. Disagreement ensued, however, on where to move to. Jevons attempted to reduce the question of value solely to the utility embodied in the consumption of goods. This had the effect of highlighting the significance of the moment of exchange and the price at which goods were exchanged. While the vast majority of modern economists emphasize the centrality of exchange relations, Menger is a notable exception. His concept of value is not epiphenomenal of the moment of exchange. For Menger, a commodity has value relative to the needs that would be left unmet were that commodity not to be consumed (Landreth and Colander 1994: 220).

For Jevons, economic activity is all about having more; for Menger, it is all about making sure that it is unnecessary to go without. The human agent who is always attempting to have more is very different from the human agent who is attempting to have enough. The intuitive utilitarian psychology of Jevons's agents is compatible with behaviour that is oriented towards ever higher levels of acquisitiveness. However, Menger's agents do not act in this way. They are thoughtful rather than intuitive, reflexive rather than instinctive. Their conduct is prefigured by introspection (Grimmer-Solem and Romani 1999: 343), whereby the decision of how to act is shaped by an awareness of what life would be like were that action not to be undertaken.

Perhaps the only way in which Jevons and Menger can be seen to be part of the same tradition is through their use of the same technique. Jevons's method was mathematical, whereas Menger's took more of a narrative form, but both adopted marginalist techniques. They studied the process through which the fixed supplies of a finite economy were allocated between competing ends (Landreth and Colander 1994: 230). From such studies, both concluded that the allocation problem has only truly been resolved if a 'maximum solution' is apparent, and this in turn occurs 'if and only if the process of transferring a unit of the dividend to a single use among all the possible uses is subject to diminishing results' (Blaug 1996: 280). Jevons's agents attempt to maximize utility, whereas Menger's agents attempt to maximize the needs that they are able to satisfy. In both cases, this implies a particular distribution of a given level of income. In the former, it implies that resources are allocated such that the marginal utility of the purchases made using each unit of income is equal. In the latter, it implies that resources are allocated such that the marginal satisfaction of need of the purchases made using each unit of income is equal. Both such cases conform to the neoclassical 'equimarginal principle'. However, for that principle to hold, the initial dividend which is distributed around the economy must be constant. While the classical political economists were interested in the dynamics of economic growth, the founders of the neoclassical tradition assumed that the parameters of the economic system were fixed.

The work of Léon Walras is also situated within an essentially static framework. He too used marginalist techniques, but for a still different purpose. Jevons applied marginal analysis to the way in which consumers' decisions influenced demand. Menger applied marginal analysis to both the demand and the supply side of the economy. Walras did likewise, but merely as a means to formulate a general equilibrium model. As Landreth and Colander note, 'Jevons and Menger looked for simple lines of causation; Walras saw the interconnectedness of all economic variables' (Landreth and Colander 1994: 211).

Walras's concern for stipulating the conditions of general equilibrium, in which all markets are simultaneously in a position where supply matches demand, is self-consciously presented as little more than a thought experiment. In the preface to his *Elements of Pure Economics*, he goes to great lengths to draw his readers' attention to the imaginary nature of his system. He self-deprecatingly refers to the founding assumption on which it is based as 'this fiction', which he then proceeds to carry 'through the remainder of the book' (Walras 1984 [1954]: 37).

As evidence of the purely hypothetical system with which he operates, Walras exorcizes all disequilibrium transactions and production from his analytical framework in the fourth edition of the *Elements*, now generally considered to be his definitive statement. Menger may well have argued that the limits of individual knowledge were such that it was imprudent to assume that any actual market could ever be in equilibrium (Backhouse 2002: 176). However, this supposition was of no consequence to Walras. Walras *had* to assume that the natural tendency of all markets was towards equilibrium, so that his mathematical exposition of idealized economic conditions could retain not only its purity, but its very validity (Walker 1987: 767; Ackerman 2002: 122–3). Any recognition of the existence of disequilibrium trading – for Menger, the whole basis of everyday economic life – corrupts the clarity and the precision of the mathematical model (Bridel and Huck 2002: 521).

In order to allow his economic system to operate in the manner prescribed by his mathematical equations, Walras introduces a process that is equivalent to having an economy-wide auctioneer to coordinate all demand and supply activity. The auctioneer construction is clearly a deus ex machina, designed specifically to guarantee the simultaneous derivation of prices for all commodities within the economy. Were the process of price formation sequential rather than simultaneous, this would entail disequilibrium trading; but this is ruled out by assumption.

The auctioneer is able to fulfil the tasks set because Walras assumes a basic homogeneity to the agents who constitute the economic system that the auctioneer regulates (Walras 1984 [1954]: 78). All agents must respond in the same way to the same price signal cried by the auctioneer, otherwise the simultaneous derivation of prices for all commodities is impossible. Walras's work consequently sets the context for the modern microeconomic assumption that the independent choices of all individuals can be reduced to the choice of a representative individual (Kirman 1992). As Steve Keen suggests, the Walrasian system thus allows for the study of only a single person (Keen 2001). Insofar as political economy is the analysis of the social interactions through which the economic system forms, the society that creates the context for these interactions is populated by only one individual.

The representative individual approach to political economy relies on that individual displaying inherent omniscience. In the absence of such capacities, general equilibrium could not be sustained, because the representative individual would not have the ability to compute the optimal response to the price signals cried by the auctioneer. Walras explains the means through which such computations take place using his concept of 'rareté' (Walras 1984 [1954]: 143–9). The significance of 'rareté' is derived from the contextual assumption of scarcity in which it is set, which in turn Walras adopted from the work of his economist father, Auguste. The Walrasian framework bears none of the Benthamite underpinnings of Jevons's *Theory of Political Economy*, in which the value of a commodity depends solely on the utility that can be obtained from consuming it. For Walras, by contrast, value reflects scarcity (Backhouse 2002: 170). Scarcity is a quantifiable concept, according to Walras, made manifest in 'the intensity of the last want satisfied by any given quantity consumed of a commodity' (Walras 1984 [1954]: 119). It is this intensity that Walras termed 'rareté'. In later editions of the *Elements*, Walras was content to follow Jevons in talking about 'maximum utility' (1984 [1954]: 115–31). However, optimizing behaviour designed to elicit such a state first required for the intensity of the last want satisfied to be maximized. In this, we see Walras's strict application of the techniques of marginal analysis.

This, perhaps more than anything else, is what the three founders of neoclassical economics have in common. As Terence Hutchison argues, the most important aspect of marginal utility theory, certainly for the originators of the neoclassical approach, was the adjective ('marginal') rather than the noun ('utility': see Hutchison 1994: 127–39). This insight may have been lost somewhat, both in the way that the history of economic thought has been typically presented and in the way that economics has developed subsequently as a discipline. From the end of the Second World War onwards, utility theory has tended to take centre stage in economics (Amadae 2003). Jevons, Menger and Walras all assumed that the essence of economic activity was maximizing behaviour, but the idea that individuals were specifically maximizing *utility* played only a peripheral role in their respective theoretical systems. It is a feature of later developments within modern economic thought to equate all forms of economic activity with utility-maximizing behaviour. It is this equation which I argue has been incorporated, however inadvertently, into the core of IPE. As such, it is to this that I turn in the following section.

The limits of utility-maximizing theory

Much has been made of the tendency for neoclassical economists to privilege the mathematical elegance of their models over the economic meaning that can be derived from them (see, for instance, Eichner 1983). Nowhere is this more apparent than in relation to the concept on which later developments in the history of modern economic thought are based: that of utility. As Joan Robinson contends, 'Utility is a metaphysical concept of impregnable circularity; utility is the quality in commodities that makes individuals want to buy them, and the fact that individuals want to buy commodities shows that they have utility' (Robinson 1964: 48). The concept of utility therefore has no intrinsic *economic* meaning. It cannot explain why individuals prefer particular courses of action to others, at least not in a way that highlights the economic logic underlying the behavioural decisions.

At most, utility theory can offer a post hoc rationalization of why a certain event occurred, but even this requires an analytical trick that questions the rigour of the whole approach. Today, most economists conceptualize the moment of exchange through the perspective of Paul Samuelson's theory of 'revealed preference' (Blaug 1996: 290). It is only once a preference has been revealed that they read back into the action utility-maximizing behaviour. Given the assumption that all behaviour is utility-maximizing, any preference revealed through action must be utility-maximizing *by definition*, because any action that did not maximize utility would not have been preferred. Nothing of any real significance can be learnt about the economy from this perspective. However, utility theory has survived within economics because it leads to mathematically tractable models (Mayer 1993).

It is also frequently claimed that utility theory has survived within economics because it leads to a view of the world that is consistent with the general trajectory of contemporary world politics. This argument is commonly voiced by those who position themselves at the critical edge of IPE (see, for instance, Gill 1994). Neoclassical economics is held by many to be a constraint on the development of a progressive political mindset. However, this explanation of the persistence of utility theory is less convincing than that which focuses on the ease with which utility theory provides tractable mathematical models. Neoclassical economics is much better viewed as a technique (relating to the application of marginal analysis) than as a normative statement (relating to the reproduction of inequalities through a non-interventionist stance on matters of policy). Indeed, as Mark Blaug argues, 'The nomenclature of utility and disutility... leads one immediately to ask whether a free enterprise system represents such a use of resources in satisfying wants as to insure society the greatest surplus of utility over disutility' (Blaug 1996: 286). Joan Robinson is willing to go still further. She suggests that utility theory 'points to egalitarian principles' and, in particular, provides the justification 'to interfere with an economic system that allows so much of the good juice of utility to evaporate out of commodities by distributing them unequally' (Robinson 1964: 53). Her conclusion rests somewhat uneasily alongside the rather different reading of the ideology of neoclassical economics that dominates today, since she insists that utility theory 'seems to be heading straight for egalitarianism of the most uncompromising kind' (1964: 66).

There is no a priori reason why the marginalist techniques of neoclassical economics should not be put to use for progressive political purposes. Arguably the finest intellectual achievement of the second generation of neoclassical scholars was Vilfredo Pareto's specification of the conditions of welfare maximization (Pareto 1972 [1906]). However, Pareto's welfare conclusions apply equally within the institutional framework of a pure collectivist economy as within the institutional framework of perfect competition (Amadae 2003: 241). Pareto used these results to become an important advocate of social reform (Worswick 1972: 75).

Moreover, in this respect, he was merely building upon the work of the founders of neoclassical economics, all three of whom were reformers, albeit to different degrees. The instinct towards social reform is most apparent in the work of Walras. The subtitle of Walras's *Elements of Pure Economics* is 'The Theory of Social Wealth' and, taking Walras's own reflections on this issue as their starting point, others have extended the Walrasian system to create a theory of *socialized* wealth. Oskar Lange and Fred Taylor's *Economic Theory of Socialism* used a general equilibrium framework to study allocation questions under socialist production (Lange and Taylor 1938), while Maurice Dobb's *Political Economy and Capitalism* used Walrasian mathematical equations to present a Marxist critique of economic theories that assume perfect competition (Dobb 1937). The Austrian followers of Menger may well have championed an unregulated and decentralized exchange economy (Hayek 1944; Mises 1949 [1940]), but this in most instances was merely a response to the socialist appropriation of Walrasian theory. Walras himself was happy to be identified as a socialist, and his views on the desirability of socializing the return to land through the imposition of punitive taxes on rent was very much in line with the socialism of his times (Backhouse 2002: 171–2).

From the foregoing it appears prudent to accept Mark Blaug's conclusion that utility theory, and the marginalist techniques on which utility theory is grounded, are 'ideologically neutral' (Blaug 1996: 256). There may still be good reasons to guard against the incorporation of neoclassical themes into the core of IPE, but these reasons are not due to the alleged conservative bias of neoclassical theory. Instead, they relate to the crudely attenuated view of human agency on which that theory is based. As such, it is to the ontological underpinnings of neoclassical economics that I turn now in order to conclude the chapter.

The entire edifice of neoclassical economics is constructed on the ontological assumption of rational action. As Nobel Laureate Amartya Sen has pointed out, however, this assumption, on its own, tells us next to nothing. If revealed preferences show consistent behaviour under post hoc examination, this must be deemed 'rational' behaviour, irrespective of its content (Sen 1977: 322–3). Within later neoclassical theory, revealed preferences equate with utility-maximizing action *by definition*. Therefore, any behaviour that is consistent must be consistently utility-maximizing. In turn, and once again by definition, it must also be rational.

In order to lend substance to what, in effect, is no more than a tautology, neoclassical economists tend to add the further assumption that behaviour is *instrumentally* rational. In other words, it is purely self-serving. No concern is given to distinguish between instrumental rationality (doing what one wants to do) and deontological rationality (doing what one considers ought to be done; on which distinction, see Davis 2002). As a consequence, society disappears from neoclassical theory (Mirowski 2002); social circumstance is not thought to be a conditioning factor on behaviour (McCormick 1997).

Were it to be, an individual could not be expected to act without regard for considerations of what he or she ought to be doing. Changing social circumstances tend to change the climate of opinion about what ought to be done. This means that a deontologically rational individual is likely, over time, to infringe the consistency criterion for rational action that forms the very basis of neoclassical theory. In order to preserve the integrity of that theory, it *has* to be assumed that individual choice – indeed, the whole of human agency – is unaffected by prevailing social conditions. As Sen suggests, however:

> A person thus described may be 'rational' in the limited sense of revealing no inconsistencies in his choice behaviour, but if he has no use for these distinctions between quite different concepts [of social circumstance], he must be a bit of a fool. The *purely* economic man is indeed close to being a social moron. (Sen 1977: 336)

The corollary of Sen's social moron is an individual who has an instinctive grasp for computing the algorithms that are necessary to determine global cost/benefit equations. Leaving aside the obviously unfeasible nature of such instincts, this also implies an elision between the capacity to reason and the demands for instrumentally calculative reasoning. According to Peter Winch, western anthropologists have falsely conflated intelligibility (as the means through which we reason) and instrumental rationality (as a form of reasoning: P. Winch 1972). As a consequence, all those who relate to their social surroundings using cognitive processes other than instrumental rationality tend to be grouped together under the heading 'irrational' (Fay 1996: 92). However, the notion of intelligibility is neither a fixed nor a universal concept. Different groups of people will reason in different ways and will display different forms of intelligibility, depending on the traditions of the societies of which they are a part.

It is not enough to attribute all seemingly 'irrational' acts to mistakes committed by the individual undertaking the act (Pettit 1978). This is merely to engage in ethnocentric analysis, assuming that all those who do not bear the same behavioural characteristics as 'we' do are somehow less rational than 'us'. It may well be the case, as Winch suggests, that instrumentally rational activities reflect patterns of integration into an industrial form of life, which demands that control is exercised over the imagination in order to enhance the efficiency of systems of work (P. Winch 1972). However, not all feasible forms of social organization require such demands. It is therefore necessary to move beyond the assumption that those who are integrated into forms of economic life at odds with advanced industrial capitalism are somehow 'irrational'. It is necessary instead to understand the social basis of different forms of rationality.

This point is completely lost within modern neoclassical economics, but it is nonetheless essential for understanding the economy. There are important differences between learned and innate patterns of behaviour. Neoclassical economics, in its predilections for instinctive optimizing behaviour, completely ignores the learning processes through which actual conduct is formed. Behaviour is shaped by the fact that social interactions take place repeatedly. As a result of this, individuals tend to adapt their behaviour on the basis of the prior experience of watching others respond to their conduct (Fehr and Falk 2002: 28). Whatever dispositions we have are socialized into us (Dupré 2003: 130–44). Habits are acquired through the process of acting in irreducibly social contexts.

Moreover, there is a long history of studying the dynamics of socialization within political economy. On the very first page of *The Wealth of Nations*, Adam Smith outlines the operation of a modern pin factory in order to demonstrate the advances in productivity that follow from institutionalizing a division of labour (Smith 1970 [1776]: 119). This example relates to the acquisition of habits of work through socialization, but it is not just in relation to work practices that political economists have highlighted the significance of habituated action: as with the pin factory in Smith's division of labour, so too with consumption (Veblen's 'conspicuous consumers') and investment (Keynes's 'animal spirits'). It may not be an exaggeration to say that all political economy, at least that which is untainted by neoclassical assumptions about the human agent, is focused on the socialization process.

Three important points follow from such a focus. First, and perhaps most obviously, it liberates the study of the economy from the mathematical method. Socialization processes are simply too contingent to be collapsed into the rigid formalism of mathematical equations. Causal connections framed by mathematical logic acquire a sense of necessity. As Martin Hollis explains, 'Mathematical truths have the interesting feature that they not only *are* true but *could not possibly* be false' (Hollis 1994: 35). However, there is nothing necessary about the constitution of economic relations, which rather reflect the underlying balance of power within society at a particular moment of time. As such, mathematical equations can tell us little, perhaps even nothing, about the way in which socialization pressures lead us either to conform with or contest the balance of power within society.

Second, by focusing on socialization processes it is possible to move beyond the neoclassical conflation of individual and group behaviour, whereby the group takes on the characteristics of the representative individual (on which see Kirman 1992). John Davis draws an important distinction between 'we' language and 'I' language – what 'we' want, what is important to 'us', etc., versus what 'I' choose, 'my' beliefs, etc. – before saying that 'the philosophical explanation of intentionality has been almost entirely associated with the explanation of individual intentions associated with the use of "I" language' (Davis 2002: 11). Neoclassical economics offers an obvious example of such a tendency. However, if we accept the existential premise that the economic phenomena we wish to explain arise from social interactions (Oakley 2002: 191), we must treat individuals as being socially embedded within groups. As a consequence, we can say with a degree of certainty that purely instrumental rationality is unlikely ever to be the sole motivation for economic activity.

Third, by focusing on socialization processes it is possible to highlight the difference between, on the one hand, having a reason to act and, on the other hand, the reason that leads to action. The former refers to a psychological state, whereas the latter refers to the content of such a state (Fay 1996: 96). An individual can *have* a reason to act in a particular way, but the *reason* that they may or may not act in this way is more complex than simply possessing the corresponding psychological state in the first place. My argument in this book is that neoclassical economics focuses solely on thinking through the logical propositions associated with a particular psychological state: that of utility-maximization. It does not focus on understanding actual economic activities that may or may not reflect such a state. In other words, neoclassical theory provides arguments about having a reason for action, rather than attempting to explain why people act in particular ways in particular circumstances. Moreover, reasons in themselves cannot explain the actual actions. It is only possible to begin explaining actions once the social context in which the reason takes shape has first been understood.

Conclusion

The foundations of International Political Economy must reflect an underlying ontology that acknowledges the social basis of all economic activity. Robinson Crusoe consequently constitutes a poor description of the typical economic agent. However, it is Robinson Crusoe who provides the model individual within neoclassical economics (Tabb 1999: 27–30). For neoclassical economics, the agent is literally '"a man", a Robinson Crusoe, an individual with his tight, impermeable, insulated equipment of desires and tastes' (Robinson 1964: 51). Yet to be Robinson Crusoe is, in an important sense, to be beyond society. It is to exist in a solitary state, in which neither the formal rules nor the informal norms of social engagement apply. As such, there are no socially regulated constraints on individual behaviour.

It should go without saying that this strict asociality is not evident in the economic circumstances in which we are called upon to act in everyday life. The economy is not, and never can be, experienced in isolation from the experiences of other people. As soon as we recognize the significance of other people to the process through which we meet our economic needs, it is impossible not to be struck by the fact that these other people also have needs. All economic relations imply mutual dependence between individuals. In such circumstances, economic activities cannot be modelled convincingly on the basis of an individual acting alone.

The task for IPE is to understand the way in which routinized forms of behaviour are situated within individuals' tacit knowledge of the world and, in particular, within their tacit knowledge of the rules, norms and conventions through which society is institutionalized (Lawson 1997). The assumption of instrumentally rational utility-maximizing behaviour is clearly not suited to this task. Nobody other than a contemporary Robinson Crusoe could bear such behavioural characteristics. Only a purely isolated individual, devoid of all social stimuli, could have no basis for action other than their own preferences (Davis 2002: 19–20). Those working within IPE must therefore be cautioned against incorporating the assumption of utility-maximizing behaviour into their analyses, as it is clear just how restricted the circumstances are in which that assumption holds. Instrumentally rational behaviour is at one extreme of all possible types of human conduct, and it captures only a fraction of the essence of our everyday economic activities. It speaks of a world in which duties, obligations and the moral requirement to exercise self-restraint do not apply. In order to speak of any other world, the assumption of utility-maximizing behaviour must be rejected, and alternative foundations for IPE must be put in place.

Chapters 4–6 concentrate on this latter undertaking. Before that, however, I deepen the general case for providing IPE with foundations that are drawn from the classical tradition of political economy. My aim is to show that, although the classical tradition is a broad church in terms of competing theoretical perspectives, it proceeds from a united position on basic ontological questions. In particular, there is consensus on the important issue of what it is in the relationship between the individual and the economy that should be the focus of study for political economists. For those working within the classical tradition, the economy is not a system that runs to its own internal logic, in some sense beyond the sphere of human agency. In other words, the individual matters. Moreover, these authors operate with a conception of the individual that is markedly different to that of neoclassical economics. The individual is socially constituted and, as such, makes decisions that are contingent upon the precise characteristics of the socio-economic relationships in which they are involved. It is to this classical conception of the relationship between the individual and the economy that I now turn.

Chapter 3

The Classical Tradition of Political Economy: New Foundations for IPE

Introduction

The term 'classical political economy' has something of a chequered history. In this book, I draw positive associations from the term. To me, to invoke the work of the classical political economists is to invoke a style of analysis which was all-too-hastily discarded by the economics profession, and which still has much to offer to the community of IPE scholars. As was argued in the previous chapter, the systematic neglect of the style of analysis of the classical tradition is to the detriment of the political economy that tends to find its way into the pages of IPE books.

However, the term 'classical political economy' has not always had positive associations attached to it. The term was first coined by Marx, and in a derogatory sense at that, to describe the tendency towards logical deduction to be found in the economic theories of David Ricardo and James Mill (see Mill 1826; Ricardo 2002 [1821]). Keynes also used the term in a derogatory sense, to argue that the tendency towards logical deduction still dominated economics and, as a consequence, was still holding it back at the time at which he wrote *The General Theory* in 1936 (Keynes 1997 [1936]). Keynes attributes responsibility to Francis Edgeworth, Alfred Marshall and Arthur Pigou, each of whom was a standard bearer for the economics profession in the early decades of the twentieth century, for deepening the grip of Ricardian methodology on economics (see Edgeworth 1881; Marshall 1920; Pigou 1920). He imposes the label 'classical' upon the work of all of these authors, but they are classicists only in the sense of having followed Ricardo's methodological preference for logical deduction.

Fortunately for my argument, the antipathy of Marx and Keynes towards Ricardian methodology does nothing to undermine the position being developed in this book. Indeed, in the sense to which I appeal to a classical tradition, both Marx and Keynes can be counted as classical political economists. It is true that the classical political economists were divided over the relative importance of logical deduction versus inductive theory building based on direct observation. However, this dispute does not concern me here. Much more important for current purposes is that the classical political economists shared a common ontology. They agreed on what the economy was, as well as on what it was about the economy that warranted study from a social scientific perspective. It is on basic ontological propositions that the classical political economists are united, and it is this that recommends the classical tradition as a suitable basis for IPE, despite differences within that tradition on how best to develop specific economic theories.

Even though each of the classical political economists attempted to develop abstract theories of the economy, none lost sight of what it was, exactly, that they were trying to theorize. Abstract principles of economic development tend to treat 'the economy' as a system that operates to its own internal logic. While the classical political economists may have disagreed on the precise specification of such a logic, each knew better than to present that logic as self-generating and self-sustaining. It is not an entity that exists beyond the sphere of the social relations which serve to sustain it. As such, to whatever extent that we are able to point to an underlying economic logic, such a logic relates solely and exclusively to the social conditions from which it originates. 'The economy' has no identity of its own; it exists only as a manifestation of the prevailing pattern of economic relations (on which point, see Chapter 1). To think in terms of 'the economy' per se threatens to reify a particular theory of economic relations, rather than trying to identify the specific factors that lead us to observe such relations.

Such reification was not an error that the classical political economists were willing to commit. At all times, they attempted to understand the economy as a social process, involving individuals who bear the full range of human characteristics, besides those that are associated with the purely 'economic' act of utility maximization.

Their focus was on the manner of these sentient beings' incorporation into the prevailing pattern of economic relations, such that 'the economy' could appear to operate on the basis of a series of abstract principles. Such incorporation was studied as a social process, rather than simply as serving the needs of the economic system.

This is the style of analysis to which I suggest we turn if we are to place IPE on true political economy foundations. To demonstrate what I mean by this, the chapter proceeds in four stages. In the first section, I investigate in more detail the underlying ontology of the classical tradition, showing in particular how this was consistent with important broader shifts in the whole nature of scientific explanations in the second half of the eighteenth century. I then move on to examine how the ontology of the classical tradition translated into a theory of the economy. In the second section, I show that the role of the pure economic theorist is only one of three adopted by those who work within the classical tradition. It was important for the classical political economists that economic theory shed light on the abstract workings of the economy, but it was equally important that theory provide both a platform for programmatic reform and a vision of the good society. In the third and fourth sections, I move from the general to the particular. I move from arguing that contemporary IPE theorists have much to gain from adopting the general style of analysis of the classical political economists, in order to develop a particular position which is consistent with the classical tradition and which can be used within IPE today. In the third section, I outline two possible ways of using classical political economy as the foundation for IPE, one based on the work of Keynes and the other on the work of Marx. However, neither of these represents the alternative that I endorse in the remainder of the book, which provides the content of the next section. My favoured approach is a synthesis of the insights of three classical political economists: Adam Smith, Thorstein Veblen and Karl Polanyi.

The ontology of classical political economy

The aim of the classical political economists was to study economic and social problems from the broadest possible perspective. In this way, the audience they sought to address consisted of more than merely the scholarly community. They made a conscious effort to write in a manner that made their work accessible to the intelligent lay reader (Hunter and Muscatelli 1997). In this respect, I am reminded of a much more recent intervention into the IPE debate by Roger Tooze and Craig Murphy. They note with concern how the use of abstract theoretical language within IPE acts in a gatekeeping role to limit the number of participants in the discussion to those with suitable training in that language. 'Much writing in IPE', they comment, 'contains powerful rhetorical moves that often succeed in silencing other views, groups, and arguments' (Tooze and Murphy 1996: 697). In the place of such deliberate acts of exclusion, they advocate a 'democratic' dimension to studies of economic relations, whereby the thoughts of scholars are presented in a language that the widest number of people possible can comprehend. This is a standard to which the work of the classical political economists most definitely conformed.

What can be seen initially in the writing of Adam Smith, and subsequently in that of those who followed in the classical tradition, was a concern to understand real processes and problems, and to do so in a way that allowed readers to connect their own experiences to those processes and problems. Smith, in particular, advocated a plain style of communication, whereby to read an author's work is immediately to develop a familiarity with the world that they are describing (Brown 1994). He believed that the popular reception of scholarly work contributed significantly to its future course (Skinner 1979: 25). As such, for a theory to be successful and gain longevity, it had to talk about the world in terms that its audience could readily relate to.

Economic theory was no different in this respect. In order to be successful, it had to be attentive to the importance of language, not just as a means of expressing abstract ideas, but also as a means of capturing the essence of the human experience of economic relations. As a consequence, Smith's understanding of the economy was set within the context of 'polyhistoric knowledge', in which economics per se 'was only a part' (Schumpeter 1994 [1954]: 182). Smith's domain covered human nature, history and social psychology, for these were the elements that directed philosophical enquiries into the relationship between the economy and society (Heilbroner 1986: 1). In his position as founder of the classical tradition of political economy, Smith established a style of analysis in which the aim was to understand the philosophy of social organization. To do this, he looked first at the individual, because it was within the complex constitution of the individual that he identified the mechanism that held society together (Heilbroner 2000: 53). Much, however, has changed in this respect, as modern economists have increasingly been content to work with an asocial conception of the individual and, as such, an asocial conception of economic relations. As Amartya Sen, the Nobel Laureate in Economics, has lamented: 'The narrowing of the broad Smithian view of human beings . . . can be seen as one of the major deficiencies of contemporary economic theory' (Sen 1987: 28).

The classical tradition, which has its origins in Smith, is therefore more an approach to theorizing, plus an approach to the relationship between theory and everyday political issues, than it is agreement on the content of theory. In contrast to the closed system approach of modern economics, whereby the economy is treated as an independent and autonomous aspect of the social world, the classical political economists worked with an open system, whereby they considered economic relations to be co-constituted with other social relations (Hunter and Muscatelli 1997). Whenever it was appropriate they linked economic analysis to other types of thinking and, in addition, their economic analysis reflected contemporary developments in scientific explanations more generally.

Looking back, an epistemological shift is evident in the natural sciences in the second half of the eighteenth century (Jacob 1993). Before that time, progress in scientific knowledge proceeded through the ever more intensive and elaborate classification of visible phenomena. After that time, however, the focus changed, such that an increasing amount of scientific endeavour was devoted to trying to understand the hidden order of organization that binds nature together. While the human senses are only capable, in the first instance, of comprehending the immediacy of surface appearances, increasingly scientific attention turned to specifying the abstract relationships that rendered these surface appearances more than merely isolated events, but as elements of an integrated system of life. As Michel Foucault has shown, the political economy of Adam Smith and, as such, that of the classical tradition more generally, is a reflection of broader shifts in scientific discourse at the time at which he was writing. In particular, it reflects the greater emphasis that came to be placed on 'invisible' relationships, which can be assumed to exist between abstract categories, and which can also be shown to have logical implications for life within the real world. In Foucault's terms, the development of theory within the classical tradition of political economy was based upon 'a principle of order' (Foucault 1989).

This, of course, is a very different sense of 'order' from that which currently underpins much of IPE (on which see Chapter 1). From a perspective that treats IPE as a sub-field of International Relations, the question of order focuses on the political interventions that are necessary to institutionalize stability at the heart of the international economy. By re-rooting IPE within the classical tradition of political economy, however, the question of order takes on a different complexion. From this latter perspective, the search for order is a theoretical preoccupation. It is about specifying the logical propositions that allow us to understand how the economic relations we experience are constitutive of 'the economy' as a whole. That is, the classical political economists attempted to explain how a multitude of economic relations fitted together and cohered into the apparent experience of a single social system.

To do this, the classical political economists followed Smith in arguing that their endeavours, as with scientific explanation more generally, could not be reduced solely to the study of visible interdependencies (Smith 1980). Their aim was to uncover the hidden structures of coordination which allowed them to create theoretical models of economic relations. As Stefano Fiori has suggested, the visible and the invisible are integrated at the theoretical level on the assumption that the elements of the visible universe, taken on their own, cannot constitute an autonomous economic discourse. At the same time, it cannot be assumed that the purely abstract elements of the invisible universe have an independent meaning beyond their connection with their visible counterparts (Fiori 2001: 430).

As such, the classical political economists wrote grounded theory, insofar as their abstract concepts related directly to everyday economic experiences. The abstract concepts, which lay beyond the realm of immediate sensory perception, have explanatory content, precisely because they speak so clearly of actual experiences. Indeed, for Smith, the visible universe could not be explained solely through reference to itself. Instead, it could only be explained through appeal to an invisible universe which ties together our immediate sensory perceptions, and thus renders them meaningful in relation to one another.

According to the classical political economists, our immediate sensory perceptions of the economy are condensed into three sets of social relations. In the abstract, these are relations of production, relations of distribution and relations of exchange. These three sets of social relations constitute the underlying ontology of the economy.

1. Starting with the relations of production, the classical political economists treated production as a fundamentally social activity, which involves the incorporation of individuals into broader patterns of human interactions. The results of those interactions are goods, which are saleable assets to be traded within the economy. The satisfaction of all provisioning needs within society relies, in the first instance, on the organization of production relations such that essential provisions are made available. Following the classical tradition, the production relation is understood as the relationship between the individual and the social institution of production (see Chapter 7). The individual is central to the activation of the production process, albeit not by acting alone. Individuals act in concert to create the goods that circulate around the economy and, as with all social institutions, these actions are regulated by a combination of formal rules (such as labour law) and informal norms (such as those relating to corporate governance).

2. The relations of distribution reflect the underlying political character of the economy by determining who gets what as the reward for their contribution to the productive process. As such, the relations of distribution condition the precise character of the provisioning that takes place within the economy. In particular, they determine whether the dominant pattern of provisioning is oriented towards the wants of the individual or the needs of society. In that sense, it is the relations of distribution which shape the exact balance between the chrematistic and the oikonomic content of economic relations (see Chapter 1). The character of such relations is the outcome of the process of political struggle, as competing social forces seek to harness the economy for their own ends. Those who hold the balance of political power within society tend to be able to harness the authority of the state to embed relations of distribution which operate to their advantage.

3. The relations of exchange govern the conditions under which goods and services circulate within the economy. They

provide a link between the separate activities of production and consumption. In all but the most self-sufficient of economies, the production process is based upon a division of labour, whereby a single product has many producers (see Chapter 4). For basic provisioning needs to be met in such circumstances, an individual's consumption cannot be restricted to what they produce, for the simple reason that they will not be involved in the production of all the necessaries of life. As a consequence, exchange relations are enacted in order for provisioning needs to be met. The relations of exchange are regulated, on the one hand, by a body of law which establishes the act of exchange on a contractual basis and, on the other hand, by the trust that one party to the exchange has in the other to honour the contract.

While the underlying ontology of classical political economy focuses on the relations of production, distribution and exchange, the ability to theorize all three in a holistic sense rests upon the connection between the economy's 'invisible chains' and the visible interdependencies to which they relate (Smith 1980). The relations of production, distribution and exchange exist in a manner that renders them susceptible to direct observation. However, the task that the classical political economists set themselves was to do more than merely engage in such observations. They also sought to understand the conceptual links between directly observable phenomena, which involved entering a purely abstract world. In the classical tradition, knowledge of the economy was a combination of empirical knowledge drawn from the real world and theoretical knowledge drawn from this abstract world.

Writing specifically about the work of Adam Smith, but in a comment that applies equally to the classical tradition as a whole, Knud Haakonssen labels these two forms of knowledge 'concrete knowledge' and 'system knowledge' (Haakonssen 1989). 'Concrete knowledge' refers to all those things that we can know about observable phenomena. By contrast, 'system knowledge' refers to all those things that we assume we know, but which are derived solely from our commitments to particular theories about how the world might work. 'System knowledge' is premised upon logical deduction from presumed systemic dynamics, while 'concrete knowledge' provides the means of corroborating the rigour of such deductions. It is 'concrete knowledge' that captures the essence of the human input into the economy, whereas 'system knowledge' is a product of the human mind designed specifically to try to impose coherence onto those inputs. In the following section, I show how the classical political economists combined 'concrete knowledge' and 'system knowledge' in their theories of the economy.

The purpose of theory within the classical tradition of political economy

If the previous section focused on what the classical political economists meant by theorizing the existential conditions of the economy, this section will focus on the classical political economists' view of the *purpose* of theory. It will become clear that much of that purpose is political. This was perhaps stated most frankly by Karl Marx, who famously disparaged those who thought that the objective of theory was merely to understand the world in which we live. For Marx, this was almost entirely to miss the point. He believed instead that one should seek to theorize the existential conditions of the economy as a means of changing them in the name of social progress. Marx was adamant that our knowledge of the economy should be praxiologically based, in that it should provide both the rationale and the impetus for social reform (Marx 1938). The concept of 'praxis' is derived from the Greek, and its literal translation refers to the act of 'doing'. For Marx, then, the purpose of theory was to inspire political activities that altered the material conditions of existence within the economy.

Moreover, in this respect, he should not be seen as being out on his own. Indeed, despite his numerous objections to the *content* of the theories of other classical political economists, on the question of the *purpose* of theory Marx was very much in the mainstream of the classical tradition. The idea that theoretical knowledge was an important constituent of attempts to change the world has been an established part of the classical tradition ever since its inception in the writings of Adam Smith.

Taking Robert Cox's distinction between problem-solving and critical theory as the standard reference for discussions of the purpose of theory within contemporary IPE (Cox 1981), it is clear that the classical political economists can be thought of as forerunners of contemporary critical theorists. For those engaged solely at the level of problem-solving, theory begins from the initial premise of taking the world as given. From this perspective, the task of the theorist is to understand how systemic disturbances can be resolved so as to restore the status quo ante. In this sense, much of the work that treats IPE as a sub-field of International Relations is problem-solving in its underlying orientation. At the very least, it tends to understand the need to preserve the stability of the existing order as the *raison d'être* of theory (see Chapter 1). For those engaged at the level of critical theory, however, a different set of priorities becomes evident. Critical theorists attempt to transcend the context in which they are located, on the assumption that this context is historically contingent and arises only because of the dominance of a particular combination of ideas and power relationships. The task of the critical theorist is to uncover the specificity of such dominance, in the hope of rendering it a merely temporary feature of the world by undermining the institutional supports that serve to sustain it (see Chapters 4–6). The purpose of critical theory is to highlight potentially feasible political strategies that, if enacted, would subject historically contingent conditions of existence to pressures for change. This is an ultimate goal that was shared by those working within the classical tradition of political economy.

This much is evident if we look in more depth at the objectives that conditioned the form and function of the theories of the classical political economists. We are helped in this regard by a recent article by Andrew Gamble, who points to the co-existence of three constitutive discourses within classical political economy. These three discourses relate, first, to how the economy is presumed to work; second, to how the economy can be made to work through strategic policy interventions; and, third, how the economy should work if the needs of society are to be met. Gamble refers to these, respectively, as the scientific, practical and normative discourses of classical political economy (Gamble 1995). I now turn to look at each in turn.

Beginning with the scientific discourse of classical political economy, this very much maps onto Haakonssen's notion of 'system knowledge', as discussed in the previous section. The scientific discourse relates to theoretical knowledge that is drawn from an abstract economic system. The aim here is to stipulate a series of internally consistent logical propositions which, when taken together, specify how an ideal-typical economic system operates.

Note, however, what the scientific discourse presupposes. It assumes that it is possible to talk about 'the economy' as a whole.

This in turn suggests that what is being discussed is an organic entity that has both a life and a logic of its own which exist beyond those of its constitutive elements. This is very different from analysing economic *relations*, whereby it becomes immediately apparent that the subject matter under review is the human interactions that underpin all economic activities. The difference between studying economic relations and 'the economy', then, is the difference between, on the one hand, studying the human basis of economic activities and, on the other hand, studying the coordinating logic that imposes systemic coherence onto those activities (for more on this distinction, see Chapter 1). The scientific discourse of classical political economy favours the latter over the former.

In this respect, the scientific discourse should be understood as pure theory. It is privileged in those moments in which the political economist reflects on what it means to deal solely with questions of an abstract nature, such that attempts are made to advance the intellectual frontiers of the subject field. The goal is to be accepted as the theorists' theorist and, as such, the audience for the scientific discourse tends to be limited to those who share the concern for pure theory.

Had the classical political economists been interested only in the scientific discourse, it would not be possible to sustain the claim that they should be considered as the forerunners of contemporary critical theorists. However, their concerns were always wider than this. A core feature of those concerns was to assess the relative advantages of different policy regimes in an attempt to specify the most appropriate institutional structure for meeting stated policy goals. This is the practical discourse of classical political economy.

The practical discourse is political in the straightforward sense that it relates directly to questions of government intervention. In particular, it tackles the issue of how best to use the policy apparatus that state officials have at their disposal in order to promote and regulate the creation and distribution of wealth. In this way, the practical discourse of classical political economy departs from the scientific discourse, insofar as its subject matter is the human impact of economic relations and not the abstract notion of 'the economy' per se.

The practical discourse should therefore be understood as policy prescription. It is privileged in those moments in which the political economist reflects upon how best to apply the lessons to be learned from the scientific discourse to actual economies, rather than to merely hypothetical circumstances. The practical discourse tends to be oriented towards the derivation of an optimal policy solution, which will operate in the interests of society as a whole. As such, it deals explicitly with distributive issues of who gets what and how much. The goal of the political economist when working within the parameters of the practical discourse is to be accepted as an authority on policy. The appeal to be considered in this light is typically directed at governments and other policy officials, but it is important also to have the support of interest groups who can legitimately claim to speak for large sections of society.

Taking the practical discourse in isolation, it appears as if the classical tradition of political economy is problem-solving in its underlying attitude towards the purpose of theory. However, what allows us to view classical political economy as a forerunner of the critical theory approach is the emphasis that is placed on the third discourse, which Gamble calls the normative discourse. To my mind, the scientific and practical discourses are merely a means of providing a rigorous framework in which to introduce the most important arguments to be found within the classical tradition: namely, those that highlight the essentially normative characteristics of the tradition. For the modern economists discussed in Chapter 1, rigour is an end in itself. This was not so, however, for the classical political economists. If there is a hierarchy of the three constitutive discourses of their field of study, then it is one that sees the normative discourse come out on top.

The normative discourse relates to the ideal form of social organization and, as such, the analysis focuses on the particular form of economic relations in evidence within society. Within the terms of the normative discourse, there tends to be no talk of 'the economy' as an abstract system embodying an equally abstract logic. From this perspective, it is always possible to expose the prevailing pattern of economic relations to both political arguments and political pressure for change. Contemporary critical theory perspectives are visible within the classical tradition precisely because of this refusal to take the prevailing pattern of economic relations as a given. Instead, economic relations are viewed as a historically contingent phenomenon (on which point, see Barber 1991: 17–22; Blaug 1996: 1–9; Backhouse 2002: 132–6).

There can be no politically neutral theory of the economy, at least not to the extent that the subject matter of those theories is economic *relations*, because all theories of the economy seek either to affirm the prevailing pattern of economic relations or to challenge it. For instance, the Polanyian critique of modern economics, which will be reviewed in Chapter 6, concentrates on the way in which modern economic theory reifies historically contingent economic relations that adopt a distinctively market form (Polanyi 1982: 50; see also Stanfield 1986: 41–7). Thus, modern economics seeks to affirm a particular pattern of commodified economic relations, whereby ever more aspects of social life are subjected to a logic of commercial exchange, while the Polanyian critique of modern economics seeks to challenge such commodification.

According to Robert Heilbroner, all theories of the economy are underpinned by 'vision and ideology' (Heilbroner 1988: 185). 'Vision' refers to pre-analytical cognitive acts that are essential to the task of initiating theoretical reflection. It is that which produces the first recognition that there is an issue to be explained. However, such recognition is not purely instinctive: it is guided by the way in which the world is understood in the first place. As such, it is framed by the ideological lenses which provide the theorist with the sense of what is important and what is not. Writing specifically about modern theory, Heilbroner states that 'vision and ideology' lie 'behind the veil of economics' (1988). By contrast, there was no such veil in the classical tradition of political economy. The classical political economists' explicit reference to their normative discourse was sufficient to ensure that the belief systems animating their work were always out in the open. Their concerns for specifying the ideal form of social organization led them to speculate about the preferred relationship between economy and society. Moreover, their theories were consciously constituted as a political call-to-arms to enact their image of the preferred relationship in daily life.

Such concerns are by no means alien to all authors working within IPE. Indeed, they correspond directly to a new standard for appraising IPE theory which has recently been advanced by Roger Tooze and Craig Murphy. Tooze and Murphy advocate the development of an 'ameliorative epistemology' (Tooze and Murphy 1996: 696–8): that is, knowledge production within IPE should be oriented towards the promotion of strategies designed specifically to make life better for those who are least advantaged.

This is a recognition that knowledge informs action and that all knowledge production has a preferred course of action embedded within it. From this perspective, there is no such thing as purely problem-solving knowledge in the social sciences, because no social scientific knowledge is simply a descriptive reflection of the way the world is. By contrast, all knowledge is based upon a conception of how the world should be. No matter how submerged such conceptions are, they are always present. As a consequence, all knowledge is directive and, therefore, it contains critical elements. What makes knowledge distinctly ameliorative is that the directive capacity of such knowledge is aimed at alleviating conditions in which basic social provisioning needs cannot be met.

Thus, there is a clear link between Tooze and Murphy's plea for IPE scholars to engage explicitly with an ameliorative epistemology and the oikonomic perspective being developed in this book. The oikonomic perspective developed here provides foundations for IPE which are rooted in forms of knowledge that prioritize the provisioning needs of society over wealth creation for personal advancement. A positive commitment to an ameliorative epistemology leads to exactly the same priorities. These priorities reflect an explicit recognition that the individual lives life within society. The individual is not an isolated atom with given characteristics; rather, the individual is socially formed. The critical dimension of classical political economy emerges from the focus on how best to create social institutions that allow the individual to flourish. By 'flourish', the classical political economists meant not only in an economic sense, but also to develop more broadly as a human being. The scientific, practical and normative discourses of classical political economy come together in this single aim: to promote forms of knowledge about the economy that enable each individual to reach their full human potential.

From the general to a particular case for classical political economy foundations for IPE

The previous sections of this chapter have focused on the general contribution and method of argument of the classical political economists. We can plausibly think in terms of a classical *tradition*, given that there is general agreement on both the underlying ontology of the economy and the underlying purpose of theories of the economy. But this conception of a tradition should not be allowed to disguise the significant disputes that arose between different authors on matters of theory. There have been many seminal individual interventions, a number of which are direct theoretical challenges to one another.

It is therefore necessary to move beyond making the general case for providing IPE with foundations drawn from the classical tradition of political economy, in order to specify exactly what those foundations should be. There are a number of different foundations for IPE that it is possible to construct out of the classical tradition. In the final section of this chapter I turn explicitly to my chosen approach. Before that, I present two alternative 'classical' approaches, one of which has recently begun to make headway in IPE debates, the other having always been present within IPE, albeit somewhat at the margins of mainstream debates. The former is associated with the work of Keynes and the Cambridge economists who followed in his stead; the latter is associated with Marx and the Ricardian themes out of which Marx's distinctive political economy was fashioned. Let me now take these alternative approaches one at a time.

Starting with the 'Keynesian' approach, Keynes's work clearly fits within the classical tradition, insofar as he operates with a fundamentally social conception of the economy. It is economic *relations* that count for Keynes, rather than the economy per se (see, for instance, Robinson 1964). Keynes's political economy is a direct response to the dominant policy-making dilemma of his day and, in this way, his concern was to show how particular policy decisions led to a particular pattern of economic relations and, in turn, to a particular experience of economic life (Keynes 1997 [1936]: 372–84). The experience that drew most of his attention was that of unemployment. Keynes studied the uneven incorporation of the individual into the economy, such that the policy-making process appeared to render some individuals necessary to economic activity but others entirely superfluous to it (Keynes 1937).

In Keynes's writings, it is the policy-making process that creates employment opportunities and, as a logical corollary, it is also the policy-making process that creates unemployment (Keynes 1997 [1936]: 245–54). This very much represented a departure from the received economic wisdom of his day, which depicted the experience of unemployment very much as a voluntary affair. Unemployment, in short, was deemed to be the fault of the unemployed. Following Jevons (see Chapter 2), it was argued that the individual was subjected to the pressure of two contradictory forces. Life was about managing the trade-off between the utility that could be derived from consumption and the disutility that was the necessary artefact of work (Jevons 1970 [1871]: 101–25). From this perspective, unemployment could be seen as a conscious choice to attempt to maximize overall levels of utility by minimizing the disutility from work.

Keynes would have nothing of this line of reasoning, which shifted the responsibility for unemployment from policy-makers to the unemployed themselves. He argued that there were historical reasons for the experience of unemployment, which were rooted in the policy-making process, and which had nothing whatsoever to do with the presumed psychological dispositions of the unemployed (see Stewart 1972: 78–115). He also argued that policy-makers had a duty to change for the better the material conditions of life for the unemployed (see L. Klein 1968: 165–87). In this regard, Keynes's work fulfils two of the criteria posited here for an IPE that replicates the style of analysis of the classical tradition of political economy. First, he develops a historicized theory of the economic relations that lead to the experience of unemployment. Second, he develops a critical theory of that experience, pointing to future economic conditions under which unemployment might be eliminated.

While there is much in this 'Keynesian' perspective that fits the broad conception of IPE that I have in mind, I choose not to construct my favoured 'classical' approach on the basis of Keynes's political economy. The reason for this is primarily ontological. My preferred approach to IPE is one that captures the sense of individual economic agents *in action*. It is also one that emphasizes the constitution of the individual as an autonomous moral being (see Chapter 1). Both of these aspects tend to be underplayed from a 'Keynesian' perspective, because Keynes's theory incorporated a different ontology of economic life. His ontology of the economy is consistent with that of the classical tradition as a whole, in that his work focuses on the significance of economic *relations*, but his ontology of economic *life* differs from the approach that I am advocating. The individual largely disappears from Keynes's work, and is replaced by an analysis of the policy-making context in which individuals find themselves as workers. Keynes's political economy relates to the impact upon economic relations of the technical settings of public policy (Coddington 1983: 24–49), rather than to the constitution of the individual economic agent.

Despite being centred so clearly on the public policy-making process, there is much in the 'Keynesian' perspective that will be of interest for those attempting to construct a classical political economy approach to IPE. My concerns differ from those of neoclassical economists insofar as I attempt to specify the precise historical conditions under which individuals are constituted as moral beings who are predisposed to see themselves as self-interested utility maximizers. By contrast, neoclassical economists take it as given that all individuals necessarily bear those character traits. Keynes's concerns also differ from those of neoclassical economists. Indeed, he famously described the frustrations of attempting to articulate those concerns in the face of the prevailing neoclassical orthodoxy as 'a struggle of escape from habitual modes of thought and expression' (Keynes 1997 [1936]: xii). Yet, instead of seeking to ascertain how individuals could be consciously re-made in the image of *homo economicus* (on which see Williams 1999), in his later work Keynes flatly refused to entertain the possibility that the economic agent could ever take the form of the self-interested utility maximizer. In Chapter 12 of the *General Theory* (Keynes 1997 [1936]: 147–64), Keynes challenges the very notion that the economic agent is imbued with an innate economic rationality (Bellofiore and Silva 1994: 1). As George Shackle puts it, economic activity for Keynes 'is not motivated by calculation and a case made out of data, but is the manifestation of a surge of the restless human spirit' (Shackle 1989: 58). This radically subjectivist account of economic activity (see Robinson 1964; Hicks 1979) has already been picked up on as a potential starting point for a constructivist theory of IPE (Widmaier 2003), and many more applications of this nature are likely to follow.

It was also this subjectivist account of economic activity that Keynes used in his analysis of the policy-making process. He pushed for the state to become actively involved in the management of private sector expectations, in the belief that the state should create a context in which private sector expectations are consistent with the conditions for full employment. Keynes argued that unemployment was caused by inadequate levels of private sector investment and, in his decisive break with neoclassical orthodoxy, he further argued that the decision to invest was merely a matter of the confidence of the investor. He referred to this as the problem of 'animal spirits': if investors lacked confidence in the ability of their investments to secure satisfactory returns, then they lacked the 'animal spirits' to invest, and no amount of good news about economic fundamentals would persuade them to make their capital assets available for productive investments. Whenever 'animal spirits' are deficient, the public policy-making process should be oriented towards instilling investors with the confidence that their investments will pay dividends.

From a 'Keynesian' perspective, then, the state is the dynamic agent that allows the private sector to thrive. A similar conclusion emerges from a 'Marxian' perspective, which represents another possible classical political economy foundation for IPE, where the prosperity of the private sector is also conditional upon the interventions of state officials. Here, however, such interventions are not merely focused on increasing the level of output of the economy; they are constitutive of the very possibility of reproducing the economy in its capitalist form. From a 'Marxian' perspective, the state is required to do nothing less than resolve the contradictions which arise from the capitalist economy, and which threaten to undermine the social conditions of its existence (see, for instance, Poulantzas 1978; Jessop 1990).

As with Keynes and, indeed, as with all of the classical political economists, Marx operates with a fundamentally social conception of the economy (Mészáros 1970). Marx's political economy is framed by his views on the structure of society, which he believed divides into two classes on the basis of the ownership of the means of production. For Marx, the individual was socialized into one of two basic identities depending on their objective class position. There were those who owned the means of production (the bourgeois class) and there were those who were employed within the production process (the proletarian class). Marx's concern was to show how the class structure of society led to a particular pattern of economic relations and, in turn, to a particular experience of economic life (Marx 1973 [1952]).

For Marx, the identity of any particular individual was determined by whether they were socialized into life within the bourgeois class or whether they were socialized into life within the proletarian class. There are social dynamics, then, that serve to reinforce the class divide. However, it is for purely *economic* reasons that the class divide is imbued with fundamental social antagonisms. Such antagonisms result from the accumulation imperative which arises from a technologically progressive economy. Heightened accumulation of capital is necessary to ensure the economic survival of the bourgeois class within an increasingly competitive system (Marx and Engels 1998 [1848]). Competitive impulses emerge from the need to continually modernize the technological base of the production process. Yet this can only be achieved by reserving for re-investment an ever higher proportion of the monetary rewards that accrue from production. As a consequence, fewer rewards can be made available to labourers, even in circumstances in which the accumulation imperative forces ever greater levels of effort onto them.

The class structure, then, which is rooted in the historical development of economic relations under a capitalist mode of production, provides the context for the extraction of surplus value from the proletarian class. For Marx, the task of political economy was to demonstrate that this experience – one of systematic economic exploitation – was a *necessary* feature of the capitalist economy. By showing that a capitalist economy must always create exploitative conditions in order to sustain its very existence, Marx believed that he had developed the rationale for introducing an entirely different system of economic relations. In this regard, his work clearly meets two of the criteria which I believe are essential for an IPE based on the style of analysis of the classical political economists. First, he develops a historicized theory of the economic relations that lead to the experience of exploitation. Second, he develops a critical theory of that experience, insofar as he also talks of a model society of the future in which exploitative economic relations are transcended.

As with Keynes's work, though, while there is much in Marx that is consistent with the type of IPE I am promoting, my preference is not to follow a 'Marxian' perspective. Once again, the reason for this is primarily ontological. In the *Communist Manifesto*, Marx and Engels reveal a theory of human nature that is determined at the level of economic experience. 'Does it require deep intuition', they ask, 'to comprehend that man's ideas, views and conceptions, in one word, man's consciousness, changes with every change in the conditions of his material existence [meaning the relationship between the individual and the means of production]?' (Marx and Engels 1998 [1848]: 58). This leads to a theory of individual action, as outlined in the preface to *Capital*, which is also economically determined. 'My standpoint', Marx admits, 'from which the evolution of the economic formation of society is viewed as a process of natural history, can less than any other make the individual responsible for relations whose creature he socially remains' (Marx 1912 [1867]: 15). It is difficult from this to understand the precise characteristics of the constitution of the individual as an autonomous moral being. The moral essence of the individual tends simply to be read off as a manifestation of their objective class position. Marx's political economy relates to the necessary antagonism that operates between economic agents of different class positions (G. A. Cohen 1978), rather than to the constitution of the individual economic agent.

Despite important ontological differences between my favoured approach and that of Marx, it would be churlish to deny that a significant contribution to IPE debates has already been made by those operating from a 'Marxian' perspective. Much of this follows from an attempt to apply Marx's basic insights about class relations to an international economy exhibiting the traits of uneven development (see, for instance, Wallerstein 1979). In turn, this is rooted in Lenin's observation, made early in the twentieth century, that exploitation within the international economy was not simply a matter of a global bourgeoisie exploiting a global proletariat (Lenin 1988 [1902]). He argued that the experiences of the proletarian class were divided between workers in advanced industrialized economies (the core) and workers in economies at rather different stages of development (the periphery). Lenin showed that governments in the core were able to harness the economic dimensions of their imperial pretensions in order to provide living standards which were of sufficient comfort as to have a politically deradicalizing effect on their own proletarian classes. However, this process of buying the acquiescence of their own workers came at the expense of increasing the exploitation of workers in the periphery.

Much work in IPE continues to be undertaken in line with these same basic themes: from studies of sweatshop working conditions in developing countries, to studies of the worsening terms of trade for agricultural products (exported primarily from the periphery) as against manufactured goods (exported primarily from the core). The only major difference in the contemporary literature is that it is no longer imperial pretensions that act as the catalyst for core/periphery exploitation. Instead, it is the structure of the international economy that results from the regulatory influence of international institutions such as the World Trade Organization, the International Monetary Fund and the World Bank.

Foundations for International Political Economy based on Smith, Veblen and Polanyi

Having acknowledged the possibility of constructing a classical political economy approach to IPE out of the work of Keynes and Marx, but having rejected those alternatives on ontological grounds, I now turn explicitly to my own approach. The following three chapters enable me to develop the case for my chosen approach by introducing the complementary contributions of the three authors whose work underpins my approach: Adam Smith, Thorstein Veblen and Karl Polanyi. Before embarking on that task, however, I conclude this chapter by explaining why I choose these three authors in particular to provide my chosen foundations for IPE.

This perhaps first requires that I state my objectives in as straightforward a manner as possible. My intention in the chapters that follow is to advocate both an IPE that is constructed in the style of the classical tradition in general and also a particular variant of that style. The classical tradition is a broad church which does not reduce to a single approach. As such, the specific approach that I develop in Chapters 4–6 must only be read as being indicative of the classical tradition more generally. The style of analysis of the classical political economists is not synonymous with the single critical synthesis of Smithian, Veblenian and Polanyian ideas developed here. One may choose not to follow my particular approach, then, whilst still accepting my general argument that it is desirable to re-root IPE in the style of analysis of the classical political economists. Table 3.1 attempts to systematize some of the key dimensions of my approach as compared to Keynesian and Marxian alternatives.

My particular approach has its origins in the recognition that many previous attempts have been made to advance heterodox forms of knowledge production within IPE (see, for instance, Burch and Denemark 1997; Gill and Mittelman 1997; Cerny 1999; Underhill 2000). Such attempts may be considered, at one level, to be a direct engagement with Tooze and Murphy's plea for the

TABLE 3.1 *Three classical political economy approaches to IPE*

	Classical approach 1: a 'Smithian' perspective	*Classical approach 2: a 'Keynesian' perspective*	*Classical approach 3: a 'Marxian' perspective*
Draws upon	Adam Smith, Thorstein Veblen, Karl Polanyi	John Maynard Keynes, Joan Robinson, John Kenneth Galbraith	Karl Marx, Vladimir Ilich Lenin, David Ricardo
Key analytical themes	Division of labour; conditions for moral propriety; habits of thought; significance of economic institutions; social embeddedness of economic activity; historical contingency of market relations	Dominance of neoclassical economics; political conservatism of neoclassical economics; relationship between economic theory and economic interest; role of the worker; orientation of public policy; idle resources	Historical dominance of the capitalist mode of production; international division of labour; class analysis; surplus value extraction; alienation of the individual under capitalism; exploitation of workers
Analytical priority	To assess the choices available to the individual economic agent within everyday life	To define the state's regulatory role over economic relations and its influence over public policy-making	To map the historical manifestation of economic class formation under a capitalist mode of production
Notion of the individual	The individual is an ostensibly autonomous moral agent, who must nonetheless accept limits on that autonomy as a condition for living within society	The individual is an input into the economic system, where expected material conditions of life depend on the government's success in getting the technical settings of economic policy correct	The individual is constituted by his or her relationship to the means of production, provided that there is a robust political defence of the existing pattern of economic ownership

TABLE 3.1 *(Continued)*

	Classical approach 1: a 'Smithian' perspective	*Classical approach 2: a 'Keynesian' perspective*	*Classical approach 3: a 'Marxian' perspective*
Status of moral enquiry	Political economy is indistinguishable from other forms of moral enquiry and the task of theory is to explain the constitution of the economic agent as a moral being	Political economy relates to the public policy-making process and, as such, the limits of moral enquiry are to hold the government to account if it enacts economic policies that are harmful to society	Political economy is only moral enquiry insofar as morality is ascribed by the individual's economic position and the focus of theory is to uncover the laws of economic development
Theory of history	History is a contingent process, dependent upon the broad belief systems to which society is mobilized at any particular moment of time	History is a contingent process, dependent upon the institutionalization of a particular style of policy thinking and particular policy outcomes	History is essentially determined, and depends upon the working through of immutable economic logics
Notion of history-makers	History is made by individual economic agents pursuing their everyday lives	History is made by governments and other state officials pursuing their economic policy goals	History is made by the bourgeois and proletarian classes acting out their predestined economic roles
Process of historical change	Follows prior changes in the constitution of the individual as a moral being	Follows prior changes in the dominant policy-making regime	Follows the necessary move through successive modes of production

Theory of political conflict	Conflicts arise within the self, between the choices that the individual wants to make for themselves and the choices they feel they should make for the good of society	Conflicts arise between countries, when the policy choice of one government has a detrimental, 'beggar-thy-neighbour' effect on the policy choices of other governments	Conflicts arise across the class divide, as accumulation imperatives enforce an exploitative relationship between the bourgeoisie and the proletariat
Key works	Adam Smith: *The Theory of Moral Sentiments, An Inquiry into the Nature and Causes of the Wealth of Nations*; Thorstein Veblen: *The Theory of Business Enterprise, The Place of Science in Modern Civilization and Other Essays*; Karl Polanyi: *The Great Transformation*	John Maynard Keynes: *The General Theory of Employment, Interest, and Money*; Joan Robinson: *Economic Philosophy, Economic Heresies: Some Old-Fashioned Questions in Economic Theory*; John Kenneth Galbraith: *The Affluent Society, Economics and the Public Purpose*	Karl Marx: *Grundrisse: Introduction to the Critique of Political Economy, Capital: A Critical Analysis of Capitalist Production, The Communist Manifesto*; Vladimir Ilich Lenin: *What is to be Done?*; David Ricardo: *The Principles of Political Economy and Taxation*

development of an ameliorative epistemology, since they seek to challenge the conception of world order implied by the current orientation of the international economic system. They ask the question, 'Why are the many poor?', and they identify asymmetries of power which enable them to answer that question directly. Yet, at another level, they do so from within an analytical framework that reinforces much of what I consider to be currently wrong with IPE. It is an analytical framework that continues to overlook the political economy roots of IPE, preferring instead to treat IPE merely as a sub-field of International Relations. As a consequence, it is an analytical framework that continues to privilege the interaction between 'states and markets' in the production of world order, while the conceptual categories of both 'state' and 'market' are taken as ontological givens.

My point of departure, then, is not a wholesale rejection of anything that would resemble a critical tradition within contemporary IPE. It is merely to point out that the conceptual basis of such a tradition has yet to be placed firmly upon political economy foundations. To repeat what I believe to be an important issue, which was first outlined in the Introduction, there is no need to deny the presence of much critical commentary within contemporary IPE. However, it is necessary to highlight the limits of the criticism currently in evidence within IPE. These limits are synonymous with a focus purely on the *outcomes* of the interaction between 'states and markets'. Furthermore, as the conceptual categories of both 'state' and 'market' tend to be treated as ontological givens associated with utility-maximizing behaviour, this corresponds to a critique of outcomes generated by the disposition towards utility-maximization.

However, an IPE founded upon the style of analysis of the classical political economists enables us to proceed beyond this level of critique. It also allows us to challenge the *assumption* of utility-maximizing behaviour from first principles. We are therefore provided with a more holistic critique of current economic conditions than if we follow most of IPE, even that which is consciously positioned at the critical edge of the subject field, in working within the confines of such an assumption. As argued in the Introduction, the assumption that economic behaviour maps onto a rational calculus of utility-maximization has been internalized to a greater extent, as well as across a greater cross-section of the subject field, than is commonly acknowledged.

It is worthwhile comparing this position with both the economic ontology of the classical political economists and their conception of the purpose of economic theories, for there is nothing in either that draws a necessary link to the assumption of utility-maximizing behaviour. Indeed, the whole style of analysis of the classical tradition focuses on the social *relations* of the economy, from which perspective it is largely meaningless to think in terms of purely utility-maximizing behaviour. To act in such a manner is to act within the context of a life lived alone, which is directly to contradict the relational character of economic life presupposed within the classical tradition. Moreover, the normative dimension of classical political economy is sufficiently important to suggest that, even if life could be lived alone in the manner of the pure utility-maximizer, this would create an unacceptable level of anomie for the individual. It would also lead to a socially dislocating lifestyle for the individual who was offered nothing but utilitarian contact with other people, hence denying that individual the opportunity to develop fully as a human being.

There are good reasons to think, then, that an IPE whose foundations are located in the classical tradition of political economy would be a more critical subject field. Those reasons begin to look compelling when we unpack the basis of contemporary attempts to emphasize heterodox forms of knowledge construction within IPE. Such attempts tend to focus on three arguments: first, the need for a theory of economic action which recognizes the ethical dimension of human behaviour; second, the need for a theory of economic structure which recognizes the institutional dimension of habituating influences on human behaviour; and, third, the need for a theory of economic dynamics which recognizes the social dimension of the accumulation process and the incorporation of particular types of human behaviour into that process. These three dimensions feature prominently in the following three chapters, as they explain why I construct my particular classical political economy approach to IPE specifically from the work of Smith, Veblen and Polanyi. From Smith I take the concern for an ethical theory of economic action; from Veblen I take the concern for an institutional theory of economic structure; and from Polanyi I take the concern for a social theory of economic dynamics.

First, the case for an ethical IPE is made most forcefully by those who seek to theorize the relationship between thought and action.

From such a perspective, IPE is about the clash of normative positions on the questions of how one should act and how one should be encouraged to act. Naeem Inayatullah and David Blaney suggest that the task of the IPE theorist must be to 'confront social meanings, relationships, and practices by conducting intrinsically ethical enquiries that (may) affirm or challenge our most basic commitments and taken-for-granted social practices' (Inayatullah and Blaney 1997: 75–6). I agree. In order to ground such an endeavour within the classical tradition of political economy, I appeal to the work of Adam Smith. For Smith, the role of economic institutions was to provide a context in which human interactions could take place on the basis of the principles of the good society. As a consequence, the role of economic theory was irreducibly ethical, in that it must envision the conditions within which the good society becomes a possibility.

Smith therefore provides us with a theory of economic relations which prioritizes justice within society. As Raphael and Macfie argue in their introduction to Smith's *Theory of Moral Sentiments*, command of the self dominates the whole of the Smithian notion of virtue (Raphael and Macfie 1982: 6). In the absence of individuals leading a virtuous life it is not possible to sustain the conditions for ensuring justice; moreover, in the absence of justice it is not possible to regulate society in a manner that can ensure its survival.

To use Smith's own words, 'Justice is . . . the main pillar that upholds the whole edifice [of] the great, the immense fabric of human society' (Smith 1982 [1759]: II.ii.3.4). Justice requires restraint – in the economy as elsewhere – and, for Smith, the goal of the political economist is to theorize the moral basis of restraint within economic relations, for fear that society would be placed in danger if such restraint was not forthcoming. Accepting this most basic of Smithian perspectives, it is necessary for the political economist to produce theories of the economy which assert the moral autonomy of the individual to act justly within economic relations. Otherwise, the actions of the individual will undermine the social basis of the reproduction of economic relations.

I suggest that the goal that Smith set the political economists of his day is also a suitable standard for those working within IPE today. Much has been written recently, in the context of modern consumer lifestyles, about the subjugation of individual identity to the consumption of the brand (see, for instance, N. Klein 2000;

Hertz 2001). In this way, the autonomy of the individual is increasingly sacrificed in the interests of being seen to consume particular brands. The global advertising industry is big business in its own right, and it both spends and makes significant sums of money seeking to create and sustain the imaginary wants that propel the global economy. What Smith termed the 'deception' and 'vanity' of intrinsically worthless desires (Smith 1982 [1759]: IV.1.9) is a principal driver of economic globalization. Furthermore, in the attempt to satisfy such desires, Smith believed that an essential element of the self had to be forgone, which would lead subsequently to the loss of moral autonomy and the corruption of the good society (1982 [1759]: I.iii.3.1). At the very least, such attempts provide tacit legitimation for the work practices that lie behind the production of brand items and, where work practices of this nature infringe fundamental criteria of justice, such attempts also provide legitimation for unjust outcomes within the global economy. The IPE developed here uses basic themes of Smithian analysis in order to ground critiques of unjust outcomes.

Second, I attempt to move beyond a binary distinction between economic activities that are just and economic activities that are unjust, in order to demonstrate that all economic actions are subjected to pressures of habituation which impact upon the likelihood of just activities. It is one thing to label an outcome 'unjust' on the basis of abstract criteria for justice; it is another thing altogether to show how deeply such criteria are embedded within the economic practices of everyday life. Whilst the former is clearly a far from inconsequential undertaking, the IPE developed here is one which is also able to fulfil the latter task. In order to make this possible, I appeal to the institutionalist tradition associated with the work of Thorstein Veblen.

The case for an institutionalist perspective is made by many who have argued for heterodox forms of knowledge production within IPE (for reviews, see Strange 1997; O'Brien and Williams 2004). However, the appeal *specifically* to a Veblenian institutionalism has yet to make an impact upon the subject area. Most of the institutionalist analyses that currently make their way into IPE focus on the regularities which are evident in the outcomes of the policy-making process of individual states. Such regularities arise in particular from the fact that policy-makers are assumed to face rational incentives to reproduce the status quo. This is because they owe their position as policy-makers to widely held beliefs that they already reflect the status quo. In this way, where institutionalist analysis has penetrated IPE, it tends to be a rational choice institutionalism (on which see Hall and Taylor 1996), couched solely at the level of the policy-making process of individual states.

The institutionalism of Thorstein Veblen differs markedly in this respect. For Veblen, an institution emerges out of the prior sedimentation of a 'habit of thought' (see Chapter 5). Changes in the structure of the economy revolve around, and follow, changes in the habits of thought of the individuals who make up that economy (Veblen 1919b). Importantly, then, given the broad aims here to create an ethically oriented IPE, changes in assumptions about the type of economic activities that are to be deemed unjust follow prior changes in habits of thought relating to broad criteria by which we understand the very idea of justice. From a Veblenian perspective, institutional change is a highly political act, because it requires nothing less than the attempted re-constitution of the individual, through changing the instinctive thought processes of that individual. Veblen's political economy is an attempt to understand the way in which the individual acts through first understanding the social pressures that are brought to bear upon the individual to think and to identify themselves in a particular way. Regularities of human conduct follow regularities of human thought; habituated actions come after the subjection of the thought process to habituating dynamics. Institutions, as the manifestation of habits of thought, play an important socializing role within the economy.

Veblen identified the structure of modern economics as an important habituating influence on prevailing patterns of thought (Veblen 1919a); it socialized individuals into acting in the manner prescribed by the theory. He argued that ever more aspects of social existence were being subjected to the disciplining effects of the chrematistic view of life outlined in Chapter 1. In other words, the logic of utility-maximization was becoming an increasingly pervasive feature of everyday life. Yet, for this logic to become more deeply embedded in action, it was first necessary for the individual to be re-constituted at the level of thought. In particular, such behavioural characteristics were conditional upon the individual first embodying the thought processes of *homo economicus*. The very idea of what counts as a just outcome changes within a society that is populated by nothing other than *homo economicus*.

Third, the IPE which I envision is most definitely an explanatory mode of analysis. As such, it is necessary to move beyond merely recognizing the increasing encroachment of chrematistic character traits associated with *homo economicus* in an attempt to explain the contextual factors that lead to the constitution of such individuals. In particular, for IPE, it is necessary to specify the economic conditions out of which chrematistic character traits arise. To assist me in that endeavour, I turn to the work of Karl Polanyi. Polanyian themes have made some inroads into IPE; however, this tends only to be related to his discussion of historical dynamics and, specifically, to his account of the increasing denouncement of market ideology following the collapse of the liberal international economy in the early twentieth century (see, for instance, Cox 1994a; Cerny 1995). I invoke Polanyi for altogether different reasons, in order to theorize the economic preconditions of the constitution of *homo economicus*.

For Polanyi, two generic possibilities exist, depending on the political characteristics of the historical juncture being observed. On the one hand, it is possible for economic relations to be embedded within society, such that priority within the policy process is given to the oikonomic needs of social provisioning. The individual within such a society is socialized along the lines of the moral agent to be found in the work of Smith (Polanyi 1982). It is an individual who has learnt how to act justly, who embodies the abstract criteria for justice, and who is willing to subordinate self-interest to a broader vision of the social good. On the other hand, it is possible for social relations to be embedded with 'the market', such that priority within the policy process is given to the chrematistic needs of personal acquisitiveness. Individuals within such a society are subjected to socialization pressures that deny them the traits of the Smithian moral agent. They are individuals who respond solely to their own wants, irrespective of the standards of justice that are infringed while satisfying those wants. In short, they are individuals who act as *homo economicus* (Polanyi 1957 [1944]).

The key to adopting a Polanyian perspective on political economy is to be able to identify the historical process through which *homo economicus* is constituted. This, in turn, is to identify the historical process through which social relations come to be embedded within 'the market'. Polanyi's analysis focuses, in particular, on the political determinants of the economic institutions that we associate with 'the market'. He concludes that the pattern of economic behaviour in evidence at any one moment of time is the product of the incentive structures that operate within the economy. Such structures become part of the lived experiences of the individual because they are imposed upon society by legal statute. As such, they have to be seen to reflect the law-making interventions of governments.

This is important from a Polanyian perspective, because it means that the constitution of *homo economicus* must always be understood as the outcome of political choice. In other words, the constitution of *homo economicus* is always a contingent political construction and, as such, it can be reversed. To suggest otherwise is, for Polanyi, to fall into the trap of the 'economistic fallacy' (see Chapter 6). The 'economistic fallacy' arises when the socially-produced psychological disposition towards utility-maximization is treated as encapsulating all possible forms of economic activity. Polanyi argues that this is to presume that all economic relations must necessarily take a market form (Polanyi 1982: 50), whereupon the whole realm of oikonomia is subordinated to a chrematistic worldview. The IPE developed here is one which is mindful of the 'economistic fallacy' and, as a consequence, it accepts that *homo economicus* can only ever be a contingent political construction.

Conclusion

By working with a synthesis of the insights of Adam Smith, Thorstein Veblen and Karl Polanyi, I am able to produce an IPE that is suited to critical analysis. It is an IPE that fulfils three basic conditions for being deemed 'critical', as outlined by those who have already developed heterodox forms of knowledge production within IPE. It uses the work of Smith to provide the context for theorizing an ethical International Political Economy; it uses the work of Veblen to provide the context for theorizing an institutionalist International Political Economy; and it uses the work of Polanyi to provide the context for theorizing a historicist International Political Economy.

My aim is not to establish the facts of history, such that the public management of the international economy can be shown to have created an institutional apparatus that sanctions unjust economic outcomes. While there may be much in this as a depiction of contemporary conditions within the international economy, my aim is broader than simply to describe the existence of such conditions. My hope is to construct an analytical framework that enables us to understand the process through which the individual is constituted as an agent within the structures of the international economy. The individual is constituted simultaneously as both economic agent and moral agent. At all times, then, the individual is situated at the interface between the economic ideologies of everyday life and abstract criteria for the satisfaction of justice claims. What I ask of my IPE in the first instance is that it is able to help me understand the relationship between these dual pressures, the one relating to the constitution of the individual as an economic agent and the other relating to the constitution of the individual as a moral agent. Moreover, I also demand that my IPE treats this relationship as a matter of historical contingency.

The foundations for IPE that I develop over the following three chapters are suited to such a task. They are embedded within the classical tradition of political economy and, as such, they are attentive to the need to treat contemporary conditions of existence as the product of a historical process. What is more, that process is considered to be open-ended. As a consequence, there is no necessary reason why the institutionalized incentives for constituting particular types of economic agents need be reproduced ad infinitum. All that is required to overwrite such reproduction is a decisive political intervention, as animated by an appropriate moral critique of existing inequities and injustices. The IPE I envision is designed to assist the development of such critiques. It is in this sense that it can be said to be critical analysis. It focuses on the moral challenges to the continued reproduction of the economic agent as *homo economicus*, while suggesting alternative ways in which the economic agent might be constituted in the future. I create such a perspective over the course of the following three chapters, starting with an overview of the work of arguably the most famous of the classical political economists, Adam Smith.

Chapter 4

Moral Propriety within Political Economy: The Work of Adam Smith

Introduction

This chapter is the first of three that seeks to add substance to the more abstract arguments contained in the previous chapters. Taken together, they attempt to demonstrate the historical and spatial contingency of claims that an instinctive utility-maximizing rationality is an innate expression of human nature. To do so, I make reference to the work of three political economists who are representative of the classical tradition as outlined in Chapters 2 and 3. The ideas of Smith, Veblen and Polanyi are built around different, albeit complementary, approaches to the way in which conscious human subjects act within everyday economic situations. By combining the three sets of ideas, it is possible to develop a critical theory of reflexive action suitable for IPE.

I begin by reviewing Adam Smith's work on the fundamental characteristics of economic life and, in particular, his contribution to the philosophical debate about reflexive action. The manner in which I use Smith must therefore be contrasted to the received wisdom on his intellectual legacy. There is, without doubt, a canonical view of Smith within IPE: the very mention of his name has become something of a metaphor for free market economics. Within such a view, his work is identified as the origin of assumptions about the human instinct to act unthinkingly in line with instrumentally self-interested norms. Accordingly, *homo economicus* is seen both as a reflection and a product of 'invisible hand' dynamics, such that all action reduces to an instinctive response to price signals emerging from the economy. There is no room for active human agency within such a framework. Behaviour is stripped of its reflexive character, as there is no decision to be made between alternative courses of action. Instead, conduct is guided by the structure of the prevailing economic environment, whereby the one instrumentally self-interested option is followed. Indeed, to call this an 'option' is probably a misnomer, as option implies choice, and there is no choice in circumstances in which the ends amongst which we select are known (i.e., self-interest), and so too are the selection criteria (i.e., instrumental rationality: see Shackle 1969).

However, such conclusions arise from a superficial reading of *The Wealth of Nations* and, in particular, to the single, arguably throw-away, passage in *The Wealth of Nations* that contains the idea of the market's 'invisible hand' (see, for instance, Rothschild 2001). It owes nothing to locating Smith's political economy within the wider context of his moral philosophy. Neither does it help us to construct an IPE that is consistent with the classical tradition of political economy, whereby economic relations are theorized in terms of a social existence that incorporates the human desire for both material and moral contentment within broader structural relations of production and distribution. In order to make headway on such a task, this chapter proceeds in three stages. First, I outline the core features of Smith's economic system, which are drawn primarily from the first two books of *The Wealth of Nations*. Second, I set this within the context of his reflections on method, in which he presents his view on the status of all theoretical systems (including, one imagines, his own). Third, I use his reflections on method to draw the link between Smith's economics and his philosophical concerns for propriety of action. This acts as a prelude to the following two chapters, in which I turn to the possibility of adopting Smithian propriety as a standard for understanding reflexive action within the international economy today.

Smith on economics: The Wealth of Nations

Adam Smith's economics can be understood in two ways, depending on whether we focus on what today would be called the microeconomic or the macroeconomic element of his theoretical system. At the microeconomic level, Smith focused on the use of the price mechanism to coordinate economic activity along competitive lines (Hollander 1987: 60; Fusfeld 2002: 31). But this in itself is a reflection of the perceived macroeconomic imperative of ensuring that economic growth enhanced the absolute living standards of the poorest sections of society (Campbell and Skinner 1982: 168; D. Winch 1997: 402).

Uniting these two elements of Smith's work, and providing it with its real novelty (Arrow 1979), is the emphasis he placed upon the division of labour. Under such conditions, the productive capacity of society is founded on complex patterns of economic specialization. For Smith, the division of labour, as well as the propensity to exchange that it entails, is not 'one of those original principles in human nature of which no further account can be given' (Smith 1970 [1776]: 117). Immediately, then, he distances his analysis from the assumption of an all-knowing 'invisible hand'. Rather, he says, 'it be the necessary consequence of the faculties of reason and speech' (1970 [1776]). In other words, it is a conscious decision, representing the collective wishes of a society at a particular stage of development, to establish a system of production based on specialization and trade. There is nothing automatic or predetermined about the existence of such a system; it has to be repeatedly argued for, justified and defended against criticism.

Smith himself, despite placing the division of labour at the centre of his theoretical system, was one such critic. He reflected at great length, and with great introspection, about the effects of a commercial liberalism based on the division of labour. In particular, he asked whether an economy founded on such principles would privilege certain conceptions of justice over others and, as a result, whether it would lead its participants into certain ways of life (Cropsey 1979: 165). It is clear from reading the first two books of *The Wealth of Nations* that the 'invisible hand' is not intended to portray a power in nature that acts through compulsion to secure particular patterns of behaviour. It is, at most, an organic metaphor suggesting the degree to which economic history is subject to a logic of unintended consequences (D. Winch 1997: 399). Such consequences are made manifest in the eternal dilemma of the division of labour: how to weigh its economic benefits against its social costs.

The division of labour is only treated as an unequivocal good in the opening three chapters of Book I of *The Wealth of Nations*, in which Smith presents it solely as an economic phenomenon while discussing the question of productive efficiency (on which see Arrow 1979). But this amounts to less than twenty of the 1,100 pages of the overall treatise, and Smith devotes much of the remaining pages to showing how the economics of the division of labour are infused with relations of power and powerlessness, privilege and exploitation. Two aspects of Smith's reflections are particularly noteworthy.

First, Smith's conception of the division of labour focuses on the choice that individuals make to specialize. It involves a conscious decision to restrict the scope of their economic activities, foreclosing the possibility of undertaking some activities in the interest of becoming more proficient in others. For Smith, this represents the inevitable reduction of human labour time to commodity labour power. Work consequently becomes confined to the constant repetition of a limited number of mundane, routine and entirely predictable tasks. Practice may well make perfect in a strictly economic sense but, if we look beyond the merely economic, we see the division of labour in an altogether different context. According to Smith:

> The man whose whole life is spent in performing a few simple operations, of which the effects too are, perhaps, always the same, or very nearly the same...has no occasion to exert his understanding...His dexterity at his own particular trade seems, in this manner, to be acquired at the expence of his intellectual, social, and martial values. (Smith 1998 [1776]: 429–30)

Later, he calls this 'mental mutilation' (1998 [1776]: 435).

We can therefore read into Smith's understanding of the division of labour, and certainly as expressed in Book V of *The Wealth of Nations*, thoughts that appear to be a forerunner of Marx's theory of alienation (Marx 1973 [1952]: 459–549). For Marx, the system of mass production within capitalist society required workers to sacrifice their own development as human beings (alienation of the self) in order to serve the systemic imperative of producing goods for the consumption of others (alienation from the product of one's labour). In this sense, Marx merely offered a more detailed account of a key feature of work within capitalist society that Smith had already identified. For Marx, however, alienation was a structurally inscribed logic of capitalism, owing to the particular place occupied by labour in relation to the means of production. For Smith, on the other hand, the division of labour represented the collective choice to construct a society on the basis of economic specialization.

Let us therefore return specifically to Smith's understanding of the division of labour. If the division of labour incurs such significant social costs for those whose labour is specialized, yet still such a system represents the collective choice of society at certain points in human history, what can we say about the circumstances in which such choices are made? This is the second particularly noteworthy aspect of Smith's reflections on the division of labour, for it provides a link between his philosophy and his economics. This enables us to refute the charge that is often laid against him, that his later work in *The Wealth of Nations* contradicts his earlier work in *The Theory of Moral Sentiments*.

In order to understand this link, it is necessary to turn to Smith's conception of the price system under the division of labour (this is to be found in chapters 5–7 of Book I of *The Wealth of Nations* – Smith 1970 [1776]: 133–66). Crucial in this respect is the distinction that he drew between 'natural' prices and 'market' prices. By a commodity's 'natural' price, Smith meant that which was sufficient to pay the wages of the labour used in the production of the commodity, the profits of the stock employed in its production, and the proportion of the rent of the land on which the production process took place. In his own words, 'The commodity is then sold precisely for what it is worth, or for what it really costs the person who brings it to market' (1970 [1776]: 158). However, Smith's definition of the 'natural' price assumes that the profits of the stock employed are merely the equivalent of the stock owner's subsistence needs (1970 [1776]). This is a condition that we know to be a poor approximation of the circumstances we experience today, as an elaborate structure of rentier interests impacts upon the level of profit, and serves to bid it up in excess of subsistence needs. Moreover, it was also a condition that Smith knew to be illusory at the time he was writing *The Wealth of Nations*.

Smith's denunciations of the activities of the business classes are well known amongst historians of economic thought. Indeed, the following observation is one of the most frequently cited passages from *The Wealth of Nations*. The business classes, he says, 'seldom meet together, even for merriment and diversion, but the conversation ends in a conspiracy against the publick, or in some contrivance to raise prices' (Smith 1998 [1776]: 129). In other parts of the text, he writes of the 'mean rapacity' and the 'monopolizing spirit' of business people, who set out to 'deceive and even to oppress the public' (cited in Sowell 1979: 6):

> Our merchants and master-manufacturers complain much of the bad effects of high wages in raising the price, and thereby lessening the sale of their goods both at home and abroad. They say nothing concerning the bad effects of high profits. They are silent with regard to the pernicious effects of their own gains. They complain only of those of other people. (Smith 1970 [1776]: 201)

Smith highlights in great detail the social dynamics of price-setting within modern economies. It is an exercise in identifying the locus of economic power, and Smith is unequivocal about where power is concentrated under the division of labour. He sketches, albeit only very briefly, the theoretical possibility of what neoclassical economists would today call equilibrium price-setting dynamics (1970 [1776]: 160). But it remains only that: a theoretical possibility. The power of the business classes – Smith's 'merchants and master-manufacturers' – allows them continually to extract 'extraordinary profits of stock' from the production process (1970 [1776]: 163).

A system of 'natural' prices exists in logical time only, as an illustration of what a pure price-adjusting economy would look like, were it possible to create the social institutions necessary for sustaining such an economy. It is not a set of conditions that has ever been experienced as an actual economy set in real historical time, and neither are they ever likely to be experienced in this way. There are structural constraints within the process of price formation that enforce a continued divergence between 'natural' prices and 'market' prices. While Smith attributes such constraints to the exercise of power by the business classes, he is quick to argue that this is a historical 'accident' (1970 [1776]: 160).

This is an insight that is of fundamental significance, certainly insofar as it informs much of the analysis within the remainder of the book. It suggests that price-setting dynamics are socially constructed, shaped by and reflecting the prevailing balance of political forces within society. There is nothing automatic or predetermined about the form that price-setting dynamics take at any particular moment of time or space. There is no underlying essence of 'the economy' in this respect. Rather, all social systems of price formation should be seen as temporary phenomena, conjunctural moments in a much longer economic history. They are defined in particular ways, to reflect particular exercises of political power. But this means that they can always be redefined, so that they can respond to normative critiques of the existing balance of political forces within society. This historical 'accident' of the price-setting power of the business classes may well come complete with self-perpetuating effects, in that it forecloses the possibility of a quick and untroubled transition to a qualitatively different social order (Jessop 1990). Yet it does not preclude the possibility of a successful normative critique of existing conditions mobilizing support for price-setting dynamics that embody a more equitable distribution of wealth within the international economy.

This, however, is not the usual emphasis that is placed on Smith's analysis of the process of price formation. Such is the influence of the canonical interpretation of his work that a single line in chapter seven of Book I tends to have captured most of the attention of historians of economic thought. Out of respect for the explanatory force of Newton's *Principia*, on numerous occasions Smith appropriated Newtonian terminology in order to present his arguments in as comprehensible a manner as possible. This is certainly evident in his analysis of 'natural' prices. 'The natural price', he wrote, 'is, as it were, the central price, to which the prices of all commodities are continually gravitating' (Smith 1970 [1776]: 160). Should the allusion to gravitational effects be treated literally rather than metaphorically, the impression can take hold of a predetermined trajectory for prices within the economy. Misread through the perspective of the neoclassical focus on equilibrium prices, this translates into an automatic predisposition for the economy to arrive at a set of prices that are both economically efficient and socially just. Empirical analysis of whether actual prices are indeed efficient and just are rendered superfluous to the task of reiterating the assertion that observed prices are equilibrium prices.

We are therefore presented with two different understandings of Smith's distinction between 'natural' and 'market' prices. For Smith himself, the 'market' price is that to be observed in actual economies suffused by asymmetric distributions of power, whereas the 'natural' price relates to a hypothetical set of conditions only. The distinction looks rather different when set within the context of neoclassical economists' concern for the relationship between short-run and long-run prices. Here, the 'market' price is treated as the short-run price, and the 'natural' price as the long-run price on which short-run prices will converge at their equilibrium level.

The significance of Smith's distinction between 'natural' and 'market' prices, to my mind, is that it represents a decisive refutation of the smooth relationship that exists between short-run and long-run prices in neoclassical theory. It suggests that there is no such thing as purely economic determinants of price, with everything else being assumed to remain constant. Therefore, prices cannot simply be read off from the underlying contextual assumption that each and every individual within the economy will be guided in all instances by instinctive utility-maximizing behaviour. The pricing mechanism of the economy must be understood as a social process that reflects relationships of power and powerlessness, privilege and exploitation. Such relationships can only be understood by attempting to unpack, and uncover the dynamic evolution of, those 'other things' that neoclassical theory allows to be treated as constant.

It is here that we can see how Smith's work can be used to formulate an alternative conception of economic relations to those that dominate the current pedagogy of economics. Consider the thoughts of Paul Samuelson, Nobel Laureate, and the man whose textbooks have provided the core introduction to students of economics for over half a century. According to Samuelson, Smith does not qualify as a modern economist because, relative to the standards of neoclassical analysis, his price theory is bedevilled by 'too many endogenous unknowns' (Samuelson 1992: 3). But this is precisely the point. Smith's price *theory* contains a number of endogenous unknowns because the *process* through which prices form in modern economies contains a number of endogenous unknowns. In other words, the process of price formation contains many contingent factors which are internal to the process itself. These features, put simply, are the politics of the political economy of prices. If we are to understand the economy as being embedded within wider political dynamics, these are things on which we cannot remain silent.

Two points follow. The first is that there is little, if anything, within Smith's reflections on the nature of political economy to sustain the canonical interpretation of his work. His economic theory is much more subtle, and provides the basis for a more diverse political practice, than is implied by focusing solely on the dynamics of the 'invisible hand'. Smith is not the high theorist of a simple instrumental rationality, as is so often maintained by those who accept the canonical interpretation of his work, and as is lamented by those like Samuelson who wish to draw a direct lineage from classical political economy to neoclassical economics. As Donald Winch observes, the concept of instrumentally rational action was introduced into political economy by Ricardo and Mill, not Smith. Smith's concern was to understand the social institutions in which particular types of economic relations were embedded, in an attempt to construct a post-hoc rationalization of the overall social system in relation to the underlying moral principles on which conduct was enacted in such a system (D. Winch 1997: 390). This is the focus of the third section of this chapter.

Before that, however, I turn to a rather different question. In arguing for a reading of Smith that emphasizes the social determinants of the economic system, it is necessary to ask what role remains for pure economic theory, for it is clear that a large part of *The Wealth of Nations* is devoted to discussions of the internal logic of ideal-typical economic conditions. Smith himself wrote extensively on the problem of method, which he saw as the tendency of the human mind to confuse hypothetical thought experiments with real-life observations, treating the former as if they were aspects of the latter. It is to this issue that I now turn.

Smith on method: The History of Astronomy

Adam Smith's reflections on method are to be found primarily in his *Essays on Philosophical Subjects* and, in particular, in his account of the *History of Astronomy* (Smith 1980). Smith can clearly be situated within the wider tradition of the Scottish Enlightenment, in both his dismissive attitude to the notion of a universal truth and also in his focus on conventional behaviour (Heilbroner 1986; Dow, Dow and Hutton 1997). I now review very briefly these two features of his thought.

First, Smith viewed the task of theory as the identification of general principles. But, following Hume, he recognized that the problem of induction meant that there was no guarantee that these general principles could ever be said to be 'true'. From this perspective, Smith cautions against those who attempt to objectify theoretical systems, however convincing their underlying narrative structure (Smith 1980: 66). As a consequence, he reduces all theoretical systems to mere inventions of the imagination (Raphael and Skinner 1980: 11) and all scientific statements to the level of the hypothetical (Olson 1975: 123).

Smith thus constructs a human, as opposed to an absolute, standard for judging the value of scientific interventions. Economics, whether Smith's own or some other theorist's, is no different to physics in this respect. All must be judged against their ability to talk about the world in terms that mirror our perceptions of experiencing that world. Theory is distinct from experience, but the value of theoretical exposition is linked in a most immediate manner to its ability to be used to provide lived experiences with a sense of familiarity. Moreover, such familiarity can be created in one of two ways. Theoretical formulations can reflect real world experiences, in which case the experience precedes the construction of the theory. Equally, however, experiences can be reshaped so that the way in which the world actually works more closely fits the way in which the theory predicts the world should work. There is nothing in Smith's reflections on method to adjudicate between these two possibilities. We might begin to experience the world described by neoclassical theory, then, but only because our economic relations have been deliberately structured to make that experience possible.

Second, this view of the role of theory complements Smith's wider notion of human agency, which he explains by emphasizing the conventions that underpin human behaviour (D. Winch 1997: 384). Smith viewed human actions as the product of the social environments in which human beings are called upon to act (Rosenberg 1979: 27). Our behaviour, he says, 'does not arise so much from the view of the passion, as from that of the situation which excites it' (Smith 1982 [1759]: 12). The desire for routine in such situations is assumed to impose on human action a bias towards the habitual.

This is evident in Smith's economics as well as in his reflections on method. As Kenneth Arrow argues, Smith's conception of the division of labour differs markedly from Ricardo's later work on the same issue in one fundamental respect. For Ricardo, natural differences in human endowments provided the foundations for the division of labour. For Smith, by contrast, the division of labour resulted from the decision of individuals to specialize in an attempt to impose an element of the habitual onto their everyday practices (Arrow 1979: 157). No assumption of rationality is necessary in order to explain the conventional aspects of human behaviour. Indeed, the assumption of a simple instrumental rationality is incompatible with Smith's focus on conventional behaviour.

These two aspects of Smith's thought – the suspicion of universal truths on the one hand, and a focus on conventional behaviour on the other – are intimately related. That relationship is founded on his view of how scientific knowledge evolves. For Smith, the human desire for conventions to inform behaviour is satisfied most obviously in circumstances in which behaviour is underpinned by knowledge that satisfies a further desire for order, so the task of theoretical formulations is to provide ordered knowledge that can inform routine actions which can be reproduced increasingly instinctively. It is in this sense that Smith talks about the way in which knowledge 'represent[s] the invisible chains which bind together all the disjointed objects [of nature]' and, hence, allays the 'tumult of the imagination' (Smith 1980: 45). The mind, in other words, has a propensity for wanting to see connections between appearances in the real world (Skinner 1979: 18). The mind of the theorist is no different, and experiences this propensity for regularity and association every bit as much as anyone else's.

Significantly, Smith works to a scientific standard of psychological, rather than literal, truth (Smith 1983: 7; for a commentary, see Heilbroner 1986: 14–15). If the mind wants to see connections then it is given connections to see. As a consequence, theoretical systems do not necessarily 'explain' real-life events, at least not in the orthodox understanding of explanation. Their task is rather to allow observers of those events to avoid feeling disoriented and troubled by having nothing to help them understand what they have just witnessed. The development of theoretical systems is thus about allowing the mind to be at peace with itself by increasing the range of phenomena with which we feel familiar, and therefore comfortable, even if our only experience of certain phenomena *is within the framework of the theoretical system itself*.

This is a significant qualification. It has profound implications not only for the status of economic theory in general, but also for the canonical interpretation of Smith's economics. Before I attend to these points in turn, it is first necessary to understand Smith's insistence that scientific progress is driven by the fear of *not* knowing rather than by the need *to* know (Smith 1980: 37). Theories are subjective constructs designed to satisfy both the psychological needs of the theorist, and those of the theorist's audience, in terms of reducing the surprise of encountering new events. If this invokes the image of theory as comfort blanket, then this is not far from what Smith had in mind. However, one further point has to be added in this respect. There is no requirement for the theory to predict forthcoming events that will provide us with feelings of moral or material comfort. The sense of comfort written into Smith's reflections on method is purely psychological, in that a successful theory eliminates concerns about not knowing what will happen next. As Heilbroner observes, 'It is not an abstract drive for truth that impels the search for theory, but the concrete promptings of anxiety' (Heilbroner 1986: 15). The passions of the observer are pacified by their ability to see events – whether good or bad – unfold in front of them in a largely predictable manner.

Of course, none of this tells us which theory will become the received view at any particular moment of time. For Smith, the main criterion for establishing a system of thought is that the theories which emerge from it must have an immediately comprehensible link to both reason and experience (Raphael and Skinner 1980: 1). In short, theories must be believable.

Moreover, this is not just believable in the sense of being logically plausible. Given the need for theories to eliminate the element of surprise that unpredictable events can elicit, there is a related need for some degree of correspondence between theory and observed reality. But reality itself is only ever seen from within socio-psychological understandings of what reality actually is, with reality in this respect being linked to familiarity (Dow, Dow and Hutton 1997: 378). This all appears somewhat circular. The theory provides familiarity for the observer, but the observer only accepts the theory in the first place because it talks of things that are already familiar. In Smith's words, 'we observe, in general, that no system, how well soever in other respects supported, has ever been able to gain any credit on the world, whose connecting principles were not such as were familiar to all mankind' (Smith 1980: 46). Causal investigation revolves around the search for a bridge between the unknown and the known; 'causality' itself is therefore little more than a believable analogy to more familiar objects (Wightman 1980: 14).

Smith assumes that the attribution of causal status to certain theories and not to others is a result of the relative persuasiveness of the way in which those theories are presented. For him, the demonstrative logic of the methodology of economics is less important than the rhetoric that economists use in order to persuade (Smith 1983). Smith's theory of rhetoric places a high value on intuitive knowledge, but intuitive knowledge is itself linked to that which is already thought to be 'true'. There is thus an in-built bias towards the status quo within rhetorical structures that emphasize the intuitive. Placing rhetorical stress on the familiar reinforces that which is already held to be known.

So what do Smith's reflections on method tell us about the status of economic theory in general? For a start, it implores us to treat with reticence any claim in relation to the objective nature of economic theories. Economics is no different from any other branch of theoretical exposition, in that the theory relates not to an irrefutable sense of how the world is; rather, it is a means of apprehending how the world might be, such that it becomes possible to gain some psychological comfort from connecting personal experiences to a wider explanation of social interaction.

Connection implies familiarity, but familiarity itself can have many different sources. If we view the international economy as a whole, the range of diverse experiences that co-exist suggests that different groups of people will be familiar with different forms of economic life. No economic theory can therefore be generally applicable without regard to context. No economic theory can do more than to narrate a particular set of experiences that are familiar only to a limited number of people.

Operating in line with Smith's reflections on method, we must restrict ourselves to modest claims about the scope and applicability of theoretical models. This is no bad thing; for, if we guard against the dangers of false universalism, we will be in a better position to challenge the methodological ethnocentrism of much contemporary economic theory. As explained in the introduction, methodological ethnocentrism ensues from the assumption that all forms of economic life are the same, and that the theory which allows us to connect our experiences to one set of economic relations is sufficient to explain all experiences of the economy.

It is perhaps ironic that I have used Smith's reflections on method to reach this conclusion, since it is the canonical interpretation of

Smith's *Wealth of Nations* that is typically presented as the universally applicable theory of the economy. However, the theory of instinctive utility-maximizing behaviour, made manifest in neoclassical economics, is not a logical extension of Smith's work. It is possible to construct a link between the two, by appealing to a particular reading of the 'invisible hand' metaphor, but this requires an entirely superficial reading of Smith's wider thought (Macfie 1967). It is this to which I turn in the following section. My aim is to show that Smith's reflections on method hold the key to uniting his philosophical and economic thinking. Recast in this way, Smith is presented less as a pure economic theorist searching for the abstract principles that underpin all economic interactions. What emerges in its place is a style of economic theory that is much more sensitive to the contextually specific nature of different forms of economic life. It also helps us to understand the process through which different forms of economic life become institutionalized in everyday practice.

Smith on philosophy: The Theory of Moral Sentiments

Adam Smith's philosophical reflections attempt to demonstrate the way in which moral principles are derived (Sowell 1979: 16). While the language that Smith uses in his *Theory of Moral Sentiments* suggests that there is something essential in human nature that informs our moral principles, his wider scepticism of universal truths implies something else. His concern was to elucidate a *particular* set of moral principles, those associated with the dynamics of everyday life in a commercial society. As Robert Heilbroner notes, Smith's conception of human nature is one 'that placed a vast confidence in the educability of humankind' (Heilbroner 1986: 2), and our socialization into certain specific economic roles is an important aspect of that education.

Our moral principles are therefore related to our experiences of the world, with the economy representing a crucial constituent of those experiences. It is through our experiences that we discover which types of action pass the moral judgement of others, and this interactive learning process allows us to reflect critically on our own understanding of what is morally just. As a consequence, the derivation of moral principles is an irreducibly *social* process. It is the fact that we live in society that both gives meaning to our moral judgements and also forces us to be attentive to the moral consequences of our actions. As Daniel Fusfeld argues, such a process 'amounts to an early "other-directed" theory of human action' (Fusfeld 2002: 24).

In this respect, Smith's economic agents could hardly be more different from those of modern neoclassical theory. The latter respond instinctively to a pleasure/pain calculus that is a purely individual phenomenon, whereas the former cannot escape the way in which their actions will impact upon others. Smith's philosophical emphasis in the *Theory of Moral Sentiments* must therefore be seen as an analysis of commutative justice (Young and Gordon 1996). In other words, he focuses on justice within individual exchanges, arguing that a just moral order between consenting individuals is a necessary condition for making possible a functioning social life. This applies to all imaginable economic systems, and no less so to life within a commercial society.

Smith followed his teacher, Hutcheson, and his friend, Hume, in arguing that pure calculable reason was not the basis of the moral principles that inform our actions (Skinner 1979: 46–7; Heilbroner 1986: 2; Fitzgibbons 1995: 63). Rather, moral judgement arises from 'immediate sense and feelings': Smith's shorthand for the 'passions' we experience in our 'fellow-feeling' for the condition of others (Smith 1982 [1759]: Part I). The key to the link between our concern to act with propriety and our concern for the feelings of others lies in the role of the imagination. In Smith's words:

> it is by the imagination only that we can form any conception of what are his [i.e., other people's] sensations…[T]his is the source of our fellow-feeling for the misery of others, that is by changing places in fancy with the sufferer, that we come either to conceive or be affected by what he feels. (Smith 1982 [1759]: 9–10)

Smith tells us that we feel pain when imaginatively reconstructing in our own minds the pain we assume others to feel. Within his *Theory of Moral Sentiments*, to act rationally is to act in a manner that is sensitive to the imaginative reconstruction of the feelings of others. To ignore the moral consequences of our actions is to ignore the potential pain that our actions can bring to other people. But to ignore their pain is also to be inattentive to the pain that we feel once our imagination allows us, in effect, to change places with those who are adversely affected by the choices we make. As Athol Fitzgibbons puts it, 'since we can sympathise with others, we can also see ourselves through their eyes' (Fitzgibbons 1995: 63). Our imagination can therefore be expected to reveal to us the blame that will be directed towards us should our actions have adverse consequences on the lives of others, and should those actions have been undertaken in a manner that was unthinking, unreflexive and without a view to their wider social impact.

We are consequently left with an interesting, moreover profound, contradiction when reading Smith's work alongside the stylized truths of neoclassical theory. In the latter, the actions of economic agents are entirely instinctive, they are directed purely at individual gain, and there is no concept of social context within the broader explanatory framework. This is what it means to be rational within neoclassical theory. However, if we choose to accept Smith's conception of the economy as a social process guided by the moral principle of propriety, it is entirely irrational to be rational in the modern-day meaning of the word. Instinctive gain-oriented action, the very essence of action within the neoclassical framework, must necessarily in some instances be at the expense of others' sense of well-being, unless we assume the unlikely circumstances in which interests are universally complementary. Yet it is precisely this sort of instinctive action that causes others to experience pain, which through the effects of our imagination brings pain to us as well. So, these are also the sort of instinctive actions that we will seek to avoid, in order to satisfy the interest that we have in avoiding pain. This applies whether the pain we feel is directly experienced, or vicariously experienced through our imaginative reconstruction of the pain felt by others. As a consequence, we are left with the following conclusion: to satisfy our self-interest in Smith's sense requires precisely that we do not satisfy our self-interest in a neoclassical sense.

For Smith, economic self-interest is about more than individual acquisitiveness, material possessions and personal wealth. Indeed, it is about restraining whatever urge we may have to use such stimuli as the guide for behaviour, in order to act with propriety. Our ability to exercise such self-command is once again the product of our imagination (Smith 1982 [1759]: 134–56). It is the passions that Smith assumes are in need of command (Levine 1998: 37), and we are able to judge what that command requires in practice because of the human capacity to reflect on the feelings that our passions elicit – in particular, those of honour and shame (Campbell and Skinner 1982: 99). To inflect Smith's thoughts with more modern language, he argues that we have second-order desires (those that relate to the well-being of others) that enable us to pass judgement on our first-order desires (those that relate solely to ourselves: Rizvi 2002: 245).

In order to emphasize his argument that the passions work on two different levels at the same time, Smith operates with a conception of human consciousness that mirrors this distinction. We are simultaneously conscious, he says, of both the self and the other. It is within this context that Smith introduces his notion of the impartial spectator (Smith 1982 [1759]: 109–34).

The impartial spectator is part of the self, but it is that part which allows us to sympathize with the condition of others, and which requires us to act in a manner that is appropriate to the emotions that our sympathies evoke. The impartial spectator therefore becomes a means of explaining how moral principles are formed (Campbell and Skinner 1982: 101). The very fact that we are able to pass moral judgement results from our capacity for reflexive self-evaluation, which in turn allows us to play two roles at once. First, we are the agents of our own decisions; we interpret our passions so that they may be able to show us our preferred sentiments and conduct. Second, we are the spectators of the decisions that we would like to take; we can temporarily suspend our passions, in order to 'leave' ourselves and to be able to reflect on the propriety of our sentiments and intended conduct. In Smith's words, we are to 'suppose ourselves the spectators of our own behaviour . . . I divide myself, as it were, into two persons; and that I, the examiner and judge, represent a different character from that other I, the person whose conduct is examined into and judged of' (Smith 1982 [1759]: 112–13).

Smith's social world is governed by duty, and it is the twin concerns of wanting to act dutifully and wanting to be acknowledged for having acted dutifully that provide the conditions for social stability. As Campbell and Skinner note, 'Smith argued that the merit or demerit of a given action would depend upon a judgement as to the propriety or impropriety of both the action taken and the reaction to it' (Campbell and Skinner 1982: 102). From this observation we can begin to see what Smith has in mind when he suggests that we carry society within ourselves (Schneider 1979: 58). Here, Smith comes close to conflating duty and conscience: we can only satisfy our desire to have dutiful behaviour recognized as such when we act in a knowingly conscionable manner.

This is not only an important insight for interpreting Smith's work and, in particular, his *Wealth of Nations*; it is also significant in relation to the main themes of this book. Smith's view of the moral basis of purposive action departs substantially from that of more modern economists, who have focused their attention on instinctive utility-maximizing behaviour. For Smith, behaviour could only be instinctive if it took place in some sense 'beyond' society. Given that all economic relations form within society, however, this was not a possibility that he took seriously. Economic behaviour does not precede wider social engagement, and it is the impartial spectator – acting as 'the judge within', 'the tribunal within our own breast' (Smith 1982 [1759]: 134, 129) – that guides the way we respond to any given set of social circumstances. According to Smith, the impartial spectator appears initially to each individual as an external observer. Over time, though, due to the educability of the human subject, the characteristics of the spectator become progressively internalized, as a real and dynamic element of the self (Fitzgibbons 1995: 102). Duty and conscience, the lifeblood of Smith's social world, must therefore be seen as learned phenomena. They are definitely not an aspect of the state of nature; they reflect life within society, and they can be constituted in different ways depending on the prevailing norms of different societies.

Within Smith's philosophical framework, there is no single defining essence to economic behaviour. Our actions will be conscionable if we are to satisfy Smith's concerns for an economy that is founded on moral principles of commutative justice (Young and Gordon 1996). What counts as acceptable behaviour, however, can be recast under the influence of decisive political interventions. Smith provides an important point of departure, insofar as he shows that decisive political interventions change the nature of the social institutions within which the economy is embedded and, as such, they change what is treated as proper or improper behaviour. The task for future chapters is to specify more precisely the character of the most important interventions in shaping such sentiments of propriety.

Conclusion

This chapter has been divided into three sections, to cover Adam Smith's three major contributions to social science: his reflections on economics, method and philosophy. It is unusual to read Smith holistically in this way, but much can be gained from doing so. It is a particularly fertile exercise when approaching the primary task of this book, that of developing a theory of human agency from the history of economic thought to serve as a suitable foundation for contemporary IPE.

Smith develops a theoretical model of a pure price-adjusting economy in the opening book of the *Wealth of Nations*. However, he does so primarily to demonstrate that this is not the type of economy that we routinely experience in everyday life. Moreover, it will never be so, as long as the economy is suffused with political relationships of power and powerlessness, privilege and exploitation. The system of 'natural' prices is a hypothetical system only; it is a product of the mind, nothing more. What we experience in practice is a system of 'market' prices, where the price we pay for the goods we consume reflects more than simple economic determinants located at the level of the costs of production. The 'market' price is a partial embodiment of the social power of those who bring the goods to market. If the 'market' price of a good is significantly above its costs of production, the producer can be said to be exercising power over the consumer. If, on the other hand, the 'market' price of a good is at or below its costs of production, the consumer is exercising power over the producer.

But can we say for sure which one of these situations we will experience in any particular instance? Should we choose to accept Smith's views on method, then the answer is 'no'. According to Smith, there are no a priori grounds by which economic theory can predict the outcome of social situations that are irreducibly contingent. Indeed, there is no such thing as an a priori truth relating to any aspect of the social world. The task of economic theory is not to predict outcomes on the basis of known truths: rather, for Smith, it is to identify general principles, in an attempt to provide a guide for action in the unlikely circumstances in which it is possible to create the social institutions that sustain an ideal-type economy. Crucially, Smith operates to a scientific standard of psychological, rather than literal, truth. We ask only of our theories that they provide a link to those things with which we are familiar.

An important distinction is therefore apparent between modern neoclassical theory and the political economy of Smith. Modern neoclassical economics revolves around the assumption that all agents are purely self-interested, in an instinctive utility-maximizing sense. The link to the familiar in this respect comes from the current dominance of political ideologies of possessive individualism. The ideology provides a post-hoc rationalization for forms of behaviour that the theory states are, in any case, entirely natural. By contrast, Smith's political economy dismisses the very notion of pure self-interest, being grounded in his prior philosophical reflections, in which he argued that our own interests are inextricably tied to our knowledge of the condition, and therefore interests, of others. The link to the familiar in this latter respect comes from our internalization of the commands of the impartial spectator. Such commands require that we act in a manner that we deem to be dutiful, and that we can expect will be deemed to have been dutiful by others.

It is now time to draw a definitive connection between Smith's economics of price formation and his philosophy of duty. This is relatively straightforward to do. In any circumstances in which 'market' prices diverge from their 'natural' price, the burden of dutiful action is shouldered asymmetrically within the economy. Some will be responding to the exhortations of the impartial spectator to act conscionably; others, by contrast, will be relying on the ability to exercise raw economic power in order to bypass what Smith saw as the necessity for conscionable action. It is therefore clear that the duty that Smith had in mind as a guide for economic action has no fundamental underlying essence. It is a social construction and, as such, it is open to political manipulation. At any moment of time, the economy is embedded within a particular set of social institutions. Such institutions reflect the prevailing balance of political forces within society; some will require a much more equitable distribution of the burdens of dutiful behaviour than others.

The task of the following two chapters is to review developments in the history of economic thought subsequent to Smith, in which the authors have conceived of the economy as institutionalized practice. I turn in the next chapter to the work of the most noted of all institutional economists, Thorstein Veblen.

Chapter 5

Institutional Analysis within Political Economy: The Work of Thorstein Veblen

Introduction

Two developments of crucial importance to the major themes of this book occurred between the times at which Smith and Veblen were writing: one relates to the structure of the economy, the other to the structure of economic theory. First, it is clear that what had been established in practice was not a manifestation of the theoretical system which Smith believed approximated the ideal economy. The duty that Smith argued was the moral basis of all social interactions had not been manifested in a pure price-adjusting economy based on a system of 'natural' prices. Second, academic economists had distanced themselves increasingly from the style of political economy that Smith had pioneered. No longer for them did analysis centre on the search for the moral principles on which a just economic order could be constructed; instead, their aim was to uncover the scientific principles on which a functioning market economy operated.

The methodology of economics changed in order to reflect the changing emphasis of economic theory. At the turn of the twentieth century, when Veblen was making his major contribution to the history of economic thought, economics was being increasingly exposed to the disciplines of mathematical argument. By reducing economic relations to a series of mathematical equations, the promise of a truly scientific economics was raised. The introduction of a mathematical method imposed a strict uniformity on all economic relations, enabling them to be modelled in a manner that approached the standards of scientific rigour. At the same time, though, abstract mathematical formalism restricts our understanding of economic relations to a study in pure logic. These are not economic relations that exist in any real historical sense; they exist only within the logical framework of the theoretical model itself. Within the terms of such a framework, all conceptions of dynamic human agency are eliminated.

What we have by the turn of the twentieth century is a dominant conception of the economy as a purely abstract space, devoid of the impact of purposive human agency, and susceptible only to the force of routine reproduction. It is against such a conception that Veblen concentrated his critical writings. He dismissed any understanding of the economy in which the human subject was reduced to the mechanical bearer of an a priori economic rationality. In its place, he offered a theory that emphasized the relationship between reflexive individuals and the structure of social norms with which they are faced when they make their choices in everyday life. In Veblen's theory economic agents can truly be said to *act*, in the sense of being conscious both of the choices that lay in front of them and also of the consequences of the choices they make. In this respect, Veblen can clearly be seen to be operating in the intellectual tradition established by Smith. In neoclassical theory, by contrast, there is no conception of action, strictly speaking. Rather, economic agents *behave* purely mechanically, in an unthinking and unreflexive way, responding to no social stimuli other than their perception of their own material gain.

The chapter proceeds in three stages. In the first section, I outline the basis of Veblen's attack on orthodox neoclassical methodology, focusing in particular on his sceptical reception of agentless economic theory. I extend this critique in the second section, in which I present Veblen's view that competing forms of rationality can be made to co-exist in any advanced economy. In the third section, I show that multiple rationalities arise from, and then proceed to reinforce, the very different ways in which individuals relate to, and respond to, the prevailing structure of social norms within which the economy is embedded. I close the chapter by reviewing the significance that Veblen attached to these norms, which provided the core of his theoretical system of economic institutions, and which he called 'habits of thought'.

Veblen on economic method: beyond taxonomy

Thorstein Veblen remained on the margins of the economics profession throughout his lifetime, and his intellectual legacy continues to be that of an outsider. His academic interests marked his distance from his colleagues, and the core of economics is still no closer to asking the questions for which Veblen attempted to supply the answer. Veblen wanted to understand economic agents *in action* (Landreth and Colander 1994: 339). To do so, he attempted to chart the process through which the institutional structure of the economy formed out of the habits of thought of individual economic agents, in order to demonstrate that economic activity is shaped by the way in which we think about the economy. This could hardly have been more different from the orthodox methodology surrounding neoclassical theory. As Robert Heilbroner notes, 'Economics for Veblen had no relation to the mannerly and precise game of the Victorians in which the ways of the world were justified by the differential calculus' (Heilbroner 2000: 221). The introduction of mathematical techniques into economists' explanatory frameworks reduced economic activity to the purely perfunctory exercise of following behavioural rules that are an essence of nature. Thus cognition, awareness and reflexivity disappear as potential explanations of economic activity. For Veblen, though, these aspects of human life are the very essence of economic explanation, as they are constitutive of the economic *relations* out of which economic activity arises. Within Veblenian accounts of the economy, the thoughts that we have about the most appropriate way in which to act subsequently inform the actions that we undertake.

Veblen would not accept that the route to understanding economic relations lay in appropriating the static theories of Newtonian physics in order to provide a scientific explanation for instinctive utility-maximizing behaviour (Perlman 2000: 16). To his mind this was not economic theory at all, so much as an exercise in taxonomy. In so being, we arrive at the seemingly contradictory situation that the neoclassical framework is at odds with, and alienated from, the one object of study over which it could plausibly claim special knowledge: *actual* economies (Dyer 2000: 41). Veblen's position, in short, was that neoclassical theory bequeaths an economics that can tell us very little about the economies that we experience in practice.

Veblen distinguished between the taxonomist (what he thought economists had become) and the scientist (what he hoped they might be) by arguing that it is not the role of the taxonomist to ask 'why' (Veblen 1919a: 60). Neoclassical economics, thus accused, is about classification without explanation (Backhouse 2002: 198). In this way, it appears to reverse the epistemological shift evident within scientific thought in the second half of the eighteenth century (Jacob 1993; see also Chapter 3), out of which arose Adam Smith's distinctive style of analysis and the classical tradition of political economy more generally (Foucault 1989). This epistemological shift ended prior concerns to treat science as a purely classificatory endeavour. From such a perspective, scientists were restricted to the description of directly observable phenomena. In other words, science could talk only of the visible universe. The epistemological shift of the second half of the eighteenth century saw scientists become increasingly interested in explaining the invisible connections which coordinated observed effects within the visible universe (Fiori 2001).

Veblen's attack on neoclassical economics consists of two charges. First, it returns us to a world in which intellectual endeavour is oriented more towards classification than explanation. But this should not be seen as the complete reversal of epistemological priorities because, second, the pre-eighteenth-century scientist focused on the classification of directly observable phenomena, whereas to Veblen's mind the neoclassical economist did not. Veblen accused the neoclassical economists of his day of practising mere taxonomy, because their models spoke of a world that was divorced from the realm of direct observation.

For Veblen, this distinction between taxonomy and science was important. The taxonomist operates solely at the level of logic, making conditional statements and charting the nature of hypothetical relations that exist in a timeless space. By contrast, the scientist operates at the level of practice, making empirical statements about lived relations that exist in concrete historical time. It is, of course, necessary to respond with caution to claims that economics should be treated as a science, unless the boundaries of the scientific endeavour are also clearly specified. But it is evident, at least when working with the above definitions, that Veblen had a preference for economics to be scientific rather than taxonomic. As he put it, 'The outcome of the [taxonomic] method, at its best, is a body of logically consistent propositions concerning the normal relations of things' (Veblen 1919a: 67).

For Veblen, then, the issue was not that economists were increasingly claiming scientific status for their discipline, but that they were doing so on entirely fallacious grounds. The economics profession was charged with conflating scientific enquiry and the adoption of a mathematical method. But the two must be seen as distinct. Science, to Veblen's mind, was all about explanation of the real world, whereas a mathematical method only provided internal consistency for a logical model of a hypothetical world. As Bertrand Russell observes in his seminal book, *Principles of Mathematics*:

> The a priori truths involved in Dynamics [the mode of reasoning in physics on which neoclassical economics is based] are only those of logic: as a system of deductive reasoning, Dynamics [and, therefore, neoclassical economics] requires nothing further, while as a science of what exists, it requires experiment and observation. (Russell 1992 [1937]: 488)

Doubt must consequently be cast about the extent to which neoclassical economics provides 'a science of what exists'. Those that work in this tradition do so to the principles of syllogistic enquiry (Perlman 2000: 19), in which deductive inferences reaching a given conclusion are made on the basis of a small number of starting premises. The standard to which they work is immanent critique, in that the internal logic of the model is open to challenge, but not the fundamental predicates of the model itself.

This may approach Thomas Kuhn's specific, albeit somewhat jaundiced, conception of the operation of a scientific community (Kuhn 1970). Within the Kuhnian framework, science is constrained by paradigmatic norms, whereby adherence to a set way of thinking is more important than the development of new forms of knowledge. Science is therefore to be seen as a social process, in which the personal relationships that socialize scientists into working within tightly specified parameters of study in turn lead to research that is marked by its conformity and its conservatism. But this is not what Veblen had in mind when he argued that economics needed to become more scientific. For Veblen, science was to be progressive, both intellectually and politically (Veblen 1919b: 59–60). As a consequence, the test of a scientific economics was whether it could generate new forms of knowledge that were capable of animating transformative social activity (Lawson 2003: 204). In Sebberson and Lewis's words, Veblen's overall contribution 'is an exercise in critical social science whose goal is social action in general and emancipation in particular' (Sebberson and Lewis 1998: 252).

The goal of creating a critical social science is frustrated by the distinctive conception of causality that dominates neoclassical economics. With the methodological framework of neoclassicism increasingly focused on a purely mathematical logic, Veblen argued that economics suffered from a lack of true causal statements (Lawson 2003: 196). Veblen distinguished between a methodology of 'sufficient reason' and a methodology of 'efficient cause' (Veblen 1919b: 58–63). The latter he viewed as emblematic of true scientific explanation, although it was the former that he identified with neoclassical economics.

The neoclassical methodology of 'sufficient reason' is able to construct relationships between economic phenomena to give the impression of causal statements, but it does so at the level of logic only. What is missing is any real sense of cause and effect among those aspects of the economy that impact upon our everyday lives. As Veblen notes, the methodology of 'efficient cause', which attempts to understand economic relationships through the perspective of cause and effect, begins with observations of past actions and asks how these actions result in present occurrences. By contrast, the methodology of 'sufficient reason' understands present occurrences in terms of their ability to realize future goals. In Veblen's words, 'The relation sought by [neoclassical] theory among the facts with which it is occupied is the control exercised by future (apprehended) events over present conduct' (Veblen 1919a: 237). The methodology of 'sufficient reason' can only tell us whether an individual can plausibly be said to have had a reason to act in a particular way. As first argued in Chapter 2, though, to be said to have *had* a reason for acting in a particular way is not necessarily the same as *the* reason for having engaged in such actions. The former is a post-hoc rationalization of the action, couched at the level of psychological disposition (Fay 1996: 96). It is only by concentrating on the latter that genuine explanation becomes possible. Consistent with the IPE I am developing here, this requires a historicized understanding of present occurrences. Importantly, it also requires that we reject all alternative accounts in which the present is functional to the satisfaction of some future state of the world.

Neoclassical economists tend to present such accounts. As Veblen made clear, within neoclassical theory, it is not the past that acts as a guide to current behaviour so much as the future. In other words, neoclassical theory pays no attention to the way in which the historical development of the economy's accompanying social institutions privilege particular patterns of behaviour in the present. Instead, such behaviour is explained by the combined assumptions of instrumental forethought and material self-interest, which together are deemed sufficient to guarantee that knowledge of a certain future will condition current conduct. Conduct in the present is therefore to be explained in a purely functional manner. Action occurs in the way it does because it has to occur that way if it is to lead to the derivation of utility-maximizing outcomes and the satisfaction of self-interest. Only one course of action can produce such results and, as such results are the manifestation of a universal behavioural psychology, that course of action must be chosen *by definition*. The future is epiphenomenal of a behavioural psychology that situates the individual in a context in which there are no social constraints on a crude instrumental rationality, and the future therefore represents a convenient telos which determines present undertakings.

The future-oriented methodology of 'sufficient reason' allows us to understand the significance that is attached to the concept of equilibrium within neoclassical theory. For Veblen, equilibrium is a normative, rather than an explanatory, concept (Landreth and Colander 1994: 330). It is used as a justification for organizing economic relations in a manner consistent with, and appropriate to, the development of a market society: the argument being that markets in equilibrium generate socially beneficial outcomes. However, this argument can only be sustained because the prior commitment to a methodology of 'sufficient reason' requires no empirical investigation of the social consequences of market equilibrium, and neither does it require empirical investigation of whether a particular market is in equilibrium at any given moment of time. Equilibrium is simply assumed, as are the social benefits of equilibrium, and the prevailing methodology mandates proof of neither assumption. The significance of Veblen's contribution to the debate on economic methodology lies in his insistence that equilibrium theorizing be abandoned in favour of historical studies of actual processes (Hahn 2000: 122).

The task for Veblen is to liberate the analysis of individual economic action from the shackles of the teleological framework of neoclassical theory. In his own words, neoclassical economics cannot 'deal theoretically with phenomena of change, but at the most only with rational adjustment to change which may be supposed to have supervened' (Veblen 1919a: 232). Clearly, however, there is no scope for understanding the reflexive element of human agency within such a framework. Indeed, the very idea of conscious and reflexive human agency is eliminated from the prevailing mode of explanation. The economy is conceived as an arena in which individuals interact with one another, yet the nature of those interactions is by no means contingent. It is predetermined by the teleological assumption that the economy forcibly imposes a logic of self-interested and purely self-serving behaviour onto all its participants. We are left with a conception of the economy in which individual actors are important, but there is no choice involved in the actions they undertake. Certainly, there is no room for a theory of conscionable action within a methodology of 'sufficient reason' founded on the hedonistic principles of neoclassical economics (Veblen 1919a: 239).

In order to facilitate the development of such a theory, which restores a dynamic conception of conscious human agency to economics, Veblen made the case for 'a theory of a process, of an unfolding sequence' (Veblen 1919b: 58). That sequence is non-teleological in character, requiring a contingent and contextually-specific understanding of economic rationality. Veblen pointed to the possibility of introducing alternative rationalities within a given set of economic circumstances: in effect, to reconstitute 'the economy' by reshaping the behavioural traits through which economic relations form. Individuals may respond in many different ways to the structure of social norms within which their economic relations are embedded, depending in large part on how their understanding of these norms leads to different reactions to the moral consequences of their intended actions. It is to the question of potentially re-making economic rationalities that I turn in the following section.

Veblen on human nature: beyond hedonism

The basis of Veblen's insistence that a single economy sustains many potential rationalities was the straightforward observation that different people occupy different positions within the economic system and, as a consequence, perform different roles. Rationality, for Veblen, was not an innate property of human nature, but a learned response to the socialization process that attends particular economic roles. Some identify themselves primarily as workers, and are socialized as such. Others see themselves as producers, or owners, or consumers – the list is lengthy. Moreover, these roles are not mutually exclusive, certainly not over anything other than the shortest of short runs. The same person can identify themselves in different ways, depending on the social circumstances in which they are called upon to act at any particular moment of time.

The primary target of Veblen's attack on the orthodox conceptual framework of neoclassical economics was the conception of human nature on which the orthodoxy is founded. Within such a framework, action is abstracted from the social circumstances in which all human relations are situated in practice. As a consequence, the motivations for action are homogenized around a single, invariant conception of human nature. Veblen was apt to use the label 'hedonistic economics' for neoclassical theory, in order to capture the essence of its understanding of the way in which humans act. He identified in neoclassical theory the internalization of a crude behavioural psychology in which all acting human subjects are compelled, as if by a force of nature, to maximize their own utility regardless of the social consequences of their actions.

Adam Smith's impartial spectator, who insists on self-command so as to control 'the violence and injustice of our own selfish passions' (Smith 1982 [1759]: 157), has no place in such a theory. According to Smith, it is the impartial spectator 'who, whenever we are about to act so as to affect the happiness of others, calls to us, with a voice capable of astonishing the most presumptuous of our passions, that we are but one of a multitude, in no respect better than any other in it' (1982 [1759]: 137). But it is this impartial spectator that neoclassical theory banishes to exile. Smith suggests that it is only '[i]n solitude [that] we are apt to feel too strongly whatever relates to ourselves' (1982 [1759]: 153), and it is this solitary condition that neoclassical theory imposes upon all human agents.

Given this starting assumption, the task of economic theory is merely to deduce the logical corollaries of a crude instrumental rationality (Veblen 1919a: 233–4). Moreover, set within the context of such an assumption, neoclassical economists proved themselves to be capable logicians. As Harry Landreth and David Colander note, 'The logic was impeccable, but' – and this is a big 'but' – to Veblen's mind at least, 'the assumption was wrong' (Landreth and Colander 1994: 332).

For Veblen, human behaviour was a response to circumstances that were encountered in everyday life, not a response to questions of pure logic (Backhouse 2002: 195). The human condition escaped the neat packaging that was imposed upon it by economic laws that operated behind the back of the individual by placing all explanation solely at the level of a priori rationalization. For economics to retain the humanistic mode of enquiry that Veblen advocated (see Seckler 1975: 53), it is necessary to forsake the imagined certainties of law-like predictions. Adopting a Veblenian position, human behaviour is instead to be explained through a method that was more familiar to psychology and anthropology. The aim for Veblen was to traverse the boundaries between these two disciplines and his own by asking – as would psychologists – what shapes human motivations to act in particular ways, but always to understand these motivations – as would anthropologists – in relation to the social context in which they were made manifest. In following such a method we are led to Veblen's principal insight. This is, in Heilbroner's words, 'that the motives of economic behaviour can be far better understood in terms of deep-buried irrationalities than in terms of the nineteenth-century prettification of behaviour into reasonableness and common sense' (Heilbroner 2000: 233).

The nineteenth-century tradition against which Veblen argued is perhaps best encapsulated by Edgeworth's reduction of the individual economic agent to a simple 'pleasure machine' (Edgeworth 1881). His objections were twofold. First, he dismissed on normative grounds the suggestion that rationally calculated self-interest was sufficient to provide the basis for harmonious economic relations and a just society. He argued that this assumption acted as an ideological justification for a status quo that was, in practice, grounded in very different behavioural traits. Second, he dismissed a purely hedonistic understanding of human behaviour on analytical grounds. He argued that the preference functions on which neoclassical behavioural theorems were based contained no explanation of how preferences form and how they are acquired in the first place (Hodgson 2001: 141).

Preferences, according to Veblen, are inseparable from the socializing influence exerted by the institutional context in which economic relations are set. Given the possibility of changing the character of that context through decisive political interventions, it is always necessary to think of preferences and, as such, of the actions they inform, as potentially dynamic. They are part of, and reflect, the political fabric of society; therefore, they mirror its contingent characteristics.

Veblen consequently castigated the vast majority of the economics profession for allowing themselves to work with a conception of agency that rendered human nature 'passive and substantially inert and immutably given' (Veblen 1919b: 73). The irreducibly human element of economic relations cannot be conceived through this perspective as the realization of a structure of propensities and habits that unfold in concrete historical time. Rather, they must be presented as an instinctive manifestation of desires, which are experienced, made sense of and acted upon in a single moment of time (Seckler 1975: 53).

In what is arguably Veblen's most frequently cited passage, he satirizes the subsequent basis of neoclassical theory in the following way:

> The hedonistic conception of man is that of a lightning calculator of pleasures and pains, who oscillates like a homogeneous globule of desire of happiness under the impulse of stimuli that shift him about the area, but leave him intact. He has neither antecedent nor consequent. He is an isolated definitive human datum, in stable equilibrium except for the buffets of the impinging forces that displace him in one direction or another. Self-imposed in elemental space, he spins symmetrically about his own spiritual axis until the parallelogram of forces bears down upon him, whereupon he follows the line of the resultant. When the force of the impact is spent, he comes to rest, a self-contained globule of desire as before. (Veblen 1919b: 73–4)

While academic appraisals of Veblen's work have tended, perhaps understandably, to concentrate on the highly evocative depiction of the neoclassical subject as a 'globule of desire', for present purposes the more important part of this passage is that which states that the neoclassical subject 'has neither antecedent nor consequent'. It highlights the tendency within neoclassical theory to understand the actions of one person in isolation from the actions of all other people. The theory must therefore remain silent on the very essence of political economy: namely, how economic relations are forged in and through human *interactions*. If the neoclassical subject is to be understood as having 'no antecedent', then it is impossible to historicize the subject's motivations for action. Without historicizing motivations, however, the social forces that help shape the individual's conception of 'needs' and 'wants' are eliminated from the analysis. If the neoclassical subject is to be understood as having 'no consequent', then behaviour cannot be regulated by individuals' concern for the moral implications of their actions. An analytical framework cast in these terms erodes the basis for a theory of conscious and reflexive action in its wholesale – albeit implicit – dismissal of the very notion of society.

Veblen identified a certain tension within neoclassical theory 'in respect of [theorists' understanding of] the alertness of the response and the nicety of adjustment of irksome pain-cost to apprehended future sensuous gain' (Veblen 1919a: 235). In other words, debate arose about how quickly the equilibrium outcome ensues. Nonetheless, 'on the whole, no other ground or line or guidance of conduct than this rationalistic calculus falls properly within the cognizance of the economic hedonists' (1919a: 235). That is, the assumption of an eventual equilibrium outcome was not challenged. The methodology of 'sufficient reason', coupled with the ontological assumption of material self-interest, simply will not allow anything else. They are truly conceived to be 'how things are', a part of the nature of things.

Veblen argued, however, that the grounds on which to argue that the hedonistic calculus reigns supreme as the arbiter of human conduct are entirely spurious. He wrote that, 'it is the characteristic of man *to do something*, not simply to suffer pleasures and pains through the impact of suitable forces' (Veblen 1919b: 74, emphasis added). He moves on to draw a crucial, although often overlooked, distinction between behaviour and action. For Veblen, the purely hedonistic neoclassical subjects merely behave. No actual action is required on their part. Their choices are revealed to them by the hedonistic calculus, and the motivational force of instrumental self-interest necessitates that they overlook any thought that they may have to conduct themselves in a manner that does not conform to purely rational calculations of utility-maximization. This is not action, strictly speaking, according to Veblen, because to act first requires one to be conscious of the alternative courses of action that are available in a given set of circumstances.

Yet it is precisely such a notion of alternative courses of action that adherence to the dictates of the hedonistic calculus rules out by definition. As Colin Hay notes, conceptual frameworks founded on the hedonistic calculus substitute a crudely constructed utility function for conscious human agency (Hay 2004b). Rational choices are therefore not choices at all in the conventional sense of the word. Choice requires thought and conscious reflection about how to act in particular conditions. However, the hedonistic calculus eliminates thought from action, as conduct is determined in a wholly predictable manner by the opportunity structure of the hedonistic calculus itself.

As a counterpoint to the behavioural traits of the neoclassical subject, Veblen outlined what he considered to be a true theory of humans *in action* (for the significance of such a theory to IPE, see Chapter 1). Within this conception, thought and action are deemed to be inseparable. He argued that:

> human activity . . . is not apprehended as something incidental to the process of saturating given desires. The activity *is itself the substantial fact of the process*, and the desires under whose guidance the action takes place are circumstances of temperament which determine the specific direction in which the activity will unfold itself in the given case. (Veblen 1919b: 74, emphasis added)

In other words, agents must be conscious both of the actions that they undertake and the state of mind that promotes such actions, before they can be truly said to be acting. Veblen's social world is one of a process in motion, and that process is animated by the reflexive actions of conscious human subjects.

As Tony Lawson argues, by working with a conception of human nature that emphasizes the reflexive characteristics of acting subjects, Veblen advocates a transformational social ontology (Lawson 2003: 204). Within such an ontological framework, each aspect of everyday life that conditions future choices, be they economic or otherwise, is either reaffirmed or challenged by actions in the present. The economy must therefore be seen as an arena for present and future social action, which is continually experiencing twin pressures, for routine reproduction on the one hand and for qualitative transformation on the other. Significantly, these pressures are themselves the result of past and present social action.

It is through human activity, and the thought processes that both attend and precede human activity, that the structures of the economy are first created, and then recreated, in either their extant or a different form. It is also through human activity that individual subjects can be transformed by changing the stimuli to which the thought process responds. For Veblen, the key to comprehending the way in which the economic system was bound together lay not in proffering some supposedly immutable law of economic being; instead, it revolved around understanding the habits of thought that shape particular forms of practice, which in turn create relatively settled patterns of behaviour. By implication, then, the transformation of the economy first requires a decisive and wholesale shift in established habits of thought. I turn in the final section of this chapter to Veblen's analysis of the process of economic habituation, in order to assess the possibility of translating a theory of conscious and reflexive action into political praxis.

Veblen on institutions: understanding habits of thought

Veblen's focus on the significance of institutionalized habits and conventions has its origins in his analysis of the machine process of his day. Those that spent their working lives attending to the machine process were assumed to be subjected to the acculturating influence of an industrial way of thinking. They had to learn how one part of the machine process impacted sequentially on all succeeding parts, increasing their awareness of the way in which their decisions affected other people. As a consequence, this led to the habit of explaining in terms of cause and effect (Backhouse 2002: 196–7).

However, this form of rationality was assumed to apply only to those who spent their days engaged in making goods to meet social needs. By emphasizing social provisioning as the principal role of economic activity, Veblen assumed a similar normative position to that of one of the founders of the neoclassical approach, Carl Menger (see Chapter 2). But the economy of Veblen's day was also an arena for those whose primary goal was to make money. Veblen attributed to this latter group not the rationality of the machine process, but the rationality of business enterprise (Veblen 1965 [1904]). Far from inculcating an industrial way of thinking, the rationality of business enterprise privileges purely pecuniary motives, irrespective of their impact on the overall provisioning needs of the economy. To return to a distinction outlined in the opening chapter, the rationality of the machine process corresponds to the realm of oikonomia, while the rationality of business enterprise corresponds to the realm of chrematistics. Veblen's concern was that the provisioning needs of oikonomia were becoming increasingly subservient to the money-making wants of chrematistics, both in economic theory and the practices of everyday life. As Alan Dyer observes of the ensuing trend towards individual acquisitiveness, 'Veblen identifies an inherent tendency to confuse economic need with commercial expediency in business culture, which transforms ordinary economic life into a ceaseless competition for pecuniary symbols of success' (Dyer 2000: 42).

For Veblen, the ultimate goal of industry is to meet the needs of society, while that of business is capturing markets at someone else's expense (Veblen 1965 [1904]). Veblen thus draws a stark, and politically charged, distinction between industry and business. In doing so, he alludes to two entirely separate processes that modern economies sustain. First, the economy serves the somewhat routine process of meeting the demands of everyday life. Second, it also serves fundamentally non-economic ends, such as the search for social status, power and authority.

The different ends that the economy serves both reflect, and are a reflection of, the competing rationalities of industry and business. Note, however, what is missing. Veblen describes two different processes of habituation, which in turn lead to different modes of behaviour, yet neither approximate those associated with the hedonistic calculus. The hedonistic calculus may well dominate the intellectual habits of neoclassical economists, but Veblen finds no basis to argue that it also provides the habits of thought of the subjects that neoclassical economists purportedly study. Neoclassical theory is thus presented by Veblen as, at best, an interesting experiment in logic and, at worst, a wholly insignificant contribution to the study of economic affairs. At the very least, it has nothing to say about Veblen's distinctions between machine process and business enterprise, and between industry and business more generally.

The economic dichotomy between machine process and business enterprise is inseparable from the human dichotomy that Veblen outlines between the benevolent propensities that motivate creative behaviour and the malevolent propensities that motivate destructive behaviour (Hill 1998: 157). Within Veblen's framework, those working in the machine process are acculturated with benevolent propensities, insofar as industrial rationalities are organized to serve the social good. By contrast, those working in business enterprise are acculturated with malevolent propensities, insofar as commercial rationalities are organized to serve the individual acquisitiveness of the business classes (Veblen 1965 [1904]).

However, such is the starkness and the stringency with which Veblen draws the distinction between benevolent and malevolent acts that he sets up a deterministic trap, into which the unwary will fall. The implication in this part of his work is that we can simply read off behaviour from the economic logics that different subjects bear. This clearly creates a tension with the more careful distinction he draws between behaviour and action, whereby subjects can only be deemed to truly act in those instances in which conscious thought is involved. Yet no such reflection is required in circumstances in which behaviour is predetermined by the prevailing economic logic.

Veblen's theory of history is largely at odds with his theory of human nature – indeed, to the point at which David Seckler identifies 'two Veblens' (Seckler 1975: 52). History, in both *The Theory of the Leisure Class* (1970 [1899]) and *The Theory of Business Enterprise* (1965 [1904]), is driven by techno-industrial forces. The 'leisure class' plays an important role in reproducing extant economic conditions, as do the business classes. But neither can truly be said to be history makers in Veblen's analytical schema (Mills 1970: xvii). It is the technological innovators who are the history makers, through their impact on the structure of the economy, and through their ability to incorporate ever more people into the machine process and, as a consequence, to socialize ever more people into set ways of thinking consistent with industrial life.

However, in his theory of human nature, socialization is itself a contingent process. The structures of the economy may exert socializing pressures, but there is no automatic correspondence between such pressures and resultant behaviour. All action is set within the context of, and preceded by, conscious thought (Veblen 1919b: 75). The reflexive dimension of human agency ensures that socializing pressures emerging from the economy can be, and are, mediated in a variety of ways, leading subsequently to differentiated forms of action. The thought/action dialectic suggests that we, as conscious human agents, are as involved in shaping the circumstances in which we find ourselves as those circumstances are in shaping us. In Veblen's words, the human agent must be seen as 'an individual, acting out his own life as such' (cited in Hodgson 2001: 141). Thus the relationship between economic structure and human agency is more complex, and less determinate, than Veblen's own theory of history implies.

Within the broader corpus of Veblen's work, structure and agency were deemed to interact through the influence of habits. The process of habituation takes two forms. On the one hand, habits may be a normative 'conception' or 'criterion', operating in the same manner as Adam Smith's 'sentiment of propriety', in order to inform the individual of the moral consequences and the social merit of the actions that they plan to undertake. On the other hand, habits may be a 'usage' or 'act', which takes place at one stage removed from fully conscious and fully reflexive human agency, being performed without due deliberation and as if by instinct (Veblen 1964 [1914]). Veblen called the normative conception or criterion a habit of thought, and the physical usage or act an institution. The prevailing institutions of the economy therefore privilege deterministic behaviour, while the habits of thought that attend conscious reflection impose a much more contingent character upon economic relations. So long as actions are set within the context of habits of thought that question their moral consequences, there is no necessary reason to believe that actions are determined at the level of economic structure.

Indeed, Veblen considered habits of thought to be prior to and more important than institutions, as is clear from his assertion that changes in the structure of the economy revolve around, and follow, changes in habits of thought (Veblen 1919b: 75). To the extent that habits of thought are always susceptible to redefinition under the influence of a decisive political intervention, the core operation of the economy is also amenable to political pressures for change. Habits of thought should be seen as the cognitive frames through which moral meanings are imputed to intended actions (Hodgson 2001: 149). They facilitate understanding of the world, but they do so in such a way as to ensure that conscious human agents are always aware of the social consequences of their actions. They represent the basis of the prevailing belief system of society, and they can often exhibit inertial tendencies, persisting after the circumstances in which they were first embedded no longer apply (Backhouse 2002: 195).

At any particular moment of time, people can become conditioned into accepting particular ideas about 'how things are', for no reason that can be reduced to a rational calculation. In Veblen's terms, such ideas should be understood as 'an outgrowth of habit' (Veblen 1919a: 241). That is, they are not strictly speaking current habits of thought, which require conscious production and reproduction, so much as the ossification of prior habits of thought, through their reduction to the level of routine and unreflexive practice. It is at the point at which behaviour becomes primarily undeliberated and unthought about that Veblen identifies the emergence of an economic institution (1919a: 243). Institutions are therefore socially formed, in that they are the result of settled patterns of behaviour. In the same way, individuals must be thought of as being institutionally formed, in that their behaviour is at least partially shaped by the institutional context in which it is set.

The task then is to identify the conditions under which contingent habits of thought harden to become everyday social practices subjected to routine reproduction. Veblen focuses on one possible social stimulus that explains such a process: emulation. He argues that emulation is not an intrinsic feature of human nature, but that it is a practice that is socially learned. He illustrates this argument through reference to the consumption patterns of the 'leisure class', a reference that is surely still apposite today:

> For the great body of the people in any modern community the proximate ground of experience in excess of what is required for physical comfort is not a conscious effort to excel in the expensiveness of their visible consumption, so much as it is a desire to live up to the conventional standard of decency in the amount and grade of goods consumed. (Veblen 1970 [1899]: 80)

The institutions of a commercial society that tolerates business enterprise can therefore be seen both to reflect the materialistic criteria of success in a pecuniary culture and also to further embed those criteria as the dominant social norm.

Veblen's most important insight into the social dynamics of modern life related to the extent to which pecuniary emulation has become a common attitude of the mass of people (Heilbroner 2000: 233). True to his broader conceptual framework, it remains necessary to understand this common attitude as having been socially produced. It has its origins in the particular structure of interests and ideologies in which the consumer society is situated. Interestingly, Veblen depicts the instinct of emulation as a distorting influence on economic activity. Not only does it divert resources away from worthwhile production at the expense of the social good, but it also creates incentive structures that inhibit our chances of realizing our potential as active social agents (Sebberson and Lewis 1998: 269–70). At the same time, however, the social institutions of a pecuniary culture enable us to understand important parts of the operation of everyday economic life, as well as the misunderstandings that are imputed to them in neoclassical theory.

First, within neoclassical theory, the price mechanism acts to coordinate production. It sends signals to consumers about the utility that they will receive from consuming a particular good, and the market demand to which producers respond is formed as a rational response to anticipated utility. Not so, says Veblen. Instead, 'the price system dominates the current commonsense in its appreciation and rating of [the] non-pecuniary ramifications of modern culture' (Veblen 1919a: 245). In other words, the price mechanism acts as a guide to the psychological gratification that can be expected by buying a product at that price in a society conditioned by the instinct of emulation. Calculations of the value of the product relative to its price are unimportant, as are calculations of the expected utility that its consumption will provide. We do not think like the economic subjects of neoclassical theory, according to Veblen. It is the symbols of social status that accompany being known to have consumed luxury goods that determines whether they will be purchased in the first place.

Second, within neoclassical theory, ownership is the fundamental condition of production. In the absence of institutionalized private property relations there are no incentives for production to take place. Not so, says Veblen. Production does not require private ownership, but when it is set within such a context it takes on a particular form and serves a particular purpose. 'Wherever the institution of private property is found, even in a slightly developed form, the economic process bears the character of a struggle between men for the possession of goods' (Veblen 1970 [1899]: 34). In other words, the existence of private property relations plays a social legitimation role. It provides an economic rationale for ideologies of individual acquisitiveness, and it reduces the moral disapprobation that can be directed against those who behave in this way.

Third, within neoclassical theory, the human subject responds to no other motivation than a purely instrumental self-interest.

Rational calculations about desired behaviour require no other basis. Not so, says Veblen. It is possible that we internalize behavioural traits that make us appear to be consciously self-interested, but this is not because self-interest is the sole arbiter of intent. 'The canons of decent life are an elaboration of the principle of invidious comparison, and they accordingly act consistently to inhibit all non-invidious effort and to inculcate the self-regarding attitude' (Veblen 1970 [1899]: 234). In other words, self-interested behaviour is a learned response to a prevailing structure of social norms, one which suggests that there is nothing improper about acting in such a way. For Veblen, self-interest is not embedded in human nature, so much as it is embedded in a dominant political project of possessive individualism.

Conclusion

Veblen's lasting contribution to the history of economic thought is to challenge the meanings of the words that define the concepts which represent the core of orthodox economic analysis. None of the neoclassical edifice escapes his critical attention. His aim is to elicit a similarly critical self-scrutiny in others, imploring them to reflect more deeply on the appropriateness, both analytical and political, of the basic premises of economics (Dyer 2000: 52). The imaginative response that he sought from others has made only limited inroads into the economics profession. However, it is much more evident in the activities of a whole host of civil society groups, who are currently questioning the very ethos of the conspicuous consumption lifestyle against which Veblen focused his analytical attack.

Veblen's attempt to distance himself from economic orthodoxy was primarily an ethical dissent from the status quo (Landreth and Colander 1994: 340–1), yet he also provided a framework for an alternative conception both of 'the economy' and of economics. Neoclassical theory, when subjected to Veblen's acerbic critique, was turned into a pale shadow of the scientific discipline that its adherents claimed it to be. He emptied its hedonistic calculus of all pretence to explanatory status. He demonstrated not only that there was no empirical basis for assuming a crude instrumental rationality, but also that there was no attempt amongst neoclassical scholars even to show that this was so. 'Logical congruity with the apprehended propensity is, in this [the neoclassical] view, adequate ground of procedure in building up a scheme of knowledge' (Veblen 1919b: 61). Neoclassical economics, argued Veblen, is detached, in an ethereal manner, from the world of everyday experience. Its theorems may well be logically sound, but they relate to lives that cannot be lived. The neoclassical theory of markets abandons the everyday language of the economy. In its place it imposes a minimal, and entirely fanciful, set of static social criteria for organizing economic life (Dyer 2000: 46). As Heilbroner notes, 'Veblen wanted to know something else: why things were as they were in the first place. Hence his inquiry began not with the economic play, but with the players' (Heilbroner 2000: 221).

Veblen's economic agents may appear to be too much in hock to the determining influence of technology. He was, after all, fascinated by the machine. Beyond this, however, Veblen bequeathed an important and instructive framework for analysis. He returned the study of the economy to the study of everyday action. In so doing, he highlighted a crucial relationship: that between conscious reflection on the propriety of action and the reproduction of routine practices in everyday life. His emphasis on conscious reflection opens a conceptual space for developing a theory of conscionable action, which in turn can inform a transformative political praxis. His emphasis on the reproduction of routine practices suggests the existence of socially produced constraints on the political transformation of the economy. The following chapter extends and deepens the analysis of such constraints by focusing on the work of Karl Polanyi.

Chapter 6

Social Embeddedness within Political Economy: The Work of Karl Polanyi

Introduction

As is clear from the two previous chapters, both Smith and Veblen operate with a theory of human nature in which the motivation to act has multiple sources, leading to a range of different, and often mutually incompatible, learned responses. The same is true of Karl Polanyi. The work of all three emphasizes the social basis of economic activity, focusing on the tensions between those actions that are directed at the social good (oikonomia) and those that appear to be entirely self-serving (chrematistics). The authors differ, however, in their identification of the social stimuli that lead to these tensions.

For Smith, they are internal to the individual, and are to be found in all individuals. They are the result of the moral ambiguities that arise when our articulation of our self-interest occurs in the presence of the impartial spectator, that part of our consciousness which reminds us of the responsibilities we bear to others in all circumstances. For Veblen, by contrast, the tension between self-serving and socially oriented action mirrors a dichotomy within society that divides us into two distinct groups, on the basis of the competing rationalities of the machine process and business enterprise. He studies the way in which the pecuniary motives of business enterprise lead to the development of a leisure class, arguing that the instinct of emulation produces patterns of behaviour that undermine the social good in favour of self-seeking ends. In effect, this is an analysis of Smithian self-love, only reconfigured by the abstraction of mutual sympathy from human nature and by the loss of self-command that the impartial spectator would otherwise invoke.

The importance of Polanyi's contribution to debates in political economy lies in its ability to help us explain this shift between

Smithian and Veblenian conceptions of self-interest. Polanyi deepens our understanding of the institutional arrangements that provide the context for all economic activities. He moves the analysis beyond Veblen's focus on the economic determinants of economic institutions. Polanyi's work focuses instead on the political determinants of economic institutions. His aim is to demonstrate that particular patterns of economic behaviour have their origins in incentive structures that are shaped by legal statutes and, as such, are the product of the law-making interventions of governments.

Polanyi's view of the economy is therefore, like Veblen's, of a process that unfolds sequentially over time. He insists that economic relations are historically produced, and so can only be understood within the framework of historicized analysis. Indeed, it is a particular historical event to which Polanyi turned his attention in his most famous work, *The Great Transformation*. His major theoretical contributions are developed to explain the breakdown and subsequent collapse of the liberal market order of the late nineteenth century, which in turn led to the political dislocations that marred inter-war Europe. Polanyi shows that the era of the self-regulating market economy was short-lived, a historical curiosity, and laden with political contradictions. It is from this perspective that he proceeds to make the case for two developments: the first a move away from neoclassical economic orthodoxy, in which monetary exchange and the market economy are treated as permanent features of human history; the second a move away from policies that enhance the scope of market regulation, in preference to those that are less destructive of the social bonds that unite individuals in a single economic system. Polanyi challenges both the chrematistic worldview of neoclassical theory and the chrematistic lifestyle that neoclassical theory serves to legitimate.

The chapter is organized in three parts. In the first section I outline Polanyi's distinctive conception of the market economy, focusing in particular on the significance that he attached to the exchange relation as the fundamental foundation of 'the market'. This enables us to understand precisely what he had in mind in his assessment not only of the market economy's historical contingency, but also of its historical novelty. The second section concentrates on Polanyi's argument that 'the market' requires economic relations to be disembedded from society, and that this only happens when the content of government policy shapes the social relations of the economy in this way. I focus here on Polanyi's conception of economic institutions, which privileges their legal dimension. In the final section I return the analysis to the predominant theme of Chapters 4–6, that of the nature of the human agent who constitutes economic relations. Polanyi's conception of human nature is shown to revolve around the assumption that we are all beings of conscience. As a consequence, we are led back to Smith's impartial spectator and his ideas about mutual sympathy.

Polanyi on the exchange relation: the market economy as historical novelty

Karl Polanyi's classic work, *The Great Transformation*, was first published in 1944. It aimed not only to explain the economic origins of the descent into war, but also to specify the political economy of more peaceable international relations. In order to do so, Polanyi trained his critical social theorizing on a historical episode that is impossible to explain from the perspective of neoclassical economics: the retreat from a self-regulating market economy in the early decades of the twentieth century. A clear moral purpose is evident throughout Polanyi's work. His insistence that we focus on the historical specificity, and therefore political contingency, of the market economy prefigures his concern to demonstrate that there is no necessary hierarchy of interests whereby distribution and trade serve the sole purpose of monetary gain.

Polanyi's contribution is therefore to liberate the very idea of 'the market' from the taken-for-granted meaning ascribed to it in neoclassical theory. *The Great Transformation* is not so much the retelling of economic history as its systematic rewriting. Polanyi adopts the conventional market metaphor, but he does so in a thoroughly unconventional manner (Lewis 1991: 476). He argues that neoclassical theory attempts to explain economic outcomes by using the market metaphor, but is limited by this use to explaining those instances, *and only those instances*, in which the metaphor accurately describes actual experiences. The applicability of orthodox economics is therefore highly restricted. As Polanyi writes in a wry observation of such restrictions, 'as should be more clearly realized than it sometimes has been in the past, the market cannot be superseded as a general frame of reference unless the social sciences succeed in developing a wider frame of reference to which the market itself is referable' (Polanyi 1982: 50).

Polanyi's major insight was to suggest that laissez-faire policies themselves required conscious planning. Such an observation, he claimed, proved an irresolvable paradox for received economic wisdom (Polanyi 1957 [1944]: 141). Neoclassical theory operates with a naturalistic interpretation of the market metaphor. As such, markets are assumed to be essential features of the human life world, being both embedded in and embedding character traits that are innate and distinctive to us as humans.

Far from the market economy being an element of nature, for Polanyi it required that social relations be forcibly embedded within 'the market' (Jessop 2001: 222–3). In demonstrating the coercive dimension of such a process (Inayatullah and Blaney 1999: 328), Polanyi was able to show that 'free markets could never have come into being merely by allowing things to take their course' (Polanyi 1957 [1944]: 139). He argued that:

> the introduction of free markets, far from doing away with the need for control, regulation, and intervention, enormously increased their range. Administrators had to be constantly on the watch to ensure the free working of the system. Thus even those who wished most ardently to free the state from all unnecessary duties, and whose whole philosophy demanded the restriction of state activities, could not but entrust the self-same state with the new powers, organs, and instruments required for the establishment of laissez-faire. (Polanyi 1957 [1944]: 140)

Polanyi depicts economic relations as the manifestation of human struggle between two competing social forces (Searcy 1993: 222). On the one side we see those who are mobilized around the theme of 'habitation', whereby their political activities are trained on protecting people, their welfare, culture and natural environment. Those acting out of 'habitation' reside in the realm of oikonomia, as outlined in Chapter 1. On the other side are those seeking pure 'economic improvement', regardless of social cost, which takes its most obvious political form in arguments for a self-regulating market, sustained by the support of political authority. Those acting out of 'economic improvement' inhabit the realm of chrematistics and exhibit Veblen's rationality of business enterprise. For

Polanyi, however, conscious human agents need to be socialized into responding, increasingly unconsciously, to market-oriented stimuli. Such socialization does not occur unprompted. It requires the coercive appropriation of political authority in order to create a socio-legal incentive structure that privileges market-oriented behaviour.

For Polanyi, the existence of such an incentive structure represented qualitatively novel conditions that were unique to late nineteenth-century industrial capitalism. He saw this period as an inherent discontinuity of development, the attempt to introduce a self-regulating market economy appearing as a distinct phase of human history, a specific structural form of capitalism (Cangiani 1994: 21–2). Polanyi's attack on neoclassical economics must therefore be seen as dissatisfaction with the way in which everyday economic practices are reconstructed using a theory of strictly limited applicability. Judgements are made, and policy advice is given, on the basis of the logical working through of the theory itself, but the theory refers to conditions that are, at best, an increasingly irrelevant historical anomaly and, at worst, solely hypothetical. The supposedly universal principles of neoclassical theory are re-presented by Polanyi as a social fiction, based on the attempted 'naturalization' of a historical abnormality.

This is not to say that market ideology is anything other than a crucial element shaping the economy that we experience today, and neither is it to say that the appeal to intuitive market logics was fully exorcized at any time between the collapse of the late nineteenth-century economic system and more recent developments; but it is to draw attention to the significance of the distinction that Polanyi made between regulated and self-regulating markets (Polanyi 1957 [1944]: 57).

The analytical tools of neoclassical theory are appropriate only for understanding the latter (North 1977: 706), whereas it is the former that dominates all economic systems except, to Polanyi's mind, for the brief interlude of late nineteenth-century industrial capitalism. There is no denying the fact, within advanced industrialized societies at least, that capital accumulation currently provides the main driving force of economic activity. However, it is important to recognize that capital accumulation is facilitated, indeed sustained, by a multitude of extra-economic regulations (see Chapter 8). The dominant regulatory form has varied over time and space, both in function and content, consistent with the changing characteristics of the ideological environment in which it has been situated. The attractiveness of free market ideology as legitimating rhetoric for political interventions has been clearly visible in certain places at certain moments of time. Despite this, in adopting a Polanyian position, none of these forms should be confused with the free market itself (Polanyi 1957 [1944]: 130). The free market is logically incompatible with successful political mobilization against it, according to Polanyi, however partial such success may seem.

To reduce the whole of Polanyi's analysis down to a single idea, the market economy does not and has never existed as a stable long-term mode of economic development, because it cannot exist in that form. All economic systems require social regulation beyond the short term. The only question confronting those in public authority is what sort of regulation they choose to introduce (Cangiani 1994: 21). Indeed, reading Polanyi literally, a true market economy is nothing more than a logical abstraction, given both the scope and the necessity of state activity in providing appropriate forms of regulation. Certainly, he imposes such a stringent set of criteria that have to be met for a market economy to truly be said to exist that it is almost unthinkable that one could be experienced in practice.

Polanyi adopts the market metaphor of neoclassical theory with sufficient vigour as to insist that a market economy, strictly speaking, must be coordinated by the supply–demand–price mechanism and nothing else. Price is considered to be the single most important aspect of the market economy. Prices must be shown to fluctuate in line with prevailing patterns of demand and, simultaneously, to act as signals to control the level of supply arising from the production process. Any other observable modus operandi is not representative of a market economy in Polanyi's terms (Polanyi 1957 [1944]: 43).

The supply–demand–price mechanism requires inter-connected markets to form a complete system: 'all inputs purchased in markets, all incomes derived from sales on markets, all purchases/sales regulated by prices *alone*' (Schaniel and Neale 2000: 93). This is reminiscent of Walras's system of general equilibrium, which, it should be remembered, he himself insisted was a purely fictional system (see Chapter 2). Notwithstanding Walras's caution against treating the conditions for general equilibrium too literally, it is only in a situation in which they apply that, for Polanyi, the three secondary criteria for the existence of a market economy are met. First, the supply–demand–price mechanism must be the sole determinant of a product's exchange value. Second, the actual process of exchange must be conducted entirely through such a mechanism. Third, the reproduction of society must occur only through the unimpeded circulation of commodities in exchange for money (Jessop 2001: 218).

We are thus led to the significance of the exchange relation for Polanyi's distinctive conception of the market economy. Polanyi identifies three 'forms of integration' that act to coordinate and impose a structured unity upon economic activity: reciprocity, redistribution and exchange (Polanyi 1957 [1944]: 43–55; Polanyi 1982: 35–45). These are heuristic distinctions, insofar as they appeal to different motivational logics through which we can understand the essence of economic behaviour. More importantly for Polanyi, they are also empirical distinctions. They define three different sets of social norms, which come complete with three equally distinctive institutional forms, and which co-exist within any modern economic system. In practice, then, reciprocity, redistribution and exchange are not wholly autonomous organizational principles. No society can be described by sole reference to one form of integration, however dominant that form may be. The institutions associated with one organizational principle always interact with, and are embedded within, those of the others (Schaniel and Neale 2000: 94).

Briefly, the three forms of integration refer to the following characteristics (for commentaries on Polanyi's position, see Hechter 1981: 408–9; Schaniel and Neale 2000: 91–3). Reciprocity occurs in social systems in which trust is the prevailing social norm. Two-way barter at a particular moment of time is not required for reciprocal relations to dominate; it is sufficient that both parties within the relationship expect the value of transacted goods to be equal over the long term. The social organization of a reciprocal economy involves symmetrical power relations between its participants. Second, redistribution occurs in social systems in which a strong governing authority is able to direct the pattern of rewards that the system exhibits. Goods flow appropriationally to the centre, before being dispersed in a manner conducive to satisfying the social good. The social organization of a redistributive economy involves general consent to centralized power relations. Third, exchange occurs in social systems in which buyers and sellers form autonomous groupings, and in which they bear no further obligations to one another other than to complete a specified transaction at a particular point of time. Interactions take an apparently random character, determined only by demand and ability to pay. The social organization of an exchange economy involves the presence of atomistic individuals, where a system of price-making markets substitutes for power relations.

Given Polanyi's wider concern to demonstrate the institutional specificity of the market economy, he focused most attention on the nature of the exchange relation. In this respect, his work speaks on the same issues as neoclassical economics, albeit with significantly different conclusions. In what remains the seminal statement of the philosophical basis of neoclassical theory, Lionel Robbins reduces the exchange relation to a purely 'technical incident', which is 'subsidiary to the main fact of scarcity' (Robbins 1969: 19–20). Polanyi's conception of exchange involved an altogether different set of philosophical commitments.

His aim was to show that exchange relations stand out from reciprocal and redistributive relations, in that they are the only way of organizing an economy that is both institutionalized in and serves to institutionalize individual acquisitiveness (North 1977: 707; Fusfeld 1994: 2). Acquisitiveness is not an a priori human characteristic, as it is in neoclassical theory, given by the prevailing contextual assumption of scarcity. For Polanyi, the social effects of individual behaviour result from the institutional arrangements in which behaviour is contemplated and, once considered legitimate, subsequently enacted (Polanyi 1982: 35–6). Individuals are conscious of the economic choices they make, but the content of their consciousness is shaped by the institutions of the economy. Exchange takes place according to the prices to be found in market-based institutions, and the presence of those institutions creates an incentive structure that rewards acquisitive behaviour. The act of exchange, the existence of price-making markets and the traits of acquisitiveness are therefore mutually constitutive; each depends on the others, and takes on a wholly different social meaning in their absence.

However, it is important not to let the argument run ahead of itself. Actually existing economies are always founded on some combination of Polanyi's three forms of integration (Jessop 2001: 214; Chang 2002: 546). To the extent that an economy experiences pressures for structural change, these should only be understood as attempts to redefine the *relative* importance of reciprocity, redistribution and exchange. The familiar market model of neoclassical economics is therefore inappropriate in all but the most unusual of circumstances, due to its underlying conception of pure exchange relations.

As a consequence, it is necessary to revisit the theory of prices. In the neoclassical framework, the process of price formation occurs solely within equilibrating markets. For Polanyi, the existence of such a process is what defines an economy specifically as a market economy (Polanyi 1957 [1944]: 43). However, the co-existence of reciprocity, redistribution and exchange within all economic systems suggests that the process of price formation is not a purely economic exercise: there are also social determinants of price. It is to this that I turn in the following section, in order to establish the terms on which Polanyi discusses economic institutions.

Polanyi on fictitious commodities: the embeddedness of economic institutions

An interesting connection can be drawn between the respective price theories of Smith and Polanyi. For Polanyi, a fully functioning market economy can only be deemed to exist in circumstances in which economic activity occurs on the basis of pure exchange relations. Prices in such circumstances reflect the fact that the economy is an operationally autonomous system, which responds to its own internal logic and nothing else. This is analogous to the phenomenon that Smith labelled 'natural prices'.

However, both men questioned whether such a situation was attainable in practice. For Polanyi, it meant that all social relations would have to be so fully incorporated into the prevailing market logic that the economy appeared to exist, in some sense, beyond society. For Smith, it meant that value alone would determine price, and that the business classes consequently could not hold a privileged position from where they could impose a price structure onto the rest of society. For both men, the social dynamics of price formation presented a potentially insuperable impediment to the 'natural prices' (Smith) that were the basis of the 'market economy' (Polanyi).

The major difference between the price theories of Smith and Polanyi is in the political complexion of these social dynamics. In *The Wealth of Nations*, Smith depicted them as overwhelmingly regressive, at least insofar as they work against the interests of society as a whole. It is the business classes who are able to suppress the introduction of progressive social regulation of the price mechanism, leaving them free to impose the price structure they choose. In *The Great Transformation*, Polanyi depicts society as an active agent, harnessing the authority of the state for progressive purposes in order to introduce the social regulation that Smith thought was beyond it. Polanyi points to this process as evidence of the essential social embeddedness of all economic relations. It was only by defending the embeddedness of 'the economy' that it became possible to control the tendency towards acquisitiveness that had led to the economic crisis and the political dislocations of the inter-war years.

Polanyi identifies two trends that explain the elevation of a purely individualistic conception of self-interest to the status of social norm. The first, which occurred before the time that Smith wrote *The Wealth of Nations*, provided behaviour oriented towards individual acquisitiveness with what Daniel Fusfeld calls its 'moral letters of credit' (Fusfeld 1994: 5). The Renaissance and Reformation came complete with new structures of socialization, which conferred legitimacy upon the value system associated with acquisitiveness, by privileging instrumental reason over moral reason (Baum 1996: 41–2). The second, which Polanyi dates to the first half of the nineteenth century, concerns the development of markets in labour, land and money. This he assumes to be a functional necessity of the introduction of Veblen's rationality of business enterprise to a commercial society that might otherwise remain distinct from overly chrematistic lifestyles (Polanyi 1957 [1944]: 75). The rationality of business enterprise required that labour, land and money – the factors of production – be readily available for incorporation into the economy. This was achieved by state action that made them available to the business classes on a commercial basis (1957 [1944]: 42).

Polanyi labelled this latter development the 'commodity myth'. Labour, land and money are 'fictitious commodities' in that they are sold as if they were commodities without first having been produced for sale (Polanyi 1957 [1944]: 72). They are routinely traded at relative prices, as determined by supply and demand. They are given monetary values at which they can be exchanged, and they can be used to the point of physical destruction, as if they were simply merchandise (Baum 1996: 4). Polanyi's concern, however, is that they are not the product of human industry. There is no sense in which any of these 'fictitious commodities' exist only in the form in which they are bought and sold: labour abstracted from the labour market retains an essential being in its human form (Polanyi 1957 [1944]: 163); land that has no commodity price attached to it remains part of the natural environment (1957 [1944]: 184); and money serves social functions other than increasing wealth through self-valorization (Polanyi 1982: 46).

Polanyi's chief concern relates to the fictitious treatment of labour as a commodity. In this, there are clear parallels between his work, Marx's concept of alienation, and Smith's lament to the human indignities enforced by a complex division of labour. While Veblen believed that the work process could have a civilizing effect, insofar as it acculturated workers into industrial ways of thinking aimed at furthering the social good, Polanyi, Marx and Smith all came to the opposite conclusion. In Polanyi's words, 'the fiction that labour is produced for sale was consistently upheld... [However], the commodity fiction disregarded the fact that leaving the fate of people to the market would be tantamount to annihilating them' (Polanyi 1957 [1944]: 131). In other words, organizing everyday life using the supply–demand–price mechanism is fundamentally dehumanizing, in that it robs people of so many of the characteristics that make them essentially human. It eliminates 'all organic forms of existence and replaces them by a different type of organisation, an atomistic and individualistic one' (1957 [1944]: 163).

For this reason, Polanyi depicted as part of a dual process society's search for protection from the ever more intrusive encroachment of market logic and market institutions into everyday life. He argued that political mobilization around the principle of 'economic improvement' led to the extension of 'the market' in relation to genuine commodities. At the same time, political mobilization around the principle of 'habitation' led to its restriction in relation to 'fictitious commodities' (Polanyi 1957 [1944]: 76).

The politics of the economy therefore reduce to a struggle between the oikonomic tendencies of the latter, in which markets are seen as an accessory of economic life, and the chrematistic tendencies of the former, in which social life is seen as an accessory of markets. Alternatively, this can be viewed as a contest over institutional design: whether, respectively, to embed the economy within social relations, or to embed society within market relations.

Reciprocity and redistribution are forms of economic integration that focus on society-building activities, relegating growth *vis-à-vis* solidarity (Hechter 1981: 424). In societies where reciprocal and redistributive systems come to the fore, the economy tends to be embedded in non-economic institutions. By contrast, in societies where exchange relations dominate, individuals tend to be disembedded from the wider interpersonal relations of trust, respect and mutual awareness of one another's life chances, which would otherwise denote the social institutions in which they operate (Jessop 2001: 223).

The process of institutional disembeddedness will clearly have an effect on the way in which individuals understand their identities, interests, capabilities and practices. Each is recast in terms of the commercial culture that emphasizes the logic of profit-maximization and material self-enhancement. As Gregory Baum suggests, disembedded social relations challenge the ethical basis of community life, in their creation of 'a devastating anomie' (Baum 1996: 9). Polanyi thus leads us to a crucial contradiction in capitalist development. On the one hand, the market economy requires workers to display an honest, diligent and responsible attitude towards their work. These are characteristics that typically are socialized into people at an early age, through the influence of family, community and society. Yet it is precisely these social institutions that are undermined by the personal alienation and dislocation wrought by the market system, hence destroying the system of socialization structures that are fundamental to its very survival (Polanyi 1957 [1944]: 168).

Polanyi described the human element of this contradiction in the following terms: 'In disposing of a man's labour power the system would, incidentally, dispose of the physical, psychological, and moral entity "man" attached to that tag...the "ideal system" of the new economics demanded a ruthless abnegation of the social status of the human being' (1957 [1944]: 73, x). The process of commodification accompanying the imposition of the market mechanism into ever more aspects of daily life therefore produces human tensions that the market mechanism alone cannot resolve.

Consistent with Gramsci's concept of resignation (Gramsci 1971), Polanyi argues that the social institutions of the market economy become most influential in those moments in which they dissolve the human capacity for imagination (Polanyi 1977: 84). This may be a familiar theme when viewed through the perspective of contemporary debates about globalization. The global economy is typically presented in public discussions as a necessitarian entity, complete with an attendant political logic of no alternative (Watson and Hay 2003), to which individuals must simply learn to respond (Kayatekin and Ruccio 1998). Adopting Polanyi's position, the social institutions of the global economy may be nothing more than a reflection of those of the market economy more generally. For Polanyi, the primary function of those institutions is to socialize the human subjects of the economy into accepting that things can be no different. It is in this sense that life within 'the market' is corrosive of the imagination. But it is the ability to exercise imagination which, for Adam Smith at least, makes it possible to live life as a truly *human* experience (Smith 1982 [1759]: 9).

It is perhaps unsurprising, then, that many have associated current globalizing trends with Polanyi's concept of disembeddedness. Embeddedness, for Polanyi, is the social control of economic relations through institutional means, where a link can be drawn between embeddedness and the social obligation to act in a morally dutiful manner. Insofar as 'the market' imposes purely functional character traits on individuals, whether it is a global market or not, the moral dimension of economic activity is increasingly dissolved. Conscionable action remains possible in such circumstances, although it is entirely self-defeating. However, for Polanyi, ethics are the most important element in the constitution of society (Baum 1996: 64–5). Set in such a context, we should expect markets and society to be mutually exclusive phenomena; the former erodes the basis of the latter.

I turn now to Polanyi's attempt to reclaim the very notion of society from the dislocations wrought by the market economy. I do so by reviewing his theory of human nature. Polanyi believed that life within society was consistent with our essence as human beings and, as a corollary, life within systems bounded by market norms was not.

Polanyi on human nature: beyond utilitarian accounts of being

Polanyi argued that differences in behaviour are in large part attributable to the institutional arrangements that define the social circumstances in which individuals are situated (Hechter 1981: 404). Individuals whose everyday lives are shaped by market-oriented institutions are therefore most likely to be socialized with characteristics that are rewarded within market society. There may well be instances in which the acquisitiveness of *homo economicus* is made manifest in pronouncements of a psychological disposition towards purely self-interested behaviour, yet this in itself is to be viewed as a reflection of the environing effects of institutions in creating self-interested identities. The institutions of the economy both support and precede present economic activities, while being the result of past economic activities.

In modern neoclassical economics social institutions are constructed as market rigidities. The early neoclassical writers were agnostic on the normative implications of such a construction (see Chapter 2). Some believed that it was legitimate to attempt to remove such rigidities, while others saw their presence as a reason to deny the legitimacy of the market economy. Yet, despite the varying implications drawn by the founders of the neoclassical tradition, today the immanent logic of the theory tends to translate into a political justification for purer forms of market relations. This, at any rate, is how it is typically read from a Polanyian perspective. However, such relations require people to think in particular ways, to behave in particular ways, and to react to the needs of others in particular ways. All of these are learned responses, arising from particular structures of socialization. The dissolution of society into isolated and atomistic individuals is itself the creation of a specific set of social institutions. Those in which a market economy is embedded are still to be seen as social institutions, even in circumstances in which they are responsible for both facilitating and legitimating fundamentally asocial behaviour.

Social institutions add an element of predictability to behaviour, in that they are consciously devised constraints to shape human interaction (North 1990: 3). In an important sense, institutional structures are the embodiment of the dominant values of the social system (Fusfeld 1994: 2). To whatever extent we can identify *homo economicus* in ourselves and in those around us, this is a product of our social environment. Polanyian political economy, in J. R. Stanfield's words, focuses on the economic system as 'a component of culture rather than a kind of human action, the material life process of society rather than a need-satisfying process of individual behaviour' (Stanfield 1986: 38). Economic relations reflect an institutional structure that shapes individual choices, which in turn lead to interdependent activities that constitute the economic process (Polanyi 1982: 32).

Polanyi consequently objects to the attempted naturalization of a purely instrumental rationality within neoclassical economics. He has few difficulties accepting the central assertion that, at the root of human activity, we find the desire to maximize. However, he argues that the determinants of what is maximized are social rather than biological or psychological (Hechter 1981: 405–6). The instrumental utility-maximizing neoclassical subject is only evident within a tightly specified set of social institutions; such subjects do not emerge on the basis of a transhistorical and transcontextual behavioural characteristic. The pursuit of material gain is assumed in neoclassical theory to be an expression of inner being. For Polanyi, though, it is more the embodiment of institutionalized compulsion, whereby individuals are required to respond to market norms using purely instrumental reason in order to secure their own futures (Dalton 1971: xiv).

Institutions can take a variety of forms and so, subsequently, can institutionalized patterns of economic activity. Such variety is obscured, however, by economic theory that seeks to naturalize the concept of a supply–demand–price mechanism as the only social institution of a market-based economy (Polanyi 1982: 48). This has the effect of also naturalizing a means–end calculus of material gain, to create the perception that all possible forms of rational action must necessarily conform to the standards of instrumental rationality (Howard and King 2001: 798).

For Polanyi, this was the same as saying that human subjects are at the whim of laws that are not human laws (Polanyi 1957 [1944]: 125). Such laws are twofold: the scarcity postulate, which is the contextual assumption on which all of modern neoclassical theory is founded; and the assertion of acquisitive behaviour, which gives life to neoclassical models by creating the impression of an economic process. Polanyi's contribution is to show that these laws are not inherent in human nature. They may be partially derived from the institutionalization of a market economy; but this, he assumes, will always remain incomplete, due to its self-destructive internal contradictions. Significantly, however, the perception that such laws hold continues to exert a substantial influence on the public consciousness, as well as on public policy, because of the certainty with which they are stated in orthodox economic theory.

It is perhaps important at this point to reiterate Polanyi's central contention that this theory applies to a unique, and tightly circumscribed, set of historical conditions. As such, neoclassical theory elevates conjunctural features of a specific institutional configuration to the level of generic and universally applicable categories of life (Stanfield 1986: 41). Polanyi demonstrates that calculative behaviour oriented towards material gain provides only one of many possible moral frameworks for economic activity. It is only when social institutions take a specifically market-based form that instrumentally rational economic concerns permeate the meaning of all aspects of social existence (Inayatullah and Blaney 1999: 324). Polanyi's aim is to review the range of possible moral frameworks for economic activity, while being careful to differentiate between those that increase and those that reduce the social accountability of individual behaviour.

In developing his own account of human nature, Polanyi embraced the themes of Aristotelian rhetoric (Polanyi 1957 [1944]: 5; Polanyi 1968; see also Stanfield 1986: 8–10). He viewed orthodox economic explanation as a constitutive element of an elaborate utopian experiment, which requires critical deconstruction using a rhetoric that is both analytically investigative and politically mobilizing (Lewis 1991: 478–81). The specifically Aristotelian element of Polanyi's rhetoric is evident in the active political response it implores: it seeks remedial interventions guided by concerns for enhanced social justice.

Polanyi emphasizes the conscionable dimension of action by arguing that there are no human activities, economic or otherwise, that do not have social, and therefore moral, consequences. We are aware of the world around us, and such awareness is prompted by the experience of day-to-day life. This may appear to be an ostensibly routine experience, but Polanyi defines it as an essentially ethical task. Our thoughts for ourselves are inseparable from our thoughts of others, what Polanyi termed the *Lebensweg* (for a discussion, see Baum 1996: 22–41). We therefore recognize in ourselves responsible agents who seek clarification about the likely consequences of our actions before proceeding to act. The subjects of economic history are therefore responsible human beings, sometimes acting individually and at other times acting collectively.

Society enters into the definition of the individual, to the extent that it provides conscious human subjects with the context through which they come to perceive their own identities. In this, there is an obvious similarity between Polanyi's theory of human nature and Smith's concept of the impartial spectator. It is possible to treat the impartial spectator as a manifestation of society, prompting concern in the minds of individuals as to how their actions will be understood and judged by those around them. It serves as a constraint on purely instrumental behaviour, by being a constant reminder that no action is ever purely economic. All economic activities carry with them cultural and social meanings and consequences. We encounter society as an ethical and interactive form of life; the ensuing *Lebensweg* entails a commitment to modesty and self-limitation (Polanyi 1977: 87).

To think and act in ways other than this first requires particular patterns of socialization that separate the characteristics embodied in Smith's impartial spectator from the prevailing sense of duty and responsibility. Polanyi identifies the structure of neoclassical economic thought as one such socializing influence. He argues that neoclassical theory has created an artificial distinction in the way in which we understand human motivations (1977: 5–11). It treats as 'real' the material motives of economic life, made manifest in economizing behaviour designed to meet self-interested ends and to maximize utility. By contrast, it treats as 'ideal' all motivations for economic action that are derived from emotions other than material gain, including concerns for the moral consequences of action. In such circumstances, it is perhaps understandable when we choose the certainties of the 'real' over the uncertainties of the 'ideal'.

Like Smith, then, Polanyi emphasizes the significance of the familiar. Actions tend to take the appearance of orderliness through repetition of behaviour with which we are familiar. Like Veblen, Polanyi suggests the more that self-interested behaviour is reduced to the level of the familiar, the more that we are likely to behave in self-interested ways. This can give the impression that purely instrumental activities are a simple reflection of human nature. But this is all it is, an impression, made evident by the socializing influence of the prevailing political, social and ideological structures.

To treat such behaviour as natural is to commit, in Polanyi's memorable phrase, the 'economistic fallacy'. This arises when one category of action, 'economizing', is conflated with an arena in which action is undertaken, 'the economy' (Stanfield 1986: 41–7). The contingency of any particular form of economic relations is consequently lost in the assumption that 'the economy' has a necessary essence, made manifest in economizing behaviour. Polanyi berates such an elision as a 'social prejudice' (Polanyi 1957 [1944]: 159), which forces 'an artificial identification of the economy with its market form' (Polanyi 1982: 50). Stanfield perhaps sums up best the disillusionment that Polanyi felt for neoclassical economics as a structured body of thought, describing it as 'patently and radically ethnocentric' (Stanfield 1986: 41). Polanyi does not wish to deny either the significance or the existence of 'the economy' in any modern society, yet he insists that economic activities can, and very often do, take place outside the context of a pure supply–demand–price mechanism. As a consequence, it is a logical error to presume that all economic phenomena can be embraced by the concept of 'the market' (Polanyi 1977: 6). The identification of an abstract model of 'the market' with everyday experience is not a matter that can precede empirical investigation. Moreover, for Polanyi, on this issue the empirical evidence is clear: the human economy cannot be reduced to its market form in any a priori manner. As such, there is no basic economic logic that compels economizing behaviour (Polanyi 1977: 117–18; see also Howard and King 2001: 737–8).

For Polanyi, we must avoid confusing 'a broad, generic phenomenon [i.e., economic behaviour]' with that 'with which we happen to be familiar [i.e., economizing behaviour]' (Polanyi 1977: 5). Such confusion leads to the reification and subsequent naturalization of current social arrangements within advanced industrialized countries, thus undermining the possibility of mobilizing around alternative forms of political praxis (Inayatullah and Blaney 1999: 326).

In order to facilitate our awareness of such possibilities, Polanyi drew the distinction between two different meanings of economic. The economy can be understood either 'substantively' or 'formally' and, according to Polanyi, the two have 'nothing in common. The latter derives from logic, the former from fact' (Polanyi 1982: 29).

The substantive meaning of economic refers to the everyday experience of interacting with others in the immediacy of social contact in order to first create, and then sustain, satisfaction in life. The formal meaning of economic refers to the logical properties of a means – end relationship in conditions of scarcity, in which behaviour is determined by an abstract situation of instinctive choice. Neoclassical theory is viewed by Polanyi as 'the application of formal economics to an economy of a definite type, namely, a market system' (1982: 32). The significance of this point, of course, is that neoclassical theory is wholly inappropriate to the task of deepening our knowledge of economic relations, in all circumstances except those in which a system of price-making markets caters for all human needs, as expressed purely in terms of a crude instrumental rationality.

Conclusion

For Polanyi, the major concern with orthodox economic explanation is its tendency to treat as given social conditions that relate only to a historical abnormality (Polanyi 1957 [1944]: 104). Neoclassical theory is constructed behind a conceptual façade that provides a post-hoc rationalization for purely self-interested behaviour, but little else. It certainly does not allow us to understand the way in which the economy is embedded as a human process situated in institutionally specific social relations. Polanyi's work, with its distinctive conception of the market and its challenge to accepted meanings of the economy, facilitates discussions that lie beyond the scope of traditional microeconomic analysis.

The crux of Polanyi's criticism of market society revolves around the way in which a market-driven culture creates new sets of human wants (Baum 1996: 48). Such wants in turn induce self-interested behaviour in an attempt that they may be satisfied and, as a consequence, they serve to undermine the interpersonal bonds that unite society at least to the extent of rendering it stable (Hechter 1981: 411). A pure market society may well facilitate a substantial increase in material wealth. However, the institutionalization of such a system would prove to be a Faustian bargain as it would privilege a set of motivations, values and norms that would themselves destroy the society in which they prevailed (Fusfeld 1994: 6).

According to Polanyi, the market economy does not occur naturally, and neither do the social conditions that bring a market economy into being. Both are viewed as the cultural artefacts of conscious political interventions enacted at the level of the state. For Polanyi, there is an inherent ambiguity in the role of the state in modern society. The policy-making apparatus of the state has simultaneously been called upon for two purposes: first, to promote the further encroachment of the structures and the logic of the market economy into everyday life and, second, to regulate their advance in the interests of the social good. To question the reification and the naturalization of the market within neoclassical economics is therefore to reflect more deeply upon the way in which market economies develop and how they are influenced by wider social dynamics (Chang 2002: 548–9). As Dennis Searcy notes, the role of public authority in this process remains 'obscured by the cultural impact of the market myth' (Searcy 1993: 221).

The analysis now changes focus. The previous three chapters have studied the way in which the economy has been understood as an integrated social system by three critical social thinkers, each of whose work falls within the classical tradition of political economy. Conscious human subjects have been shown to be the key historical agents enacting such systems. It has consequently been of particular significance to reveal the theories of human nature on which these conceptions of economic relations are founded. I have argued that the assumption of a universal human nature is misplaced. To the extent that action takes on the appearance of orderliness through routine social reproduction, this is not due to any innate human characteristics; rather, it is the contingent result of behavioural traits that have been actively and systematically socialized. In other words, it is a question of cultural conditioning. The following two chapters explore how this conclusion impacts upon our understanding of the two most important conceptual categories within IPE: 'the market' and 'the state' respectively.

Chapter 7

Understanding the Market within Modern Society

Introduction

From the previous three chapters, it is clear that there is much more to theorizing the conditions under which market relations form than we can learn from modern neoclassical economics. This would perhaps be unimportant for current purposes, were it not for the fact that the conceptual framework that underpins neoclassical economics is all too often incorporated into IPE. This is not to say that neoclassical *theory* is accepted by more than the most orthodox of IPE scholars. However, I do argue that important elements of the neoclassical *framework* re-emerge within much IPE.

Two such aspects of the neoclassical framework are particularly noteworthy. First, and the focus of the previous three chapters, is a theory of action which reduces all conduct to instrumentally rational behaviour. This ensures that actors are merely prisoners of a predetermined behavioural logic. Second, and the focus of this chapter, is the fact that the market is treated as a mechanism. In other words, the market itself is considered to be as capable of acting as those who form inter-personal relations within a market environment. In neoclassical economics, the market acts to coordinate individual activities in such a way as to produce a functioning economy. It is a mechanism that creates social order out of what might otherwise be the disorderly context of purely self-interested behaviour. In IPE, by contrast, the market tends not to be thought of as a coordinating mechanism, although it does still tend to be thought of as an actor. It is usually understood as an actor that is able to impose itself on international economic affairs, circumscribing political possibilities and thus shaping both the lifestyles and the life chances of those who operate within its environment.

My aim in what follows is to distance myself from both of these positions, which are dominant within IPE. There is a tendency within IPE to ascribe exactly the same characteristics of the utility-maximizing market actor *to the market itself*. In other words, the market is treated as an actor within its own environment. The market is assumed to have both an interest of its own and the will to ensure that its interest is secured. Such a position, while seldom explicitly stated in the stark terms outlined above, nonetheless sustains whole swathes of the academic literature. However, it is based on a double analytical fallacy. It is a mistake to reduce any action simply to the motivations that generate self-interested conduct. It is even more of a mistake to then assume that 'the market' exists in a form in which it could exhibit these fundamentally human behavioural characteristics; yet it is this assumption, albeit largely implicitly, that drives so many explanations of international economic affairs within IPE.

Much is written in IPE about market forces and the political effects of market ideology. However, despite the significance attached to 'the market' as a key explanatory variable in IPE, it remains fundamentally undertheorized as a concept. In this way, a number of entirely different conceptions of the market – some analytical, some ideological and others popular – are often conflated within academic discourse. This chapter proceeds in three stages. In the first section, I attempt to differentiate between the multiple meanings of 'the market', in IPE and beyond, focusing in particular on identifying an analytical meaning of 'the market'. I distinguish between the popular/ideological conception of the market as actor and the analytical conception of the market as an arena for human action. In the second section, I use the analytical conception of the market as an arena for human action to revisit one of the formative debates in the history of economic thought: how are individual activities coordinated in the context of decentralized market relations such that they create a smoothly functioning economy? I focus on Adam Smith's attempt to resolve the so-called coordination problem at the level of moral philosophy, and Léon Walras's later attempt to resolve the coordination problem at the level of pure economics. Walras's ultimately unsuccessful attempts set the scene for the discussion in the final section. Here I ask: if the introduction of market institutions has no justification at the level of pure economics, because the coordination problem cannot be resolved at that level alone, then how do we explain how market relations form and why market institutions are introduced? As a precursor to the analysis in the remainder of the book, I answer that question by saying, not through reference to the 'invisible hand'. Instead, I concentrate on the political activity that is necessary to shape society in the image of market relations. The imposition of market institutions is, in essence, a political decision.

The market as actor versus the market as arena for action

It is necessary to draw a number of crucial distinctions in an effort to inject analytical clarity into the discussion of markets that is to be found within the IPE literature. The first such distinction is between market actors and the market itself. It is human agents and human agents alone who can act within the context of inter-personal market relations in order to structure economic outcomes. Economic relations may or may not take the form of market relations but, either way, they are constituted by individual agents and not the market itself. As an analytical point, this may appear to be too obvious to need stating. However, this is not necessarily the case. Given the underlying progressive consensus within IPE, the debate within the literature often turns to the 'victims' of the current international orientation of market-based economics. Moreover, there are good prima facie reasons for so doing. Rampant inequalities within the international system, plus concerted attempts by the International Monetary Fund (IMF) and the World Bank to subjugate traditional lifestyles to market institutions, all sustain plausible narratives of victimization. However, such narratives often suggest that it is the market itself that creates both inequality and the pressure for societies to restructure themselves in the market's own image. This, though, is a serious misattribution of causality. It is not the market per se that generates such effects, but human agents operating within the context of market relations.

To identify 'the market', rather than those who operate within the market environment, as the cause of socially regressive outcomes runs the risk, somewhat paradoxically, of depoliticizing the whole issue. I say 'somewhat paradoxically', because it is difficult to believe that this is the intention of those who work within the critical consensus evident within IPE. The very essence of their work is to demonstrate that human relations shaped by market ideology lead to adverse social consequences. Yet the appeal to 'the market' as the sole determinant of such consequences serves only to obscure the wilful actions of conscious human agents. Indeed, they get written out of the analysis altogether.

The problem with such an approach lies in the fact that the market economy appears in the analysis as a process that has not only an internal logic, but also a will, of its own. In other words, 'the market' is assigned fundamentally human characteristics, which allow it to deliberate between alternative courses of action, before deciding on the alternative that best reflects its interests, and then imposing this alternative. Lost from the analysis is any sense of conscious human agents seeking to impose a particular type of market relations, which produce the effects that are then misattributed to the market itself. In turn, this hides from view the true political content of the effects and, as a result, protects the human agents who produce the effects from political counter-mobilization. If it is simply 'the market' that creates the effects, there are no conscious human agents to hold to account. If it is a process that takes place beyond the sphere of conscious human action, it is impossible to identify those who are to blame for the effects that the process enacts.

In order to avoid the depoliticization of market outcomes that attends such an approach, it is necessary to distinguish between the market as actor and the market as an arena for human action. In what follows, I will differentiate between the two usages by placing inverted commas around the former but not the latter. The latter usage, to my mind, is the only one that is analytically acceptable. The former sustains any number of popular/ideological positions, from those who consider themselves politically to be 'pro-market' to those who consider themselves politically to be 'anti-market'. Yet however enticing this might be as an analytical shortcut, no real analytical meaning can be derived from treating 'the market' as a wilful political actor in its own right.

This is true, despite the fact that the most popular conception of markets that we see in everyday usage is one that emphasizes the ability of 'the market' to secure its own interests. This conception, while implicit in the academic literature, receives almost constant repetition in both the written and spoken words of leading opinion formers and politicians. It is this conception, for instance, that enables globalization to be presented as a non-negotiable economic force and, as a consequence, as a structural constraint on government policy (Watson and Hay 2003). However, such a conception is only made possible in the first place by an underlying assumption that all individuals act to maximize a self-interest that is defined in all instances in purely material terms (i.e., the crude instrumental rationality postulate that receives critical attention throughout the book). With each individual deemed responsive to the same motivations for action within market environments, it is assumed that those individuals will always act in an identical manner. Viewed in this way, it is only a small, and superficially innocuous, conceptual jump to aggregate the conduct of individual market actors into a unitary whole. Once this conceptual move has been made, it becomes possible to conceive not only of individual market actors, but also 'the market' itself, as a consciously motivated agent. Of course, should the rationality postulate be challenged (see Chapters 1–6), there is no basis on which to make this move, and 'the market' cannot be seen as a strategic actor capable of imposing its will on human affairs. Instead, it must be seen only as an arena for strategic human action.

Settling on this definition of what a market is takes us beyond the generic themes of so much of the IPE literature. At the same time, though, it also raises new questions that require answers. Perhaps most obviously, if the market is to be understood as an arena for conscious human action, we must decide what counts as an arena in this respect. Do markets have to possess real physical dimensions to be treated as an arena, such that they create a context in which human relations form out of the immediate proximity of one person to another? Or can market relations form between individuals who do not, and are not ever likely to, share the same physical environment? In other words, can markets be virtual arenas of inter-personal contact and human conduct?

These are important issues to raise because markets no longer physically exist as defined marketplaces, and certainly not in the sense that all trade depends on face-to-face contact at a specified location. If we return briefly to the time of Adam Smith, references to the market were essentially descriptive; they were literal references. A marketplace actually existed, and it was a designated location that served one purpose for the surrounding community. It was a physical place in which buyers and sellers met face-to-face to trade. The language that Smith uses in *The Wealth of Nations* is highly instructive in this respect. In Books I and II, in which Smith outlines the fundamental properties of his market system, the language he adopts continually suggests that the market is to be understood as an ontological reality and not merely as a metaphor. Smith reiterates the image of goods being physically transported – from where they are made to where they are sold – in returning repeatedly to his definition of manufacturers' supply as the 'quantity *brought* to market' (Smith 1970 [1776]: 157–66, emphasis added).

The same image shines out of Jenny Uglow's collective biography of the master manufacturers of the mid- to late eighteenth century, the time at which Smith was writing: men such as Josiah Wedgwood and Matthew Boulton (Uglow 2003). Reading Uglow's account, one is struck by the distance that the master manufacturers were prepared to travel in order to make a market, particularly if they were in search of a high-profile commission. Both Wedgwood and Boulton undertook tours of royal courts and high society households throughout Europe, considering this personal touch to be necessary if they were to sell their wares. If the buyers were not willing to come to the designated marketplace, the actions of the master manufacturers seemed to be saying, then take the marketplace to them.

In Smith's day, then, the marketplace, as a physical entity, was the locus of commercial life. However, the historical purposes that marketplaces served have now been drastically reduced in significance. Eighteenth-century exchange relations, those that formed the basis of the first economic theories of the market, were restricted to the physical boundaries of the marketplace. It was face-to-face activity between what we now call the producer and the consumer. In the absence of the physical proximity of the two, market relations would not have formed and exchange would not have taken place.

However, the structure of eighteenth-century exchange relations has increasingly been overwritten. Part of the intrinsic human element to economic interaction, as embodied in the moment of exchange, has disappeared. This is not to say that exchange *relations* are any less human in nature, only that the *moment* of exchange now does not require the intimacy of face-to-face interaction. The process of exchange now routinely takes place between people who do not physically have to share a social space in order to interact economically. In most instances today, one party to the interaction is unlikely to know who the other party actually is. Indeed, in most conventional accounts, this is the very essence of the political economy of globalization: the idea that economic relations are being progressively stretched across space (Held *et al.* 1999; see also Chapters 9 and 10).

Two more distinctions therefore have to be added to the discussion. The first is between the market (understood generically as a context for human action) and the marketplace (as a specific location in which buyers and sellers come face-to-face in order to trade). The second relates to the recently reduced significance of actual marketplaces and, as a consequence, the increasingly virtual dimension of market relations. Economic activities conducted within actual marketplaces give rise to *literal* references to the market. Given that the increasingly virtual nature of market relations has done nothing to undermine the use of the language of 'the market' in contemporary political discourse, it is clear that such appeals are no longer literal. We would seem to have reached the point at which appeals to the concept of the market are more *metaphorical* than literal.

This leaves just one more issue to resolve. If we are to accept that the concept of the market is now more metaphorical than literal, in response to the changing spatial dimensions of economic exchange, we next need to ask, 'metaphor for what?' As soon as we acknowledge the metaphorical element of market-based economic discourse, we are required to render explicit the often submerged ideological content of the language of the market.

Disagreements abound on this issue within the literature, and the dividing lines for that disagreement are drawn according to the different theoretical positions that we find within IPE (on which see Chapter 1). From a Marxist perspective, for instance, 'the market' is a metaphor for the alienation that is imposed upon workers who have to sell their labour power to those who own the means of production. As it is the owners who benefit most directly from the system of forced labour, 'the market' is also a metaphor for an exploitative system that extracts surplus value from the workforce. For Gramscians, 'the market' is an important part of the rhetorical repertoire that seeks to sustain a coherent ideological underpinning for neoliberal economics. For feminists, 'the market' acts as a post-hoc rationalization of a social system that continues to tolerate systematically unequal economic treatment of women relative to men.

While these critical positions diverge on the question of for what, exactly, 'the market' is a metaphor, they are united on the question of for what it is not a metaphor. All dismiss the notion that 'the market' refers to a process through which individual economic activities cohere, in the absence of direct interventions, to create a functioning system. This, of course, is the coordination problem, successive attempts at resolving which provide the driving force for intellectual developments throughout the history of economic thought. It is to this issue and, in particular, to the ultimately unsuccessful efforts to resolve the coordination problem at the level of pure economics, that I turn in the following section.

The market economy and the coordination of individual activities

It is arguably *the* founding problem of economic enquiry: to explain how the actions of individuals undertaking the routine business of everyday life cohere to form the complex structures of advanced economies. Viewed as a black box, the economy appears as if it must have an innate coordinating mechanism if it is to sustain such structures. The task of political economy, however, is to dispense with the image of a black box, in order to specify the conditions under which coordination takes place. The coordination problem is the very lifeblood of economic analysis, and has been ever since Adam Smith made the first attempt to stipulate how the social dynamics of the market economy create a stable system.

Returning to the formative analysis of Adam Smith, it is interesting to note the level at which Smith attempted to resolve the coordination problem. For Smith, the key to understanding the conditions under which individual activities can be expected to cohere into a stable economy is to realize that this is not, in essence, an economic puzzle. The answer to the coordination problem is a matter of moral philosophy, according to Smith, not a matter of pure economics. His analysis focuses on the moral principles that underpin our socially conditioned responses to given economic circumstances, and he suggests that the coordination problem is resolved when, and only when, these responses instinctively embody the principles of justice in inter-personal relations.

To act justly for Smith is to deny whatever motivations we might experience to act in a purely self-interested manner. Smith was alert to the possibility that the price of a good represented more than simply an indication of its economic worth. Throughout *The*

Wealth of Nations, he points to instances in which the manufacturers of his day attempted to increase the price of goods above their true worth, such that the price mechanism manifested the self-interest of the manufacturers. Such observations formed the basis of his important distinction between the 'natural' price and the 'market' price (Smith 1970 [1776]: 157–66; see also Chapter 3). The 'natural' price prevails in economies in which all actors are socialized into acting justly. In such circumstances, justice in exchange is maintained, as all goods are sold at a price that corresponds to their true economic worth. The 'market' price, by contrast, prevails in economies in which some seek to secure their own self-interest, to the detriment of justice in exchange. The more that 'market' prices diverge from the 'natural' price, the more the criteria for justice are infringed. Significantly for the present discussion, the coordination problem can only be resolved when 'natural' prices are in evidence throughout the economy. Whenever prices reflect the self-interested enactment of asymmetric distributions of power, it is impossible to explain, as a matter of pure economics, how individual activities cohere into a functioning economy.

The key to resolving the coordination problem is therefore to explain how market actors may be able to restrain self-interested motivations to use whatever power advantage they might have in order to influence the structure of prices. Of course, this is not a question of pure economics at all, so much as a question of moral duty.

Smith's work is replete with references to the necessity of acting dutifully. Moreover, duty is not simply some abstract ideal for Smith. He suggests that we serve our own ends by acting dutifully. We have a genuine interest in the well-being of others (West 1976) because we not only have the capacity to display sympathy for the circumstances in which others find themselves; according to Smith, it is impossible for us not to internalize part of their feelings. We feel what other people feel (Smith 1982 [1759]: 10, 83–5), which has important implications for the decision to act self-interestedly. If, in acting self-interestedly, we infringe the criteria of justice and consequently do harm to other people, we ourselves also internalize an aspect of that harm through our capacity for 'fellow-feeling'.

Smith describes the capacity to rein in the self-interested passions, in order to satisfy the needs of others, as self-government (Smith 1982 [1759]: 76–7). Self-government emerges from a combination of duty and imagination. For Smith, we imagine ourselves in situations in which others approve of our decisions to act dutifully. This in itself increases the incentive to act in such a way. But the conception of duty only resonates with us in the first place because we have the ability to imagine our actions causing harm to other people.

It is only in circumstances in which all participants within a particular market environment exercise self-government that the coordination problem is resolved for that market. In the absence of such circumstances, the conditions will not be in place for individual economic activities to be coordinated without the intervention of an external agent ensuring compliance with a particular type of exchange relations. If the moral principles are not sufficiently embedded within society to ensure that the coordination problem is resolved, it then becomes a matter of politics if the economy is to function smoothly. At no stage in Smith's work does the smooth functioning of the economy reduce to a simple question of *economic* logic.

Attempts have been made, however, to stipulate the solution to the coordination problem in terms of pure economics. The most important such attempt was made by Léon Walras, in his *Elements of Pure Economics*. Walras's work differs from Smith's in many ways. Given the themes of this book, perhaps the most important is the theory of the individual on which their respective analyses are based. While Smith argued that it is fundamentally irrational for individuals to act out of pure self-interest, Walras was content, for the purpose of developing his analysis, to ascribe the simplistic behavioural traits of pure utility-maximization to all individuals.

In making this assumption, Walras reminds his readers that it should not be understood literally. It is a modelling assumption only, not an ontological commitment to a view of the world in which real-life economies are populated by pure utility-maximizers (Walras 1984 [1954]: 47; see also Jaffé 1980; Bridel and Huck 2002). Walras is not seeking to derive a theory of *the economy* so much as a theory of *pure economics*.

Walras attempts to specify the conditions under which exchange relations cohere into a functioning economic system. He begins with the concept of tâtonnement, which represents a theory of the determination of prices. Under the assumption of tâtonnement, the economy gropes its way towards a structure of equilibrium prices, such that all exchange relations are undertaken on the basis of utility-maximizing behaviour. As an abstract account of how equilibrium prices are formed – and, therefore, of how the coordination problem is resolved – this works fine. But it does nothing to tell us *why* such prices exist, or to explain the mechanism through which the process of equilibrium price formation is activated. In the first three editions of *The Elements* Walras attempts to solve this issue mathematically, while retaining the image of an economic process that develops over time. However, his attempts do not bear fruit. He is unable to reduce the process of tâtonnement to solvable mathematical equations, while at the same time preserving the iterative nature of the economy groping its way towards equilibrium through successive time periods (Walker 1987).

In response, Walras rethought his theory of tâtonnement in the edition of *The Elements*, the fourth, which is generally considered to be his seminal account of the coordination problem. He rules out all disequilibrium production and trading by definition. This reduces the tâtonnement process to an instant. In turn, it produces an account of the economy ostensibly groping its way to equilibrium, but in which all actual groping is eliminated. Walras's earlier theory of tâtonnement is an abstraction designed to capture the *history* of the equilibrating process. It represents a series of events that occur within the context of concrete historical time. By contrast, his later theory of tâtonnement is an abstraction designed to capture the content of the equilibrium *outcome*. The whole notion of a process, of a series of events unfolding over time, is lost. The existence of an equilibrium moment can be assumed, but the manner in which it comes to exist cannot be specified.

Within the framework of Walras's later analysis, the existence of equilibrium requires the prior existence of a character that resembles an 'auctioneer'. The 'auctioneer' presides over all known economic activity, and its task is twofold. On the one hand, it carries all market-sensitive information simultaneously to all market participants, so that they are all aware of the logical possibility of an equilibrium price structure. On the other hand, it cries out the equilibrium price as a guide for exchange relations, at which point all market participants, armed with the information to enable them to know that this is an equilibrium, undertake all possible exchanges.

The introduction of the 'auctioneer' resolves the coordination problem, but it does so at a substantial analytical cost. First, the need to rely on the 'auctioneer' to solve the coordination problem erodes the in-time interpretation of the tâtonnement process. However, in the absence of an in-time interpretation, nothing is actually being explained. The conditions under which an equilibrium exists can be demonstrated as a matter of deductive logic, but the introduction of the 'auctioneer' does nothing to explain the process of equilibration. Second, while the existence of an equilibrium can be subjected to logical demonstration, this is not a question of *economic* logic. Walras resolves the coordination problem *mathematically*, not economically. What we are left with is a market model that is able to elucidate a mathematical system, rather than a mathematical model that is able to explain the way in which exchange relations form in a market economy (Jaffé 1967).

Walras does more than simply fail to specify the economic conditions under which individual activities are coordinated to create a stable economic system. To my mind, he proves that the coordination problem is fundamentally irresolvable as a matter of pure economics. If this is true, then there is no *economic* justification for the introduction of market institutions. In the following section I explore the implications of this conclusion.

The political construction of market exchange: beyond the 'invisible hand' metaphor

The reification of 'the market' is now commonplace amongst both academic and policy-making communities. The incorporation of ever more people into structured market relations gives the impression that they are natural artefacts of life within modern economic systems. However, this is a misleading impression. As the previous section has shown, from the earliest writings in political economy, economists have attempted to derive the pure economic principles on which market institutions are founded, but each attempt has ultimately proved unsuccessful.

This may only be what we should expect, particularly if we view the development of actual economies in historical perspective. There is no instance in human history in which a pure price economy has existed, governed by nothing other than the price mechanism (Searcy 1993: 222; see also Chapter 6). However, this is not what seems to be implied in what is, almost certainly, the founding metaphor of modern economic analysis: that of the 'invisible hand'.

It is the image of the 'invisible hand' that sustains the marginalist techniques of the founders of the neoclassical tradition (on which see Chapter 2). In the absence of a mechanism resembling such a device, the discussion of equilibrating tendencies at the margin cannot be passed off as one from which any meaningful *economic* implications can be inferred. Without an 'invisible hand' there can be no explanation of *why* equilibrating tendencies arise in the first place, or why they take a form that can be analysed using marginalist techniques.

Moreover, neoclassical economists are not alone in working to the assumption that free exchange, embodied in market-based institutions, comes complete with 'invisible hand' dynamics. Much of the IPE literature is constructed on exactly the same assumption. The tendency for IPE scholars to work with a binary opposition between 'politics' and 'economics' (on which see Chapter 1) is most pronounced within the context of analyses of 'the market'. From such a perspective, 'the market' equates with pure economics and, as such, explanations of market dynamics must be situated solely at that level. From here it is but a small step to internalize assumptions about the 'invisible hand'.

Craig Murphy and Roger Tooze point to a 'tripartite pedagogical framework' within IPE, that of liberalism versus mercantilism versus Marxism, which they say is 'so often inappropriately used by scholars as something more than a tool for the beginning student' (Murphy and Tooze 1991a: 6). Within such a framework, 'invisible hand' dynamics – whether explicitly specified as such or merely acting as part of the assumptions from which the analysis unfolds – dominate the way in which liberal IPE is taught. For instance, from Jeffry Frieden and David Lake we learn that, 'Liberals believe firmly in the superiority of the market as the allocator of scarce resources' (Frieden and Lake 1995: 10); and from Robert Gilpin that, 'Economic liberals believe that the benefits of an international division of labor based on the principle of comparative advantage causes markets to arise spontaneously and foster harmony among states' (Gilpin 1987: 12). Moreover, if this is the view of liberal theory from two of the best-selling textbooks from the *IO* school of IPE, their British school counterparts are no less prone to describe the liberal view of the market in terms of the 'invisible hand' (on the distinction between the *IO* school and the British school, see Murphy and Nelson 2001; see also Chapter 1). For instance, from

Geoffrey Underhill we learn that, for liberals, 'the market' is 'self-regulating if individuals are left largely to their own economic devices' (Underhill 1994: 27); and from Robert O'Brien and Marc Williams that, 'Liberals believe that if individuals are left freely to engage in production, exchange and consumption all would benefit and that the insertion of state control distorts benefits and adds costs to participants in the market' (O'Brien and Williams 2004: 19). The 'invisible hand' lies behind all these conceptions of the market. Ngaire Woods is perhaps the most explicit of all when summing up the liberal tradition in IPE in the following way: 'The economy is oiled by freely exchangeable currencies and open markets which create a global system of prices which, like an invisible hand, ensures an efficient and equitable distribution of goods and services across the world economy' (Woods 2001: 285).

In such constructions of market relations, the 'invisible hand' is contained within the price mechanism that regulates free and voluntary exchange. Individuals are assumed to act in an instrumentally rational manner in response to price signals, thus activating the coordinating logic of the 'invisible hand' and ensuring that 'the market' manifests itself as an automatically self-adjusting and self-sustaining entity.

The 'invisible hand' metaphor originates with Adam Smith and, to be sure, Smith introduces it when discussing the relationship between the price mechanism and 'the market'. Smith used this metaphor only twice in the work that he submitted for publication during his lifetime. However, on both such occasions there is nothing in the original text to sustain the interpretation of 'invisible hand' dynamics that has subsequently found its way into IPE. Smith appears to use the 'invisible hand' as a metaphor for market failure rather than, as commonly assumed today, a metaphor for a spontaneously self-regulating market.

The first time that Smith uses the 'invisible hand' construction in the work that was published during his lifetime is in *The Theory of Moral Sentiments*. It appears in a passage in which he is bemoaning the self-aggrandizement and the luxury lifestyles of the landlords. Such displays of opulence are made worse because they occur in the presence of landless labourers, whose means of ensuring their own daily existence is much more limited. However, Smith appeals to something which is akin to a trick of nature, and which overrides the price system, in the amount of food that is consumed by the landowning classes *vis-à-vis* the landless labourers. Were consumption patterns merely to reflect the ability to pay market prices, Smith argues that the disdain the landowning classes showed the labouring classes would lead them to exploit the price system in order to consume the vast majority of the earth's natural resources. He suggests that this is not the case, however, because their consumption is limited by a finite ability to consume. The trick of nature is therefore the size of the human stomach. Despite their desire to revel in gratuitous displays of opulence, and despite having the material means to satisfy that opulence, the landowning classes can eat only what they are capable of eating. As Smith puts it, 'They are led by an invisible hand to make nearly the same distribution of the necessaries of life, which would have been made, had the earth been divided into equal portions among all its inhabitants' (Smith 1982 [1759]: 184–5). As such, the mere existence of a price system to guide exchange relations does not necessarily lead to socialization into purely self-interested forms of behaviour, and neither does it explain how market relations are constituted in practice.

The same is true, on both counts, on the next occasion that Smith uses the 'invisible hand' construction, this time in *The Wealth of Nations*. Here, Smith is discussing the reluctance of the nascent capitalist classes to invest their capital overseas, even in circumstances in which they could be reasonably sure that the returns to overseas investment would be greater than the returns to investing at home. His nascent capitalist classes are more confident investing in familiar surroundings, despite the fact that the promptings of the price system suggest that they should act otherwise. Smith argues that merchants stay close to home in an attempt to safeguard their financial interests, for fear of the unknown. Moreover, the unintended consequence of such actions is that they continue to provide a means of sustenance for domestic industry, and therefore they continue to contribute to the accumulated stock of the national economy. As Smith puts it:

> By preferring the support of domestick to that of foreign industry, he [the merchant] intends only his own security; and by directing that industry in such a manner as its produce may be of the greatest value, he intends only his own gain, and he is in this, as in many other cases, led by an invisible hand to promote an end which was no part of his intention. (Smith 1998 [1776]: 291–2)

Once again, the 'invisible hand' appears to be a metaphor for market failure.

It is, then, to disregard the intended meaning of the 'invisible hand' metaphor by attempting to reify a self-regulating market. In line with the perspective outlined in the previous chapter, it is also to ignore what Polanyi called the 'facts of anthropology' (Polanyi 1982: 40). As Jean Ensminger explains, one important difference between the way in which economists and anthropologists understand economic behaviour is what each takes to be endogenous to the behaviour itself (Ensminger 1996: 11–21). For an economist trained in neoclassical theory, behaviour is little more than a reflex response to signals, comprehended rationally, emerging from the price mechanism. The social institutions that shape the way in which prices form – ranging from the legal statutes of corporate governance law to moral norms relating to what constitutes a 'fair' price – are considered superfluous to explanations of how behaviour changes in response to price changes. By contrast, for an anthropologist trained in observing behaviour within human communities, the price mechanism alone carries little useful information about how individuals are likely to behave. What counts for an anthropologist is how social institutions shape the intentions of individuals, with prices in the economy reflecting those intentions, not the other way around. To turn all economic relations into pure exchange relations governed by price alone requires nothing less than the wholesale purification of human motivations into the single desire to act self-interestedly in all circumstances (Inayatullah and Blaney 1999: 313).

Of course, it may well be possible to point to recent political trends that have attempted to normalize acquisitive behaviour. These trends take many forms, all of which relate to a shift from public authority structures to private authority structures in the governance of the international economy. They range from a reassertion of entrepreneurial activity as the basis of the economy (Armstrong 2001), to related attempts to undermine the legitimacy of both the tax system and the payments to welfare recipients (Kitschelt *et al.* 1999); from the ever more personalized appeal to the individual as consumer (N. Klein 2000), to the related marginalization of questions of justice across borders (Caney 2005); from the reduced influence that organized labour has been able to wield over policy (Iversen, Pontusson and Soskice 2000), to the decline of collective identities more generally (Beck 2002); from the distributional effects of the tendency towards central bank independence (Watson 2002b), to the impact of IMF and World Bank adjustment ideology on the economic structure of developing societies (Fratianni, Savona and Kirton 2003). All of these changes point in the same direction: towards pressure for, and increasing social acceptance of, personally acquisitive behaviour.

It must be emphasized, however, that this is an artefact of distinctively *political* processes. There is no innate economic logic here, and certainly not an innate economic logic of 'the market'. Patterns of behaviour within market arenas are shaped by prevailing social institutions, which in turn reflect the dominant political orientation of society. It is on this distinctively political issue that I concentrate in the following chapter.

Conclusion

If we accept the writings of most academics at face value, 'the market' appears to have become a pervasive, and determining, influence on everyday life. 'The market' is variously presented as the primary institution to which we belong, the source from which we draw important aspects of our identity, and the entity to whose promptings we routinely respond. Little distinction is made between those whose experience of 'the market' follows directly from living within the institutional setting of advanced capitalist economies, and those who live beyond this core and whose experience of 'the market' is mediated by the influence of international institutions. Everyone is considered vulnerable to the social conditioning of the internal logic of 'the market'. In all instances, the will of the individual is subjected to the overriding will of 'the market'.

My aim in this chapter, however, has been to distance myself from this line of reasoning. To conceive of 'the market' as an entity that is capable of imposing its will is to treat it as an actor in its own right. I have used the foregoing analysis to stress the importance of rejecting such a view. 'The market' is not an actor; it is merely an arena for human action. It may well be possible to identify a will that is acted upon within the market environment, but this is not the will of 'the market' itself; it is the will of conscious human agents.

By treating the market as an arena for action, it is possible to restore a conception of dynamic human agency to the discussion of markets. This is rarely done in IPE, where it is more usual to ask how 'the market' shapes the choices of human agents than it is to ask how the choices of human agents serve to coordinate individual activities within market environments. The second section focused, in part, on Walras's ultimately futile attempt to resolve the coordination problem at the level of pure economics. This showed that the conditions for creating economic order are not, by nature, economic. I take up this theme in greater detail in the following chapter, demonstrating that such conditions are, by contrast, political. In order to analyse those conditions, I turn my attention to the other core concept in the 'states and markets' approach to IPE: the state.

Chapter 8

Understanding the State within Modern Society

Introduction

A tension appears to exist between those parts of the IPE literature that deal with the scope of state activities and those parts of the IPE literature that deal with the question of 'the state' itself. On the one hand, when IPE scholars are called upon to explain contemporary governance dilemmas associated with globalization, the impression they give is typically one of a crisis of the modern state. At the very least, the tendency is to suggest that the state is able to act in an increasingly limited way. Susan Strange captures such a view by arguing that globalization is synonymous with 'a fundamental change in the economic base of the world of states, in the power and even possibly the legitimacy of the state' (Strange 1994: 210–11). On the other hand, there remains an abiding attempt by many IPE scholars to locate all explanations of international economic developments at the level of 'the state'; indeed, to reduce all political activities to those of the state. Stephen Krasner's robust, but simplistic, defence of state-centric IPE is indicative of such a position. He argues that 'states are the ontological givens in the system' (Krasner 1994: 17), such that other actors are constituted by states and have their capabilities delegated to them by the decisions of states.

This apparent tension is only resolved when it is recognized that the *concept* of 'the state' tends to be undertheorized within IPE. For many IPE scholars, 'the state' has been used as analytical shorthand for political authority more generally, whereby it is assumed that politics equates with the state's pursuit of some pre-given national interest. From this perspective, the state can continue to be Krasner's 'ontological given of the system', while at the same time it can experience the loss of power to which Strange alludes, as political authority becomes more diffuse and, as a consequence, the scope of state activities becomes more attenuated.

The aim of this chapter is to transcend the conflation between 'the state' and political authority within IPE. An important distinction must be drawn between 'the state', as a policy-making body, and a state *project*, as the underlying orientation of policy. The coherence of the latter depends on the degree to which the dominant trajectory of policy is contested within society, and on the degree to which potential sources of contestation can be either undermined or bypassed altogether. As such, the output of the state policy-making process must be seen as a reflection of the balance of political forces within society. State projects are a residue of historical struggle. 'The state' has no pre-given national interest that is somehow ontologically prior to the historical process of political struggle.

The chapter proceeds in three stages. In the first section, I provide a brief sketch of the familiar argument from the globalization literature that recent processes of international economic restructuring have led to a crisis of the modern state. I suggest that, to the degree to which we should take narratives of state crisis seriously, these refer less to an objective crisis of the state per se, and more to a constructed crisis of certain forms of state action. This has led to a shift to prioritizing accumulation imperatives relative to legitimation imperatives. In the second section, I argue that this shift cannot be reduced to a question of the functional necessities of the modern state; rather, it is a reflection of a conscious state project, born of the temporary resolution of the historical struggle over the form and content of state policy. In the final section, I argue that the increasing significance attached to accumulation imperatives is built upon two prior social shifts. First, it requires ever more aspects of everyday life to be subjected to the process of commodification, in that they become subjected to the discipline of monetary exchange. Second, it requires concerted efforts to change the underlying cognition of economic agents, such that they think in a manner that is compatible with an increasingly commodified social existence. These two shifts have occurred within a political context in which the authority to make policy decisions has been increasingly delegated to unaccountable agencies, such as international institutions and central banks, so as to reduce the number of potential sites of resistance to the process of commodification.

'The state', state projects and the competing imperatives of accumulation and legitimation

In strict analytical terms, 'the state' exists only as a theoretical abstraction. While it is a legal entity, insofar as it can be held culpable for the decisions taken in its name, it is a somewhat misleading image to depict 'the state' itself as a unified collective actor. This is a caricature of a reality in which separate policy-making spheres often encapsulate divergent, even contradictory, political goals. Nonetheless, those who act in the name of the state continue to play a constitutive role in the experience of everyday life. As a consequence, 'the state' is a theoretical abstraction that continues to have intuitive appeal.

Such a point bears repetition, particularly when set alongside a discussion of the subject matter that dominates contemporary IPE, that of globalization. It has become increasingly common to use the contextual assumption of globalization to question whether 'the state' remains a *meaningful* abstraction (for a cross-section of the debate, see Drache 1996; Ohmae 1996; Douglas 1997; Mosley 2000). The argument is posed by drawing a stark opposition between 'states' and 'markets'. With the power to shape and regulate economic relations assumed to reside at any moment of time with either 'states' or 'markets', the fact that globalization privileges market-oriented economic relations is further assumed to have a detrimental impact on the state's ability to direct the conduct of economic agents. Taken to its logical conclusion, this argument suggests a crisis of the state.

The alleged crisis of the state is made manifest in the first instance as a crisis of territoriality. It is argued that the state has been hollowed out by the increasingly footloose character of capital and the increasingly cross-border character of economic relations. To the extent that 'the state' requires the integrity of national borders to remain a meaningful abstraction, the increasingly porous nature of national borders in the face of footloose capital is assumed to have undermined the ability of 'the state' to act *as* a state. Globalization is argued to be changing the nature of the spatial relationships that underpin the state's successful reproduction, in such a way as to militate against what Gianfranco Poggi calls the 'coherent expression of [its] institutional mission' (Poggi 1990: 173). In contrast to the ever more fluid spatial relationships of everyday economic life, the state remains locked into a fixed territorial configuration: the state remains fundamentally a *national* state.

Presented this way, the crisis of territoriality is an objective crisis of the state in all its manifestations. A state is defined in relation to the territory it commands. Consequently, if economic relations now form at a spatial scale that does not correspond with that of the state, the ensuing state crisis is generic in both its scope and its impact. However, this may be a misrepresentation. The crisis of territoriality may merely be the geographic expression of a crisis of rationality, which applies not to 'the state' per se, but only to particular forms of state activities. It is one thing to say that the policy-making process appears to have become less effective when it comes to enforcing particular types of regulation on economic relations, but it is a claim of an entirely different nature to suggest, as a corollary, that 'the state' ceases to exist *as* a functioning state.

Taking a Habermasian perspective, a rationality crisis exists only insofar as the prevailing state project is deemed to be beyond the scope of normal politics at the moment at which the rationality crisis is announced (Habermas 1976). In other words, all rationality crises are constructed; they exist only to the extent that they are presented in such a way. While a territorial crisis suggests a generic crisis of national space, a rationality crisis suggests only a crisis of national policy-making, and only then when the policy-making apparatus is oriented towards delivering certain outcomes which have been defined as lying beyond the limits of acceptable political action. Rationality crises therefore mark moments at which one state project is challenged, and the terms on which the crisis is constructed represent an attempt to institutionalize an alternative state project. This is not a wholesale challenge to the legitimacy of the state, only a contingent challenge to the perceived legitimacy of the current trajectory of policy. As such, the recent phase of international economic restructuring, which is so often associated with the state-replacing effects of globalization, can be linked more closely to a reconstitution of the perceived imperatives to which state policy is asked to respond than it can to a bypassing of 'the state' itself.

By emphasizing the distinction between 'the state' (as a policy-making body) and a state project (as the underlying orientation of policy), it is possible to show that the latter can change without having a necessarily detrimental effect on the scope of the former. Indeed, in order to initiate a significant departure in the underlying orientation of policy, it may be necessary to extend the reach of the policy-making process into society. A state project not only defines the prevailing structure of social norms, it also shapes the way that people think of themselves in relation to those norms, as well as the way that they act within the context of those norms. To institutionalize a new state project may therefore require the simultaneous embedding of a new form of cognition within society. As a consequence, the most useful abstract characterization of the role of the state may well be to follow the Poulantzian tradition of viewing 'the state' as a factor of cohesion in the social formation (Poulantzas 1978).

Seen in such a light, the exercise of state power tends to be condensed at the level of social formation. It is used in periods of normal politics in order to direct the organization of social relations in ways that reflect the prevailing state project. By contrast, in moments in which attempts are made to replace the prevailing state project, it is used to direct the organization of social relations in line with new conceptions of what life should be like within society (Paggi 1979). While the identification of a rationality crisis involves promoting a new set of imperatives to which 'the state' must respond, the identification of a *solution* to a rationality crisis may involve changing the way that people think of themselves and their relationship to others within society, if such imperatives are to be satisfied. This is about changing habits of thought and changing the increasingly regularized behaviour that follows the development of a particular habit of thought (on which basic Veblenian point, see Chapter 5).

The state theory literature provides an important heuristic distinction between the state's accumulation and legitimation functions. At any particular moment of time, the prevailing state project can be oriented towards accumulation imperatives, legitimation imperatives, or some combination of the two. Accumulation imperatives require the state to intervene within society, in order to promote a specific rationality amongst members of that society, a specific cognition and a specific set of instincts, all of which complement the attempt to satisfy the accumulation function. By contrast, legitimation imperatives require a different type of intervention, aimed at facilitating a different rationality, a different cognition and a different set of instincts. Let me now outline in turn the core features of accumulation and legitimation imperatives.

The fact that the modern state has an accumulation function arises from the significance of the economy and, in particular, of the health of the economy, to the cohesion of society. Given the increasingly routine nature of the conflation of social progress and economic growth, the economy, and the activities on which the economy depends, penetrate the very essence of the state. A state project that is unable to oversee the successful reproduction of the economy is unlikely to underpin a state that is able to act as a factor of cohesion in the social formation. A state actively takes responsibility for guaranteeing such success when it socializes the ownership of the means of production. However, the state is still held to account for the success of the economy even in circumstances in which the means of production are privately owned. As such, it is extremely rare for state projects to attempt otherwise than to establish the conditions under which the expanded reproduction of the private economy can be secured. This condition is often referred to in the academic literature as the state's structural dependence on capital (see, in particular, Przeworski and Wallerstein 1988).

The state's structural dependence on capital requires the state to mediate in the competition between different units of capital. Unregulated competition is likely to lead to the destruction of many units of capital, as one business expands its consumer base at the expense of others. The task of the state is to intervene within society so as to ensure the reproduction of existing units of capital, even if this means shifting the burden of the competitive imperative onto society. The state is thus charged with displacing the immediate manifestation of the contradictions of unregulated competition within an economy that is privately owned. This it does by internalizing those contradictions within society, ensuring that society is structured in a way that allows businesses to take profits out of society.

The state's legitimation function follows directly from its role as mediator in the accumulation process. In circumstances in which society is aware that it is the source of wealth creation within the economy, the state is unlikely to receive continued consent for its interventions if the product of society's wealth creation remains solely in private hands. The authority for the state to act *as* a state is a delegated authority that has its origins within society. The willingness of society to confer such authority onto the state in turn depends on the state's ability to socialize at least part of the product of society's wealth creation. As such, the consent of society for the continued interventions of the state in the sphere of accumulation is a manufactured consent. It is founded on the existence of a sufficient flow of material benefits into society, typically through the redistribution of economic rewards away from those who own the means of production.

As such, it is clear that the state's competing imperatives in the spheres of accumulation and legitimation place policy-makers in a potentially troublesome situation. To secure the accumulation function requires policy-makers to subordinate social concerns to the needs of the economy and, more specifically, to the needs of the private owners of the means of production. However, we should not expect this to occur in the absence of an ensuing impact on the perceived legitimacy of state interventions. To secure the legitimation function requires policy-makers to prioritize social concerns, even if this has potentially adverse consequences for the productive base of the economy. However, we should not expect this to occur in the absence of an ensuing impact on the state's ability to sustain the conditions for accumulation.

From the foregoing, it is possible to see why so many state theorists treat the modern state as a potentially contradictory phenomenon (see, for instance, Wolfe 1977; Carnoy 1984; Clarke 1991). At the very least, it is clear that policy-makers can do no more than attempt to absorb the tension between accumulation and legitimation within the structures of the state, with a view to displacing the manifestation of its contradictions some time into the future. The competing imperatives of accumulation and legitimation do not have a resolution per se. Their internal contradictions can only be offset into succeeding time periods. It is the state's necessary mediating role, preventing privately owned economies from undermining their own means of expanded reproduction, which explains why critical tendencies emerging from the economic system tend to assert themselves as *political* crises of rationality (Habermas 1976; Offe 1985). In such circumstances, it is the specific form of the state, plus the prevailing state project, which is most often viewed as problematic, and thus ripe for change.

It is within this context that it is necessary to view the alleged rationality crisis of the state exposed by the economic restructuring associated with globalization. To the extent that this is an actual crisis of the state, it only represents critical tendencies within a specific form of state action, following a manifestation of the contradiction between accumulation and legitimation imperatives. The economic restructuring associated with globalization is not itself *evidence* of that contradiction; rather, it is evidence of attempts to provide a temporary *palliative* to the manifestation of that contradiction, thus displacing the contradiction into the future.

Political conditions are currently such that the tension between accumulation and legitimation imperatives is set within the context of growth ideologies. Legitimation resources have increasingly taken a provisional nature (Kitschelt *et al.* 1999). Legitimation will be sourced only if it is easily affordable, and only then if it remains a secondary consideration to accumulation. The provisional character of legitimation follows from the way in which it has been tied more explicitly to the performance of the economy than previously in the postwar period. In this respect, then, the situation has increasingly become one of legitimation through growth and, by extension, legitimation through accumulation. The terms of the 'embedded liberal' settlement of the postwar period (on which, see Ruggie 1983; Marglin and Schor 1990) attempted to enforce an institutional separation between the welfare functions and the economic functions of the state, so that policy-makers could maintain two independent logics of action in the spheres of accumulation and legitimation. To the extent that attempts are now made to secure legitimation through accumulation, these logics of action have been increasingly blurred. In the following section, I suggest that this is a conscious state project, reflecting the current balance of political forces within society.

The state as the manifestation of the balance of political forces within society

The increasing tendency for legitimation to be sourced through accumulation is not a general condition of the development of the state, but a reflection of political trends embodied in the prevailing state project. Indeed, there are no general conditions of the development of the state that exist in some sense beyond politics. While it is usual within IPE to appeal to 'the state' as an organic entity, this serves to mask the essentially conjunctural character of the law-making body to which 'the state' refers. Both the form and the functions of the state are conditioned by the prevailing climate of political opinion and, in particular, by the existing structure of political common-sense.

In this respect, 'the state' is inseparable from the dominant state project that is implemented through its law-making capabilities. The former reflects the latter, rather than vice versa.

A number of important points follow from these preliminary observations. If the manifestation of 'the state' at any particular moment of time is embodied in the dominant state project, and if the dominant state project gains its legitimacy from the dominant discursive representation of reality, we can say at least two things about the nature of the state. First, the state acquires its logic of action from the way in which reality is constructed in political discourse. Second, and as a consequence, the state reflects the prevailing balance of political forces within society. The dominant representation of reality and, more specifically, the dominant representation of the functional imperatives to which the state responds, is itself a reflection of which groups are most able to define the scope and content of state activities. The law-making capacities of the state are always directed towards a particular view of society, and a concomitant view of the structure of human subjectivity which is compatible with that view of society. The image of a universal state interest disappears from such an analysis. Once such an image is rejected, the issue then becomes one of who is able to impose their favoured construction of society onto the structures of the state, and under what conditions is this possible. In turn, this is an issue of how the dominant representation of reality is formed.

Reality is apprehended from a particular subject position; the world looks different depending on the perspective we adopt from which to observe it. Our identities are open to multiple forms of construction, and at most they reach only temporary periods of closure. As a consequence, at different times we may well apprehend reality from different subject positions. Significantly, the subject position we choose at any particular moment is open to manipulation. It is not an objective position from which to view the world, but an aspect of the dominant structure of socialization. We can be appealed to in a number of ways in any specific set of circumstances. This is only the same as saying that a given event can sustain any number of narratives about it. For instance, in any specific set of circumstances, we can be appealed to as 'citizen', as 'taxpayer', as 'worker', as 'consumer', as 'producer', as 'homeowner' – or, indeed, in any manner that reflects an element of our identity. The actual way in which we allow ourselves to be appealed to is likely to reflect the prevailing character of the socialization process. It is also likely to be reflected in the character of the prevailing state project.

Such thoughts are somewhat abstract, so let me attempt to explain them using an illustration. If we are content to be socialized into an economic system that emphasizes extensive welfare entitlements as a right to be claimed against 'the state', we are likely to allow ourselves to be appealed to as citizens. In such circumstances, political mobilization is unlikely to take place against a state project that attempts to generate revenues to be used as welfare expenditures. Furthermore, in the absence of mobilization of this nature, the reproduction of the prevailing state project will be largely unproblematic. If, on the other hand, we insist on being appealed to as taxpayers, we are unlikely to be as receptive of a state project that attempts to maintain extensive welfare payments, because of the way in which 'we' will be implicated in the funding of such payments. The dominant structure of socialization in this latter instance will tend to be one that treats the individual specifically as an individual, one who enjoys personal rights but who has no countervailing obligation to act in the interests of others.

The subject position through which we understand our relationship to the economy is therefore replete with political meaning. So, too, are the appeals to which we are subjected, which seek to persuade us to understand ourselves at a particular moment of time from a particular perspective. This process is known as interpellation (see Laclau and Mouffe 1985), whereby individuals are hailed from a certain subject position to accept that position as their own. The act of interpellation is therefore an intensely political act on behalf of the hailer. By the same token, the act of being interpellated involves a moment of subordination on behalf of the hailed.

A state project develops internal coherence in proportion to the number of people who consent to being interpellated to the subject position that is consistent with it. At any moment such consent may be withdrawn, at which point the internal coherence of the prevailing state project is undermined. It is for this reason that it is a mistake to view 'the state' as the bearer of a universal interest. 'The state' acquires a specific form and function at a particular moment of time, to reflect the temporary dominance of a specific mode of interpellation. It is not possible to explain the product of the state's law-making capabilities through reference to a functionalist logic, as would be implied by the assumption of a universal state interest.

As soon as the dominant mode of interpellation proves incapable of hailing people in large numbers to the prevailing state project, that project is displaced and 'the state' acquires a new form and function.

For instance, in some circumstances, the authority of the state is secured by hailing individuals to a vision of society that is based on an extended sphere of social rights. Here, the state preserves its legitimacy by appropriating the product of the accumulation process in order to fund additional welfare payments. Individuals are appealed to as social beings, who are willing to show Smithian sympathy for those most in need of welfare. As a consequence, the accumulation process experiences extensive social regulation. In other circumstances, however, the authority of the state is secured by hailing individuals to a vision of society in which the state socializes an ever smaller proportion of the product of the accumulation process. Here, the state preserves its legitimacy by restricting the scope of its redistributive activities within society. Individuals are appealed to as autonomous beings, very much in the image of the neoclassical agent, in that they are unencumbered by responsibilities for the well-being of others. As a consequence, the accumulation process experiences minimal social regulation.

If we are indeed witnessing a restructuring of the form and function of the state, such that the prevailing state project seeks to secure legitimation through accumulation, these latter circumstances are more likely to apply. The tendency for legitimation to be secured through accumulation presupposes a mode of interpellation in which appeals to the individual as 'citizen', 'worker' and 'producer' are downplayed. All such appeals imply a structure of social rights that can be claimed against the state and require a redistributive state project. They also imply a collective dimension to identity construction, whereby individuals form their views of the world through membership of particular groups. To be a 'citizen', to be a 'worker', or to be a 'producer' suggests a social experience of life. By contrast, the mode of interpellation consistent with securing legitimation through accumulation emphasizes purely individual experiences of life. Within such a framework, those who are hailed to the prevailing state project are appealed to, amongst other things, as 'taxpayers', 'consumers' and 'homeowners'.

Each of these aspects of everyday life highlights the autonomy of the individual. They place the way in which individuals are asked to think of themselves in a context that mirrors the conception of the individual to be found in neoclassical economics. To the extent that people bear the characteristics of utility-maximizing economic agents, they have to be encouraged to act in that manner. An important part of such encouragement involves the constant repetition of the image of the individual as an autonomous being abstracted from broader social structures. This image of the individual acting alone is embedded in appeals to support policies that emphasize those elements of our identity in which we recognize ourselves as 'taxpayers', 'consumers' and 'homeowners'. Such constructions defend a social distribution of wealth that emphasizes the right of individuals to retain as much of their personal wealth as possible. At the same time, then, they also undermine the likely resonance of alternative visions of society, in particular those that seek higher degrees of socialization of the economy's wealth-creating capabilities.

All state projects are a manifestation of the balance of political forces within society (Jessop 1990). From the foregoing, we are in a position to say more about the balance of political forces that underpins state projects which attempt to secure legitimation through accumulation. Such attempts reflect a balance of political forces consistent with resistance to the socialization of wealth. In turn, this reflects a society in which the dominant political ideology is tolerant of inequality and attaches greater significance to economic than social concerns. It is also a society that understands justice in terms of the freedom of individuals to pursue lives that are shaped more by their intentions than by the directive capacity of public authority. Within such a society, the general trajectory of politics is to emphasize a binary opposition between 'the individual' and 'the state', such that the individual inhabits decision-making environments akin to those of neoclassical economics. I turn in the final section of this chapter to investigate ways in which the opposition between 'the individual' and 'the state' has recently been enforced.

The state and the commodification of the individual

The image of an increasingly impotent state, bypassed by international economic restructuring and unable to intervene as effectively as before, sits uneasily alongside the foregoing analysis. The latter suggests that the real issue to investigate is not the ostensible rise and fall of state *power* so much as the changing character of the prevailing state *project*. Prevalent assumptions concerning an alleged rationality crisis of the state are actually a misspecification of attempts to secure the state's legitimation function through establishing increasingly dynamic systems of accumulation. Attempts to enhance the accumulation process are predicated not on the withdrawal of state power, but on its *use*.

In particular, the law-making apparatus of the state has been used to intervene at the level of the individual, in order to create economic subjects whose habitual actions and habits of thought are compatible with accumulation imperatives. This has involved the increasing commodification of social relations, such that individuals respond ever more instinctively to market values as a guide to how they should conduct themselves in their everyday lives. In turn, this requires that their basic cognition be recast. There is nothing inherent in thinking of oneself as a strictly autonomous being, isolated from society and the social structure of responsibilities that rest upon it. However, in the absence of successful attempts to persuade people to think of themselves in such a way, it is unlikely that increasingly commodified social relations will take root within society. Such relations will tend to be resisted as 'unnatural', unless successful appeals can be made for people to understand their lives through reference to the ideals of a distinctively market-based society.

As a consequence, the reconstitution of the individual in line with accumulation imperatives requires some degree of consent on behalf of the individuals thus affected. However, this process has not been *entirely* consensual. The attempt to institutionalize a state project which secures legitimation through accumulation also involves coercive means. Part of that state project, however paradoxical it may appear at first, has been to use the law-making capabilities of the state in order to disperse state power beyond national borders. A range of external enforcement mechanisms for policy now exist, embodied for instance in the trend towards central bank independence and the delegation of policy-making responsibilities to international institutions, each of which increases the ostensible distance between 'the individual' and 'the state'. At the very least, they erode the line of accountability running from the latter to the former, thus bypassing the very need for consent to the increasing commodification of social relations.

Two developments are therefore important in the attempt to reconstitute the individual in a manner consistent with accumulation imperatives. First, individuals must be increasingly subjected in their everyday lives to the logic of commodification. Second, they must develop habits of thought that are compatible with the logic of commodification, such that they think of themselves as autonomous beings, driven only by the self-serving desire to act as utility-maximizers.

We may recall from Chapter 6 the link that Polanyi draws between the process of commodification and the experience of the market economy. Indeed, for Polanyi, it was to misspecify the basic nature of everyday life to frame it through reference to the market economy *unless* it could be shown that pure exchange relations existed in the 'fictitious' commodities of land, labour and money. Polanyi calls a commodity 'fictitious' when it has a monetary value ascribed to it, such that it can be traded on the basis of those values, but when it has an ontologically prior essence before being put into a form in which it can be bought and sold (Polanyi 1957 [1944]: 72). A real commodity for Polanyi is one that has been produced specifically, and for no other reason, than to be exchanged on an open market for its given monetary value. State projects that attempt to secure legitimation through accumulation are based on the further development of markets in each of Polanyi's 'fictitious' commodities of land, labour and money.

Let me start with the institutionalization of exchange relations in land. A number of points can be made here. Perhaps most obviously, the mode of interpellation that underpins accumulationist state projects is one that emphasizes ideologies of individualism, and the appeal to the individual as 'private property owner' is a constitutive element of such interpellation in advanced industrialized economies. Homeowning represents the naturalization within everyday life of the idea of private property. To the extent that homeowning is considered legitimate, so too is the idea of private property, with its attendant logics of surplus value extraction and profit-taking.

Of course, in many regions of the world the appeal to 'homeowners' has no resonance and private property relations have to be imposed, often by an external agency. The development strategies of the World Bank have tended to be based on attempts to commodify land, opening up developing economies to potential sources of foreign investment by institutionalizing private property rights within the local economy. The image of globalization that is embodied in World Bank programmes is one that attempts to transpose a system of private property rights onto a truly international scale (see Chapter 11). Within many developing countries, land has traditionally been seen as a communal good, collectively owned by the society that has its home on it. As such, this is land that exists in a completely different social context to that described by the concept of 'private property' (Bonfil Batalla 1996: 33). The forced imposition of private property rights therefore changes the relationship between the land and the people that live on it. Such developments make the former susceptible to the process of commodification, and the latter susceptible to the ideologies of individualism that underpin the process of commodification.

The susceptibility of individuals to ideologies of individualism is heightened by their incorporation into labour markets, especially in circumstances in which the dynamics of the labour market are expressed in terms of supply and demand. This tends to downplay the possibility of an oikonomic conception of labour, in which work is organized to meet the needs of the community in which that work is undertaken. Instead, those who labour do so within a chrematistic worldview, in which their work is subjected to the discipline of market logic. It is given a monetary value, as determined by those who purchase their labour, and it is judged purely on this monetary value, rather than on the contribution it makes to the community in which it is undertaken. This serves to distance workers, in their minds at least, from the social context in which they work. Their emotional attachment, as workers, is less to the society to which their labour contributes than it is to those who determine the monetary value that is to be placed upon their labour and, ultimately, to the monetary value itself.

It is more likely in these latter circumstances that individuals will think of themselves first and foremost as individuals, rather than as part of a broader social grouping. In the absence of prior processes of labour market commodification, the appeal to the individual as 'worker' is likely to affirm collective elements of individual identities (that is, the 'worker' works for his/her community, rather than for him/herself). As before, in many regions of the world, World Bank development programmes are implicated in normalizing ideologies of individualism within everyday life, in this case turning work into something that is done for oneself, rather than on behalf of the community in which one lives. Typically, such programmes dissolve traditional social structures by imposing labour market relations on work practices that previously were regulated by the norms of communal life (Cheru 1997).

International institutions have also been key players in the process through which the increasing commodification of money has taken place. It is usual within IPE to talk of 'global finance', and this refers to patterns of money commodification that increasingly transgress the boundaries of the national economy. The wholesale relaxation of the preceding structure of capital controls followed the collapse of the Bretton Woods settlement in the early 1970s. As a result, financial markets have increasingly embedded a circuit of capital that is fully contained within the financial markets themselves (Watson 1999). Finance and production have begun to operate ever more as autonomous aspects of the economy. Financial markets no longer exist solely as a means of providing capital for investment in the productive sectors of the economy. Financial markets themselves have become a genuine realm for the valorization of capital.

The IMF has attempted to truly internationalize this realm by suggesting revisions to its own articles of agreement that make fully liberalized capital accounts a prerequisite of continued Fund membership (IMF 2000). This has been backed by the introduction of a Special Data Dissemination Standard, through which the right to negotiate loans through the Fund is made conditional upon meeting international standards for full public disclosure of economic data (Watson 2002a). These changes are designed to give international investors more and better information about the likely investment opportunities available in all economies, but especially those of the developing world. The IMF's attempt to 'open up' the financial systems of developing economies is therefore an attempt to open those economies to new forms of investment. In essence, it is to incorporate them into an ever expanding sphere of money commodification.

Recent further commodification is therefore evident in each of Polanyi's three 'fictitious' commodities of land, labour and money. In each of these instances, two outcomes are apparent. First, the process of 'fictitious' commodification has taken on an increasingly international dimension. The means through which commodified social relations have been deepened has been to expand the territorial reach of such relations beyond the boundaries of the national economy. Second, such developments exist within a context in which the dominant state project privileges accumulation over legitimation. Indeed, they are the direct result of attempts to inscribe an increasingly pure accumulation strategy at the heart of the state's policy-making apparatus.

The issue then becomes one of what type of human subjectivity is required in order to sustain such a project. Any successful state project must be embedded within society; it must be compatible with the prevailing structure of social norms. Such norms ascribe particular roles to the individual, which entails prescribing certain forms of subjectivity, while actively proscribing others. The individual whose everyday life is shaped by a particular state project must be a particular *type* of individual if he or she is to be incorporated into that project.

There are a number of points that we can make about the type of individual, and the type of individual subjectivity, rendered necessary in order to sustain state projects that emphasize the accumulation function. For a start, many of the characteristics associated with Adam Smith's conception of the individual must be absent. Smith argued that economic activity was essentially social, insofar as it brought people together in both physical and emotional relationships with one another (Skinner 1979). For Smith, the study of the economy proceeded on the same basis as the study of society, and the study of society was synonymous with an analysis of the moral principles on which all social relations were founded.

Smith reduced such principles to those that exerted restraint over any elements of the passions that were directed at purely self-serving ends (Smith 1982 [1759]: 109–78). Purely self-serving actions cannot pass the moral judgement of others, from whom we seek approval of our conduct, particularly in circumstances in which those actions are known to inflict harm (see Chapter 4). Smith's economic agents therefore differ markedly from those of neoclassical theory, but it is those of neoclassical theory who fit more easily into a political context in which legitimation is secured through accumulation. These are people whose responsibilities are solely to themselves, and whose actions are directed solely towards maximizing their own utility. There is no notion of 'society' embodied in the simple demand and supply curves of neoclassical economics (see, for instance, Clower 1998; Keen 2001). As such, there can be no sense in which one individual bears responsibilities for others within society. Moreover, it is precisely such people who are implied by attempts to sustain state projects that focus primarily on accumulation. At the very least, such projects require a rational calculative subjectivity, within which the concept of gains applies only to the self. Support for attempts to secure legitimation through accumulation cannot be sustained, certainly not on a consensual basis, should appeals for such support be set within the context of a subjectivity that acknowledges, indeed emphasizes, the responsibility that each individual bears for the well-being of others.

Conclusion

Chapters 7 and 8 have attempted to reformulate our understanding of the basic units of analysis within IPE. In the previous chapter I focused on 'the market', arguing that it is inadequately theorized as an actor that embodies both an interest and a will of its own. Rather, 'the market' is, at most, an arena for action, one that encapsulates a particular type of commodified exchange relations as the basis for everyday life. In this chapter, I have focused on 'the state', arguing that it is necessary to draw a distinction that is all too rarely made in IPE. 'The state', which is a law-making body, must be differentiated from the prevailing state project, through which the general orientation of policy is established. As with 'the market', 'the state' bears neither an interest nor a will of its own; rather, policy output reflects the internal characteristics of the prevailing state project. In turn, this reflects the balance of political forces within society.

Bringing the analysis of these two chapters together, it is a mistake to conceptualize recent processes of international economic restructuring as some sort of immanent power shift from 'state' to 'market'. It makes more sense to think of the way in which state power has been appropriated in order to increase the extent and reach of commodified exchange relations within everyday life. Individual subjectivities are being actively re-made in the image of commodified economic agents. This takes place most obviously when the prevailing state project privileges concerns for accumulation over concerns for legitimation. To sustain such a project, individuals must begin instinctively to understand themselves, as well as the social relations in which they are involved, in terms of the monetary values that are placed upon them in a commodified social world.

A number of external enforcement mechanisms for commodification have recently been put in place. Many of these support structures involve the delegation of policy-making responsibilities away from 'the state'. State projects that privilege the accumulation process are founded, like all state projects, on the exercise of state power. In this instance, however, state power is called upon in order to disperse the locus of that power. In particular, it is used to avoid the concentration of state power that leaves 'the state' susceptible to capture by those who would seek to reshape existing power relations within society.

Such external enforcement mechanisms range from the extension of private property rights across borders, with the subsequent shaping of everyday life by corporate logics, to the increasing delegation of policy responsibility to international institutions, and even to the development of the popular political mantra of our times, that which equates globalization with a market-based logic of no alternative. Each of these has become an automatic pilot for policy, whereby the need for consent has been increasingly bypassed. The final three chapters offer illustrations of this trend. They chart the way in which individuals have been increasingly incorporated into a process of commodification that now extends across borders. I focus on three issues: globalization, trade and development. In particular, I seek to show how the process of incorporation into a purely commodified lifestyle remains incomplete, and how it is always open to contestation and the mobilization of counter-political movements.

Chapter 9

Applying the Theoretical Framework (1): Globalization

Introduction

The focus of the analysis now changes for the next three chapters. They offer brief illustrations of the value of reworking the underlying conceptual framework of IPE in the manner outlined in this book. This chapter focuses on the contemporary condition of globalization.

No issue has received more attention from the social scientific community in the last twenty years than that of globalization. The dividing lines in the literature are drawn across even the most fundamental questions relating to the issue: both the extent of globalization and its nature. The debate about its extent ranges from 'hyperglobalist' proclamations of the ubiquity of the global condition, to 'sceptical' concerns about globalization mythology. The debate about its nature relates to whether globalization is, in essence, an economic, a political or a cultural phenomenon (Held *et al.* 1999). My intention here is not to review academic debates about globalization in their entirety, for that would be beyond the scope of this, or any, book; rather, my aim is to show how the foregoing analysis helps us to make sense of existing academic debates, while also offering a novel characterization of the condition and experience of globalization.

To this end, the chapter proceeds in three stages. In the first section I emphasize the main differences between the dominant policy-maker discourse and the dominant academic discourse of economic globalization. Policy-maker discourses of globalization have tended to focus on the economics of competitiveness, suggesting the necessity of policy adaptation to the rigours of global competition. Such concerns are also evident in academic discourses, but these latter discourses tend also to focus on explaining the emergence of competitive imperatives in the first place. They do so typically through reference to market-clearing dynamics operating at the global level. I argue in the second section that this view of the global economy presupposes certain characteristics relating to globalization in general. It assumes that globalization has a will of its own which it can impose on other actors. In the third section, I depart from such an assumption to analyse the way in which specific forms of global economic relations have been institutionalized as a means of prioritizing the state's accumulation function over its legitimation function. In particular, global economic relations have become the backdrop for weakening the responsibility that individuals might otherwise feel for the well-being of others.

Competitiveness concerns, market ideologies and discourses of globalization

Globalization tends to be understood simultaneously as both opportunity and constraint. It empowers mobile factors of production to take advantage of profit opportunities, wherever in the world such opportunities arise. As a corollary, it disempowers policy-makers who might otherwise seek to restrict factor mobility in the interests of social policy and welfare rights. Understood in this way, globalization can be seen to have placed strict parameters around the politically possible as a result of inexorable economic processes. However, I suggest that the image of inexorable economic processes *itself* has causal effects that constrain political outcomes (Watson 2001). As such, we should be looking not only at global economic restructuring, but also at common assumptions about the 'inevitability' of that restructuring, in trying to explain contemporary economic policy-making. In this respect, there is much to gain from analysing both the overlap and the significant points of departure between the way in which assumptions about globalization inform the discourses of policy-makers and academics.

In an era of global economic relations, it is typically assumed that all economies are subjected to increasingly common economic pressures. Moreover, such pressures are further assumed to have led, if not yet strictly speaking to common political outcomes, then nonetheless to a common political trajectory resulting in increasingly similar outcomes (Hay 2004a). The one major distinction between policy-maker and academic constructions of the pressures of globalization lies in the identification of different 'bearers' of these structural pressures. For policy-makers, globalizing pressures are made manifest in a heightened awareness of competitiveness concerns. For academics, by contrast, both globalizing pressures and competitiveness concerns are more usually linked to assumptions that markets now clear in a manner consistent with equilibrium dynamics of global supply and demand.

Let us first consider the competitiveness concerns that feature most prominently in policy-maker discourses. Interestingly, notions of competitiveness significantly predate those of globalization in public policy-making debates (Hay, Watson and Wincott 1999). The context of globalization has therefore reinforced assumptions about the competitive imperative which were *already dominant*, rather than having created them from scratch. However, the contextual assumption of globalization has allowed the notion of competitiveness to be applied in a new way in public policy-making debates. In the past, arguments about the competitive imperative applied only at the level of the firm. It was only firms that were considered to be competitive (and therefore profitable) or uncompetitive (and therefore prone to bankruptcy). More recently, though, the burden of the competitive imperative has been displaced upwards in policy-making discourse, from the level of the firm to the level of the national economy (Krugman 1994). Thus the firm itself is no longer required to be competitive; rather, it is the *environment* in which firms are situated that is expected to be able to source competitiveness concerns.

This returns the analysis to the significance of the social institutions in which the economy is set. It is the form that such institutions take which shapes the outcomes of the policy process, which in turn shapes the perception of a country's competitiveness. Competitiveness tends to be linked to political conditions in which expectations of social policy and welfare rights are suppressed in the interests of corporate profits and shareholder value. We hear much of creating a 'business-friendly' economy, and this is the manifestation of such an economy in policy terms. Competitiveness concerns have been harnessed in order to impose an overriding commercial rationality onto economic policy.

Such conceptions of commercial rationality themselves require a prior assumption that all actors within the commercial realm operate solely to the standard of an innate instrumental rationality. In the absence of such an assumption, there can be no sense in which governments are 'mandated' to provide conditions for enhanced competitiveness and, as such, expanded profit opportunities. It is only in the presence of such an assumption that firms can be expected to respond in a purely instinctive manner to ensure that they will always locate where such conditions do operate. The conventional wisdom of globalization is important in this respect, for it depicts a world in which differences in national law are no longer institutional barriers that prevent businesses from relocating wherever in the world comparative advantage dictates. Footloose firms are now assumed to be able to play governments off against one another, in an attempt to seek out the lowest possible production costs. Governments are consequently thought to have become locked into competitive relations of their own, in which the winner is the one that can bid down the costs of production to the greatest extent. The more that governments can provide social institutions that lower production costs, the more incentives they can offer to instrumentally rational firms to locate in their country (see Swank 1998).

This suggests that the word 'globalization' enters the vocabulary of policy-makers most frequently to describe the emergence of a new structure of disembedded capital flows. An important element of all market relations concerns the way in which they are constantly being remade, as they are disembedded from one combination of place and time horizon and re-embedded in others (Jessop 2001; see also Chapter 6). Globalization infers a spatial mismatch between the essentially rooted social relations that underpin the economy and essentially rootless capital. The image that appears in much policy-maker discourse, and which is confirmed in much academic discourse, is that of a purely disembedded space of capital flows. In order to capture such an image, globalization has been variously described as 'time/space compression' (Harvey 1989), 'the death of distance' (Cairncross 1997) and 'the end of geography' (O'Brien 1992). At one level of abstraction, the depiction is of capital physically and permanently on the move. At another, it is of the creation of genuinely global conditions of supply and demand, interacting to ensure genuinely global market clearing dynamics.

In other words, behind every public pronouncement of the need to enhance country competitiveness lies the prior assumption that international markets now clear in line with global equilibrium dynamics. While a full articulation of this prior assumption tends to be absent from policy-maker debates about globalization, it features much more prominently in academic debates, albeit with one qualification. It is an assumption that is present in *conceptual* debates about globalization, but it does not feature in *empirical* debates.

The reason for its absence from empirically oriented debates is relatively straightforward. The assumption of genuinely global market clearing dynamics requires an attendant assumption that the process of economic adjustment within the market environment takes place instantaneously. Quite clearly, 'instantaneous adjustment' is a bold claim. It requires that spatial constraints on the development of economic relations be entirely eroded by the emergence of an economy that operates outside the context of historical time.

Not only is this a conception of the economy at odds with the one developed in this book, but it is also contradicted by all available empirical evidence. There is no reason to deny that the international economy has passed through a significant period of recent restructuring, in terms of the dominant circuit of both production and consumption. Moreover, most of these changes have resulted in an increasing internationalization of the process of economic decision-making, reflected in both the business models of producers and the choices we make as consumers. Yet none of this means that genuinely global conditions of supply and demand are in evidence. For that to be the case, our experiences of globalization would have to be determined by a mechanism akin to Smith's system of 'natural prices' (see Chapter 4). The world of 'natural prices', however, is far from the world of current experience. As the following chapter makes clear, there are important social determinants of price that move us away from a system of 'natural prices'. The ability of businesses to act as price makers in most market relations is the most obvious manifestation of the difference between 'natural prices' and 'market prices'.

However, this may not be the most significant point. It is more important for our everyday experiences of the economy that policy is informed by the *assumption* that there is an equilibrium of global supply and demand than it is that there is ample empirical evidence showing that such an equilibrium is entirely mythical. Moreover, it is more important still for the concerns of this book that such an assumption is based on particular conceptions of the market economy and of human nature. It is to these issues that I turn in the remainder of the chapter.

Globalization as actor versus globalization as arena for action

The image of globalization that dominates policy-maker discourse is that of globalization as actor. Globalization is constructed in terms of policy imperatives that its very existence mandates. Academics, by contrast, tend to be more reticent in endorsing the idea that globalization has both a will of its own and the characteristics of a conscious agent. Yet, in accepting assumptions relating to genuinely global conditions of supply and demand, the academic literature is also culpable of reifying the idea of a global market. Set in such a context, the global market appears to operate to its own internal logic, forcing adaptation to such a logic onto those whose lives are shaped by the market relations in which they are involved.

Missing entirely from such analyses is the idea that globalization is a site of political struggle. Indeed, the whole sphere of conscious human agency is dissolved when globalization is understood as the manifestation of a structural economic logic. However, globalization does not occur in a political vacuum; it is a feature of contemporary life that is rife with dissent. We have seen the emergence of a myriad of groups attempting to challenge the dominant orientation of the public management of globalization. Some have campaigned on single issues, such as 'Third World' debt restructuring (www.jubilee2000uk.org; www.waronwant.org); others have attempted to change the very ethos on which the public management of globalization has been based (www.fairtradefederation.com; www.globalexchange.org); others still have focused on challenging the legitimacy of international institutions that manage the process of global economic governance (www.50years.org; www.wbbeurope.org).

Resistance to globalization is endemic to globalization itself. Resistance is not outside the process of globalization, detached from it and impacting upon it in a purely external manner; rather, it is intrinsic to the broader process of social struggle surrounding globalization, out of which our experiences of it arise.

Indeed, globalization is not an 'it' in any real or objective sense. The language that is most frequently used to discuss the issue typically turns globalization into a thing, but we have to be careful not to be distracted by this language into reifying the whole concept. Globalization is not an 'it', a homogeneous and monolithic entity, so much as a series of tendencies that are produced through conscious human action. In addition, these will be tendencies to which counter-tendencies arise, as action occurs in a political context defined by the dynamics of social struggle. Totalizing claims about globalization must be avoided, as globalization is not some simple structural condition. At most, we are restricted to observing particular processes that produce effects which can be understood as evidence of globalization.

From the perspective developed in this book, globalization is to be viewed as an arena for action. It is an important part of the context through which actors seek to impose their intentions in order to shape the economic relations that impact upon their lives. It is an arena in which we act economically to engage in the transactions that sustain our daily lives. It is also an arena in which we act politically in an attempt to ensure that the economic relations in which we are involved meet our concerns for propriety. This may be that we seek from others a commitment that we are treated in an appropriate manner: for instance, we may mobilize politically as workers in an effort to ensure just employment contracts. Or it may be that we seek to commit ourselves to treat others in an appropriate manner: for instance, we may mobilize politically as consumers to boycott goods that are produced in conditions we deem to be unjust.

All this suggests that the focus of discussion should not be globalization per se, so much as the type of economic relations to be preferred in an era putatively understood as one of globalization, the type of economic relations to which we will consent, and the type of economic relations to which we are politically mobilized. This means that, in an important sense, our experiences of economic relations – and, therefore, our experiences of globalization – are there to be shaped. However, it is also necessary to recognize that there are significant constraints that might prevent any single person from shaping economic relations in the way they see best. Many of these constraints arise from the dispersal of state power, as discussed in Chapter 8, which is designed to provide institutional support for state projects that emphasize accumulation over legitimation.

One obvious example of such a trend is the increasing displacement of responsibility for monetary policy from the government to the central bank. This trend has followed developments in the economics literature, which have emphasized the merits of 'delegated' policy-making (see Blinder 1999). Central banks are able to provide an institutional guarantor for price stability because they are unelected and unaccountable, in a way that governments are not. Accumulation strategies favour price stability, but the same is not necessarily true of legitimation strategies, given that price inflation tends to have redistributive effects. As such, central bank independence not only provides an institutional guarantor for price stability; it also provides an external enforcement mechanism for both accumulation strategies and the defence of existing patterns of wealth within society (Watson 2002b). While the economics literature on delegation highlights the need for 'market sensitive' monetary policies within contemporary capitalism, it remains silent on a more important issue, that of the social basis of 'market sensitivity'. The value of money clearly has a significant impact on the organization of society, since the allocation of credit is a cornerstone of distributional politics. As such, the decision to cede operational autonomy to central bankers is not merely a functional response to the need for market sensitive policies; it is also a means of defending existing social hierarchies against possible redefinition.

Another way of doing this is to tie 'the state' to international accords negotiated through institutions such as the IMF, the World Bank and the World Trade Organization (WTO). Such institutions now have the authority to write laws which not only apply across national borders, but which also supersede national law. The law-making capabilities of international institutions can therefore be appropriated by domestic policy-makers, in order to introduce potentially unpopular policies, while displacing dissent against such policies onto the institutions themselves. Robert Cox has written of 'the state' increasingly acting as a transmission belt for policies that are formulated at the international level (see Cox 1994b). However, this should not be understood in any way as a straightforward diminution of state power; in fact, it represents a conscious strategy of policy delegation, designed specifically to protect the current form of state power against attempts to use it for other purposes. It allows state power to be oriented almost exclusively towards securing the conditions for accumulation, by providing another means through which the need for consent is bypassed. As is the case with central bank independence, the automatic pilot provided by policy delegation to international institutions should not be thought of in terms of policy outcomes alone. It is also a means of further embedding the structures of existing social hierarchies, and of defending those structures against possible redefinition.

The issue, then, may not be one of explaining globalization per se, but of explaining how global economic relations can be used as an arena for institutionalizing state projects that prioritize accumulation over legitimation. We can therefore do away with the conception of globalization as an externally generated process that acts upon our lives from behind our backs. What we need to understand instead are the 'hailing' strategies through which individuals are mobilized to state projects that emphasize accumulation imperatives. In particular, we need to understand how such strategies are predicated on remaking individual subjectivities, so that global economic relations reconstitute the individual as an autonomous being, abstracted from society, who hence prioritizes purely self-serving passions. It is to this question that I now turn.

Globalization as ideological justification for self-interested behaviour

The image of utility-maximizing behaviour is a persistent feature of the academic literature on economic globalization. Perceptions of a causal relationship between the two tend to take one of two forms. First, globalization is assumed to make it easier to undertake utility-maximizing behaviour, insofar as it erodes institutional constraints that once stood in the way of purely self-interested actions. For instance, institutional guarantors now exist at the international level to ensure that private property rights apply across borders. This has reduced the corporate risk involved in investing overseas, allowing the self-interested pursuit of profit opportunities to be increasingly unconstrained by location. Second, globalization is assumed to enforce behavioural adaptation in line with utility-maximization. A crude survivalist logic is invoked, whereby anything other than self-interested actions are deemed to be incompatible with the broader global environment. To follow the same example, the existence of international guarantors of private property rights provides policy-makers with incentives to create a 'business-friendly' policy environment in an attempt to attract mobile sources of investment. Failure to do so is deemed likely to lead to a haemorrhaging of investment funds as firms seek alternative locations (Przeworski and Wallerstein 1988; Swank 1998).

Set in such a context, the whole sphere of potentially conscionable action is dissolved. Globalization can still be understood as an arena for human action, but the conscious and reflexive elements of action are lost, replaced by the image of routine and instinctive behaviour that is determined by the environment in which it occurs. Let us return to Veblen's important, albeit rarely used, distinction between action and behaviour. It cannot be said that participants within such an economy are truly *acting* (Veblen 1919a: 232; Veblen 1919b: 74; see also Chapter 5). If globalization mandates certain patterns of behaviour in response, there is nothing conscious about such reactions. An account of agency disappears from the explanation of outcomes within an economy of this nature. There is no choice in how to act, and neither is there a sense of reflecting on the implications of alternative courses of action, before proceeding to choose how to act. Instead, behaviour is structurally determined by the logic of the global economy itself.

Perhaps the most notable contradiction within this understanding of globalization concerns the claim that globalization forcibly necessitates new habitual responses to prevailing economic conditions on the part of all individual actors. The purely functionalist notion of causality rooted in such a claim is sufficiently circumspect on its own, but there is more. The broader institutional apparatus, *through which habits form*, is believed to be unimportant to the process through which economic relations form. The prevailing social and political norms, which together shape the institutional context in which economic relations are reproduced, play no part in the way in which the economy is conceptualized. Instead, they are overridden by the assumption that, in Roland Robertson's terms, globalization equates with the experience of living through something that is simply 'bigger than us' (Robertson 1992).

There is thus no explanation for how behavioural traits are conditioned and produced, except for simply reading off an automatic response from a determining economic structure. As Serap Kayatekin and David Ruccio argue, human actors 'in this vision are subjects "in" globalization rather than...subjects "of" globalization'. In other words, globalization is something that acts upon us and our ability to display conscious human agency, rather than conscious human agency being something that acts upon globalization. Indeed, so one-sided is this relationship that 'subjects are "objects" of globalization insofar as processes are exerted upon them' (Kayatekin and Ruccio 1998: 80).

There is good reason to oppose on analytical grounds the suggestion that the global economy is actively and intentionally recasting all socio-economic relations in its own image. However, this is not to deny the existence of a widespread, and very real, impression that economic events are being shaped beyond the capacity of ordinary people to control them or alter their course, although this is not the outcome of globalization per se. It is the outcome of attempts to institutionalize globalizing tendencies as a means of making the reproduction of accumulation strategies appear ever more distant from the decisions of individuals. Such distance impacts upon the consciousness of the individual by deactivating the Smithian impartial spectator.

Let me provide two brief examples. First, the increasing delegation of policy-making responsibilities away from democratically elected officials has institutionalized an 'expert' culture both domestically and internationally. Authority to set domestic monetary policy has increasingly been ceded to central bankers, and authority to determine international development policy has increasingly been ceded to the World Bank and the IMF. Within such a framework, the well-being of others typically is not seen as a matter of individual responsibility, but as a matter solely to concern the aforementioned experts.

Second, the ever more intrusive encroachment of marketing and advertising industries into daily life has been engineered specifically to make the act of consumption an increasingly unreflexive, even unconscious, activity. The more that consumer behaviour is reduced to the level of the routine, though, the less we question the world that is legitimized through the act of consumption. As before, responsibility for the well-being of others is displaced from the individual.

Given the general themes of the book, which seek to embed the foundations of IPE in an understanding of human nature, this brings us to arguably the most significant aspect of globalization. Globalization is not a unified economic structure that exerts a determining influence on action, thereby mandating self-interested behaviour. However, the public management of globalization has established a reward structure that provides increasing incentives for actors involved in market-based relationships to behave in line with self-interested norms. The ideology of individual acquisitiveness has been actively promoted as the guide for the way in which globalizing tendencies are experienced. Moreover, the dominant discourse of globalization suggests that globalizing tendencies endorse self-interested behavioural traits that are, in any case, natural phenomena. This provides an added impetus for acting self-interestedly, as it lessens the sense of moral disquiet that individuals might otherwise feel when they become aware that they are acting in this manner. It is difficult to know how we can be held responsible for our actions if they are grounded in natural character traits, whatever their consequences on other people.

The crux of the matter is this. The discourse of globalization has an independent causal effect on economic relations, which extends beyond any that can be attributed to globalizing tendencies themselves. It displaces moral responsibility for purely self-interested behaviour away from the individuals who engage in such behaviour and towards a structure of faceless economic forces that requires them to behave in this way in the first place. Globalization thus becomes a convenient excuse for activities that in other circumstances might provoke moral sanction.

Individuals who do harm to others through the consequences of their actions, but who can relate those actions to the economic logic of globalization, are more difficult to censure than those who do harm purely for the sake of doing harm. In the latter instance there is a simple line of responsibility, which ensures that the perpetrator can be called to account. The individual who engaged in the harmful action is clearly culpable for the consequences that ensue. By contrast, things are much less clear-cut in the former instance, when set within the context of the economic logic of globalization. The individual who engaged in the harmful action still bears responsibility for the consequences of those actions, but culpability can be blurred by attributing the cause of the action to a determining economic logic.

Globalization is an arena for action in which much harm has been done by one person to another in the name of self-interest. I will briefly list three examples of what I mean by this. First, moments of acute financial crisis created by trading patterns in international financial markets cause widespread economic insecurity. The Asian financial crisis, for instance, is estimated to have generated

60 million new cases of poverty in the first six months after its onset (Lee 1998). Second, by guaranteeing private property rights across borders, international institutions have made it more difficult for governments to protect the natural environment against environmentally-degrading production techniques. This enables cross-border investors to fundamentally change the eco-system that sustains many local economic activities (Paterson 2001). Third, work has become more onerous in most countries of the world, as corporate managers threaten relocation in an attempt to lower unit costs of production. Amid the increasing political isolation of trade unions, workers' rights have been undermined and average working hours have risen (Coates 2000).

In each of these instances, harm has been caused to others by the actions of individuals – respectively, those reinforcing speculative dynamics within international financial markets; those choosing to relocate production activity away from established environmental regulations; and those who have redefined contractual obligations specifying the nature of work. Yet in each instance it is possible for such individuals to escape public admonishment for their actions, in a way which suggests that culpability lies elsewhere. In particular, by appealing to a simple structural logic of globalization, harmful actions can instead be attributed to a determining economic essence. This displaces culpability for the consequences of actions away from the individual whose actions they were in the first place. In conclusion, then, the dominant discourse of globalization has two main effects. On the one hand, it provides ideological justification for purely self-interested behaviour; on the other, it provides a means for individuals to avoid confronting the moral consequences of their own actions.

Conclusion

Arguably the most significant aspect of globalization is that it has served to embed a particular conception of the market economy ever more deeply within everyday economic life. The image most readily identified with globalization is one which suggests that the whole world now resembles a single unified marketplace. The fact that all the empirical evidence on the extent and reach of globalizing tendencies flatly refutes such a suggestion is largely beside the point.

The dominant discourse of globalization must be understood as part of a broader economic belief system, which it now serves to sustain. It exists in a cognitive context in which the concepts of 'market', 'market clearance', 'market forces', 'market logic' and 'market imperative' enjoy a wide degree of familiarity and recognition. Indeed, it is directly due to the extent to which these concepts *already* provided the basis on which to choose between alternative courses of action in day-to-day life that the very *idea* of globalization has been accepted so readily.

The language of the market acquires its discursive power because its use cannot simply be reduced to a crude false consciousness on the part of those who seek to accommodate themselves to perceptions of 'market imperatives'. The dominant discourse of globalization is important in this respect because it adds a further dimension to the everyday language of the market. Moreover, it also provides a means of disabling the moral critique of individual actions consistent with market ideology. In particular, it makes it more difficult to impose a standard of conscionable action as the basis for judging the propriety of individual behaviour, and it makes it more difficult to hold to account those whose behaviour is deemed to be improper.

Chapter 10

Applying the Theoretical Framework (2): International Trade

Introduction

The ability of individuals to engage in economic activities that have a knowingly conscionable dimension rests, at least in part, on the existence of social institutions that facilitate such action. Action can neither be understood nor conducted outside the context in which it is situated. If the social institutions that are necessary for conscionable action are absent from the economy, the broader economic environment will not sustain conscionable action. The political campaign for fair trade attempts to create such institutions. The fair trade movement encapsulates the activities of a number of organizations and interest groups, who highlight the way in which global economic relations connect consumers in advanced industrialized economies with producers in less privileged parts of the world. These groups are animated by the concern that the price paid by a consumer in one part of the world should, at the very minimum, cover the costs of production in another part of the world. The normative argument for fair trade is that consumer power should not be used, whether knowingly and deliberately or not, in order to depress consumer prices to the point at which producers are unable to sustain themselves. It suggests that it is legitimate to be asked to pay a price premium in the interests of social development.

The chapter proceeds in three stages. In the first section I focus on the tendency to treat trade as an exclusive phenomenon of market relations, which are formed for purely self-interested reasons. Polanyi showed that trading relations have developed in societies that are not bounded by market ideology, and this observation enables us to think of multiple motivations for trade. I extend this argument to characterize the development of global trading relations in terms of the deliberate increase in distance between producer and consumer. This increased distance takes both a geographic and a moral dimension, the latter impacting adversely upon the awareness of conscionable alternatives within the international economy. This insight informs the analysis in the next section, in which I focus on attempts to heighten consumer awareness of fair trade alternatives. Much of the discussion of fair trade focuses on the limited penetration of such products in relation to both market share and consumer preference. I challenge such a focus, arguing that it internalizes, however inadvertently, the orthodox conception of consumer preference as a purely price-related phenomenon. I suggest that the internalization of market-based economics is an inadequate grounding for a critique of market-based outcomes. I use the final section to construct an alternative theoretical standard against which to judge the campaign for fair trade. I argue that fair trade products rely for their success on the appeal to Smithian propriety as the guide for action.

The economistic fallacy and the development of global trading relations

Polanyi's attempt to historicize the social basis of the market economy reveals important insights. He suggests that trade tends to be thought of necessarily as *market* trade, and that our ability to derive the benefits of trade is treated as symptomatic of the existence of an economy bounded by market institutions and market ideology. Instead of universalizing current conditions, however, Polanyi shows that efforts to create a market economy are a relatively recent phenomenon in human history, and that the establishment of trading relations significantly predates such efforts. An important element of the economistic fallacy identified by Polanyi is that trade necessarily involves markets, yet Polanyi is able to demonstrate that this is unequivocally not the case (Polanyi 1957 [1944]: 59).

According to Polanyi, human societies have established three basic types of trade. Of these, market trade may today be the most prevalent, and it may contribute most to our sense of globalization, but it is also the most recent. Each of Polanyi's three forms of integration – reciprocity, redistribution and exchange (see Chapter 6) – has its own dominant trading relation (Hechter 1981: 409). Gift trade typifies reciprocal economies, administered trade typifies redistributive economies and market trade typifies exchange economies. It is only the market trade of exchange economies that takes place on an individualistic and competitive basis, and that therefore falls prey to purely self-interested ideologies. By contrast, trade in reciprocal and redistributive economies tends to be organized along collective and non-competitive lines (Polanyi 1982: 41–5).

The significance of Polanyi's observations for current purposes lies in the fact that, if all trade is not necessarily market trade, then trade does not necessarily have to be conducted within the context of market ideology. It is possible to impose other normative criteria onto the form that trading patterns assume. It is not a prerequisite of economic life for trade to be organized using strict monetary exchange, in which the price at which the product changes hands is the manifestation of supply and demand dynamics that reflect nothing other than pure self-interest. The price at which trade is conducted may also serve social purposes, in order that those who are short of certain necessities may receive a price that allows them to make good this shortfall. There is no necessary economic logic embedded within the properties of monetary exchange to dictate that trade takes place solely for pecuniary gain.

A market-driven culture may well create new sets of wants among its participants (Baum 1996: 48) such that trade increasingly fulfils the function of satisfying self-interest. Consumption patterns associated with globalization perhaps attest to such developments. However, outcomes of this nature are not intrinsic to trade per se. Polanyi urges us to look beyond orthodox economic assumptions in which trade, money and markets are mutually constitutive and, as a consequence, form an indivisible whole. He argues that, 'Such an approach must induce a more or less tacit acceptance of the heuristic principle according to which, where trade is in evidence, markets should be assumed, and where money is in evidence trade, and therefore markets, should be assumed' (Polanyi 1982: 40). Breaking free from the economistic fallacy, trade takes on an entirely different complexion. It is not automatically embodied with market-based ideologies of possessive individualism, competitive acquisitiveness and utility-maximizing self-interest; instead, it becomes a context for alternative, and potentially more socially progressive, forms of political mobilization.

Let me now situate these thoughts in relation to the concerns of the current chapter. It is usual when discussing the economics of globalization to do so specifically in terms of a global *market*. In the absence of a direct challenge to the economistic fallacy that conflates trade and market, all trading relations within the global economy tend to be treated as market trade. To return to Polanyi's perceptive commentary on the economistic fallacy, the very existence of global trading relations therefore tends to come complete with assumptions about the moral framework in which global trade occurs. These assumptions imply that to trade globally is to operate in a global context in which market ideology dominates, and in which self-interest is the only moral guide for action.

This implication acquires added significance given the substantial increase in the volume of world trade over the last three decades. Indeed, for many authors, this expansion in trade is the most important measure of globalization. Certainly, growth in exports as a percentage of GDP has consistently been higher than growth in GDP for almost all of the post-Second World War period (Hirst and Thompson 1999: 54). The traded sector of the international economy has been arguably its most dynamic, with output growth being less than three-quarters of export growth in the 1980s and 1990s combined (United Nations 2003: 1).

There are two ways in which we could interpret the heightened sensitivity of an increasing amount of world production to conditions elsewhere within the international economy. Ignoring Polanyi's observations on the economistic fallacy, we could conclude that global trading relations increasingly enforce strict adherence to instinctively self-interested behavioural norms. However, this conclusion would be at odds with the perspective developed here. Alternatively, we could look at the way in which a heightened incidence of world trade impacts upon, and changes, the moral basis of everyday economic life. The result may still be an increase in explicitly self-interested behaviour, although the cause of such an increase would be rooted in the changed moral basis of everyday economic life rather than in the very logic of trade itself. Let me explain.

Market relations form today beyond the physical location of an actual marketplace, where buyers and sellers meet face-to-face in order to exchange products. Indeed, the whole essence of trade is that it facilitates exchange 'at a distance'. Those with a product to sell do not necessarily have to share a physical space with those who wish to buy in order for an exchange to take place (see Chapter 7).

The market, understood in the concrete as a physical space, is not the same as 'the market', understood in the abstract as a supply–demand mechanism (Silver 1983: 815). The former requires locational proximity, while the latter does not. From this perspective, the significance of the heightened incidence of world trade is that it emphasizes the latter over the former. Increases in world trade have the effect of stretching economic relations over ever greater distances.

'Increased distance' can have two meanings in this context. First, and most obviously, an increase in the volume of world trade tends to increase the geographical separation between producer and consumer. Global trading relations connect people in ever more disparate locations. Second, and less obviously, an increase in the volume of world trade also tends to increase the moral separation between producer and consumer. Global trading relations disconnect people morally insofar as they create economic links between people who know very little about each other's lives and lifestyles, and who have few (if any) directly shared experiences.

This sense of 'not knowing' the person at the other end of the exchange masks the responsibility that might otherwise be felt for ensuring that the process of exchange does not inflict harm upon them. The cloak of anonymity masks direct recognition of the moral consequences of trading with distant strangers. Such circumstances make it less discomfiting to us morally, should we choose to use this anonymity to engage in consciously self-interested behaviour. Indeed, it is possible to characterize the political project of globalization as a deliberate attempt to create an arena for action in which there are fewer ethical constraints on acting purely out of self-interest.

As the remainder of this chapter makes clear, the campaign for fair trade attempts to remove the 'anonymous' nature of many global trading relations. It seeks to do so in order to re-state the case for conscionable action within the international economy. 'Personalized' trading relations reveal the moral consequences of economic action for exactly the same reasons as they are obscured by 'anonymous' trading relations. It is to this question that I now turn.

The fair trade market and fair trade ideology

Fairly traded products, in total, currently have global sales that are less than those of many medium-to-large corporations. They constitute a tiny fraction of global output, although the trend suggests a significant expansion in the fair trade market. Global output growth was around 3 per cent for 2002 (www.un.org), yet output growth in fair trade products totalled more than 30 per cent (Fair Trade Federation 2003). This followed a number of years in which the availability of certified fair trade products rose rapidly, accompanied by a similar increase in consumer awareness of such products. Taken together, these two developments have ensured that fair trade products have become an increasingly important part of the day-to-day choices made by ever more consumers.

The impact of the campaign for fair trade has been most marked in two sectors: foodstuffs and textiles. Sales of certified fair trade coffee showed the greatest expansion in the five years to 2002, with those for tea coming a close second (www.ifat.org). Following the successes in these commodity markets, a number of other fair trade alternatives have gained additional prominence, including those in chocolate, cocoa and orange juice. Similar trends have been evident in the clothing industry, in the wake of concerted efforts to ensure that retailers accept more responsibility for informing consumers of the conditions in which the clothes they sell were made (www.cleanclothes.org). The headline-making 'Labour Behind the Label' campaign has focused the attention of consumers on the type of factory work that their consumption choices tacitly endorse. As a consequence of the heightened visibility of both fairly traded alternatives and fair trade politics, the value of the fair trade market has more than tripled in the five years to 2002.

An analysis of the strategies employed by fair trade campaigners in their efforts to popularize the purchase of fair trade alternatives is highly instructive. It shows the way in which political mobilization is engendered specifically to re-connect consumers with the producers of the goods they buy. In particular, the campaign focuses on the moral consequences of consumption choices. Most of the politics of the fair trade issue concerns raising the consciousness of consumers. This involves a narrative strategy, through which campaigners tell stories about the lives of the producers who stand to benefit from the adoption of fair trade norms. This is not only about how such producers would benefit, and neither is it only about why it is ethically right that they should benefit. It is specifically focused on *who* benefits – putting names and faces to the process of global trade.

It is an attempt to transcend what might otherwise be the anonymity of trading relations.

This requires two things. First, fair trade campaigners have found it necessary to demonstrate that the rhetoric of free trade, which is embedded within the policy agenda of international institutions and sustained by assumptions of globalization, actually masks important asymmetries in the way in which free trade principles are applied in practice. Globalization is an arena for action, and it has been used by the governments of advanced industrialized countries to promote free trade vigorously in those sectors in which their economies specialize, while maintaining an elaborate structure of protectionist measures in those sectors in which they do not. The adverse impact on access to world markets for 'Third World' agricultural products is particularly noteworthy in this respect. The principles of free trade are allowed to operate only in circumstances in which they are to the advantage of those who are sufficiently powerful to exercise control over the agenda of international economic management. As needs no explanation, 'Third World' farmers do not fall into this category, and neither do labourers in newly industrializing economies.

Second, the issue then becomes one of introducing these farmers and these labourers into the lives of those who might be of a mind to buy their products. This involves projecting as many images as possible of their lives and lifestyles into the consciousness of consumers: beginning with their names and those of their families, where they live, the history of their area and the symbolic importance of their culture, before explaining how they are systematically disadvantaged by the asymmetric operation of the international trade regime. The image that is presented to us, as consumers, of the farmers and the labourers with whom it is hoped we will trade is not one of an abstract element of the equally abstract concept of comparative advantage, and neither are they presented as a necessary effect of an unchangeable logic of surplus value extraction and structural exploitation. Rather, they are presented as real people, with human emotions, human desires and human needs. The connection between producers and consumers that the movement for fair trade attempts to establish are irreducibly human connections.

This feature of fair trade politics is yet to be reflected, however, in the academic literature on the topic. Where fair trade concerns have made an impact on the academic literature, they have done so in a way that reflects the continuing dominance of orthodox economic thought in discussions of the economy. Most of the literature works on the assumption that the consumer will be the ultimate arbiter of the success, or otherwise, of fair trade products. As a statement of fact there is little with which to disagree in this assertion. However, the very notion of 'consumer preference' that underpins this view very closely mirrors that on which the whole conceptual edifice of neoclassical economics is constructed. It highlights the lack of market share enjoyed by fairly traded products, and attributes this to preferences that form solely on the basis of the price at which the product is traded. In almost all instances across all categories of goods, the fairly traded alternative is more expensive than those products not certified in such a manner.

In neoclassical economics, price acts as a signalling mechanism. Once more, this is a general idea that is relatively easy to accept. However, neoclassical theory is based on a more specific claim than that. Price is presumed to signal how a consumer's constrained budget can be organized in order to yield the greatest utility. Within such a framework, price is synonymous with opportunity cost and a logic of forgone alternatives. It estimates the utility that cannot be derived from other products, because the purchase of one rules out the purchase of others. The higher the price of one product, then, the greater the forgone utility involved in its consumption. Set in such a context, the higher prices that tend to be associated with fairly traded alternatives lead to an overall reduction in utility for the consumer. Of course, the core of neoclassical theory is that all economic actors, and certainly consumers, are instinctive utility-maximizers. Action is always oriented towards the derivation of self-interest, where self-interest and utility-maximization are mutually constituted, which lessens the likelihood that the fairly traded option will be chosen. Indeed, on a strict interpretation of the neoclassical framework, it is irrational to choose the fair trade alternative over a lower-priced product. At most, such actions are consistent with a deontological rationality (doing what one considers ought to be done given prevailing social circumstances) rather than an instrumental rationality (doing what one wants to do regardless of social circumstances: on which distinction see Davis 2002; see also Chapter 2).

It is only once the neoclassical theory of price has been challenged that it becomes possible to reveal the true significance of the argument for fair trade. Price is indeed a signalling mechanism, but it signals much more than merely the forgone utility associated with paying that price. The price premium associated with fairly traded products indicates a commitment to a particular type of world. It suggests that there are legitimate reasons for paying 'over the odds', so long as this can be linked directly and explicitly to social and development goals.

The impartial spectator and the fairly traded alternative

Fair trade is not solely an issue of commodity exchange: it is also an idea about justice, and a process designed to facilitate the popularization of that idea. The price that a consumer is willing to pay in order to choose the fair trade product is a signal of social intent. It is a commitment to a notion, however vaguely expressed, of a fairer world. It is also the recognition of the desirability of norm change within business culture, so that justice concerns are prioritized above pure price concerns. The question becomes one of how to theorize fair trade in IPE, such that the individual's commitment to the notion of a fairer world can be brought to the fore.

My chosen starting point, like that for the book as a whole, is Adam Smith's *Theory of Moral Sentiments* (see Chapter 4). For Smith, it is 'passions' rather than 'reason' that provide the guide for action, and which condition our response to the social circumstances in which we find ourselves (Smith 1982 [1759]: 11). It may be beyond pure reason in a calculative utility-maximizing sense to pay more for a product when a cheaper option presents itself to us. Equally, however, it may be within our passions to engage in precisely this type of activity, should doing so make us feel more comfortable with our contribution to maintaining other people's dignity and, as a consequence, with our contribution to maintaining the basis of society. We are sentient beings, according to Smith, and we call upon our capacity for imagination to ensure that our behaviour is not only reflexive, but that it also reflects a sense of duty to advance the social good (1982 [1759]: 134–56).

Fair trade campaigns, by presenting distant strangers as real people, immediately begin to break down the distinction between 'us' and 'them', and hence focus the imagination upon the constitution of society. It is less that 'we', as consumers, are united in our desire to consume, and that 'they', as producers, are united in their attempts to induce consumption, so much as a shared sense of social purpose. The economic act of trade is stripped of any lingering vestiges of an essential economic logic, and it is invested with social significance instead.

By introducing the social circumstances of distant strangers into our consciousness, the campaign for fair trade attempts to inspire particular emotions within us. The hope is that these emotions, once consciously recognized for what they are, may be sufficient to induce behavioural adaptations in line with both the principles and the practices of fair trade. The campaign for fair trade provides us with what Smith called the 'mirror' into other people's lives – even if we have never met, and are not ever likely to meet, these 'other people' – and it tends to invoke what he had in mind as a 'sympathetic' response to their circumstances.

Smith argued that, unless socialized to think otherwise, individuals will be left with an acute feeling of unease if they know that their gains are at the expense of others within society. Such unease will invoke emotions akin to guilt. They arise because we are social beings. Indeed, for Smith, we are unrecognizable to ourselves except within the context of the society in which we live. He developed his famous 'mirror' metaphor in order to establish this point:

> Were it possible that a human creature could grow up to manhood in some solitary place, without any communication with his own species, he could no more think of his own character, or the propriety or demerit of his own sentiments and conduct, of the beauty or deformity of his own mind, than of the beauty or deformity of his own face. All these are objects which he cannot easily see, which naturally he does not look at, and with regard to which he is provided with no mirror which can present them to his view. Bring him into society and he is immediately provided with the mirror which he wanted before. (Smith 1982 [1759]: 110)

In this single passage Smith provides a devastating critique of the theory of human nature that became the economics orthodoxy around one hundred years after he published his *Theory of Moral Sentiments*, and which all too often claims him as its intellectual forebear. Neoclassical economics gains its distinctiveness precisely from the fact that it conceives of the essence of human existence in terms that invite comparison with Smith's notion of 'some solitary place', in which 'species communication' is conspicuous by its absence. Such is the instinctive character of utility-maximizing behaviour in neoclassical thought that action is assumed to precede any form of interpersonal relationship. As a consequence, existence outside a context of solitude is considered simply unnecessary for sustaining human life. It is perhaps no surprise in this respect that neoclassical economists, where they specify their 'typical' agent at all, do so through reference to Robinson Crusoe (Tabb 1999: 27–30).

One interesting outcome of treating all economic agents as if they were Robinson Crusoe is that such a treatment eliminates all discussion of justice and, as a consequence, of conscionable action. Justice is a relative concept, in that to act justly is to act justly in relation to someone else (Witzum 1997: 244; Verburg 2000: 24). The first prerequisite for justice, then, is that life is lived within society. By extension, the prerequisite for being able to think about economic justice is that everyday economic life is conceptualized with respect to society. To live life like Robinson Crusoe is to live beyond society, existing in a solitary state in which the question of justice does not arise, because everyday economic life does not require interaction with other people who may have legitimate claims to being treated justly.

To return the analysis to the issue of fair trade, the implications of such a distinction are fairly obvious. Modelling consumption on the premise that economic life resembles Robinson Crusoe's serves to mask the true relationship that is contained within the act of consumption: that between consumer and producer. Rather, it anonymizes the relationship by obscuring the producer, treating the relationship instead as being between consumer and product. Understood in this way, moral standards relating to justice are inoperative. There is no conscious agent who can claim the right that the consumer acts justly in relation to them. The fair trade campaign focuses on reactivating discourses of justice, by re-personalizing trading relations, and by highlighting the fact that the very essence of such relations is that they link consumer and producer rather than consumer and product.

We find a similar emphasis on the necessarily human element of economic relations in the work of Adam Smith. We recognize, according to Smith, that we trade not with an abstract entity called the economy, but with other people. Moreover, by recognizing this, Smith argued that our economic relations would always be set within the context of our capacity to display 'sympathy' with our fellow human beings (Smith 1982 [1759]: 9–13). Smith's sense of sympathy departs somewhat from more modern usage. He focused on our ability to undertake the imaginative reconstruction of other people's social circumstances, as a means of feeling what they feel. Smith's sympathy therefore entails what Heilbroner calls 'psychic projection' (Heilbroner 1986: x). It is an emotive response to the situation in which others find themselves, and it is an emotive response that compromises what otherwise might be the tendency to behave in a purely self-serving manner (Campbell and Skinner 1982: 99; Rizvi 2002: 247). As we might recall from Chapter 4, for Smith, sympathy is 'fellow-feeling'. As he puts it in the opening sentence of *The Theory of Moral Sentiments*, 'How selfish soever man may be supposed, there are evidently some principles in his nature, which interest him in the fortune of others, and render their happiness necessary to him, though he derives nothing from it except the pleasure of seeing it' (1982 [1759]: 9).

It is to precisely such principles that the campaign for fair trade appeals. Smith was adamant that, for the distribution of goods within society to be just, the dignity of those who had to make do with an inferior distribution was paramount (Young and Gordon 1996: 19). The campaign for fair trade extends this condition one stage further. It suggests that, in order to maintain dignity as the basis of social stability, it is necessary to ensure a just distribution of rewards to those who produce the goods in the first place (Fair Trade Federation 2003). This could well entail paying more than the lowest available price for any category of good. However, the willingness to pay the price premium of the fairly traded alternative carries social and moral significance, in addition to having a straightforward economic impact in terms of forgone utility resulting from reduced purchasing power.

Conclusion

In neoclassical economics, trade is the outcome of a natural propensity to exchange, and all exchange entails the development of market relations based strictly on the principle of utility-maximization. In consequence, trade is assumed to provide a context in which all participants in the trading relation, driven ostensibly by innate characteristics, seek only to do what is best for themselves. The campaign for fair trade, by contrast, attempts to link consumers and producers at a moral level that transcends the ethics of pure self-interest. It appeals to individual subjectivities constructed on ideas of what it is best to do to further the provisioning needs of society (i.e., an oikonomic decision based on a deontological rationality), rather than on ideas of what it is best to do for oneself (i.e., a chrematistic decision based on an instrumental rationality).

However, the purchase of fairly traded goods remains a strictly peripheral economic activity. Such has been the incorporation of the orthodox economics worldview into daily life that the image of consumption as a utility-maximizing practice remains dominant. For most individuals living within societies in which the ideology of consumerism is an established part of the socialization structure, utility-maximization is truly entrenched as a primary habit of thought. The increasing visibility of fair trade products provides the means of alternative habitual practices based on alternative habits of thought, but such habits are distinct from the behavioural norms of a pure consumerist society.

In order to challenge those norms, it is first necessary to challenge the assumptions about human nature on which they are founded. The campaign for fair trade attempts to do this by transcending the anonymity of most trading relations. Within a consumerist society that conforms to the neoclassical worldview, the consumer's preferences are shaped solely by the economic characteristics of the product itself: in other words, its price relative to expectations of its quality. The campaign for fair trade attempts to shape consumer preferences, not on the basis of the impersonal characteristics of the product but by personalizing the very notion of trade. It appeals to individuals to act conscionably in circumstances in which the social good will be advanced, and it does so by putting names and faces to the producers who will benefit when consumers choose to pay the price premium of the fairly traded alternative. By removing the anonymity of the trading relation, those who campaign for fair trade attempt to invoke an emotive response in consumers, which will see them act to preserve the dignity of the producers with whom they trade. In such moments, assumptions about the universal nature of utility-maximizing self-interest are rendered meaningless. As a consequence, so too is the orthodox economics worldview that supports and sustains such an assumption.

Chapter 11

Applying the Theoretical Framework (3): International Development

Introduction

The public management of globalization has been predicated on attempts to extend a system of private property rights across borders. For most people, such attempts have been introduced, as it were, from the 'outside' – by international institutions such as the World Bank and the International Monetary Fund. Two-thirds of the countries of the world, embodying around three billion people, lack full control of their own economic policy (Pieper and Taylor 1998: 37). For the majority of the world's population, the process of policy formation takes place in decision-making arenas that operate without the need for local consent. A displacement effect is in evidence, whereby policies that are introduced in one country are actually formulated elsewhere. This has led to accusations of the coercive imposition of development policies that threaten to undermine local livelihoods and local lifestyles, in favour of a truly global economy that aspires to a single systemic logic of development.

Critics of the World Bank and the IMF, and of their role in the development process, tend to concentrate on three issues. First, they point to the highly political nature of interventions designed not only to restructure societies, but also to restructure individual subjectivities and patterns of cognition, especially when this occurs in the absence of local consent for such interventions. Second, they highlight attempts to depoliticize what might otherwise appear to be intrusive and coercive interventions, through justificatory appeal to abstract economic principles of market supply and market demand. Third, they argue that the institutions' reading of the historical development of advanced industrialized countries is a selective *mis*reading of the past, in that it prioritizes market mythology over accounts that are sensitive to the actual conditions in which the development experience was situated.

In order to assess the validity of such criticisms, the chapter proceeds in three stages. In the first section, I provide an overview of the changing development discourse of the international institutions, focusing in particular on the changes introduced in the early 1980s, which have since become a routine aspect of development practice. I analyse the increasing prominence of Structural Adjustment Programmes (SAPs), and the attempt to naturalize orthodox economic conceptions of a self-organizing and self-regulating market within SAP ideology. This provides the basis for the analysis in the second section, in which I outline a variety of forms of resistance to international institutions' development programmes. These include local level resistance, which tends to entail organized non-compliance with conditionalities imposed by the institutions, as well as resistance generated by pressure group activity in countries which are not undergoing adjustment themselves. This latter activity is resistance on behalf of others, involving the imaginative reconstruction of the situation in which others find themselves, in such a way as to invoke feelings of Smithian sympathy. Much of the pressure group politics surrounding this issue is directed at interventions by international institutions that attempt to reconstitute individual consciousness through the process of adjustment. This is the subject of the final section. I focus in particular on interventions designed to condition economic agents with a specific type of economic rationality associated with market-based institutions. I conclude with an observation that is a familiar Polanyian insight: it is unfeasible to expect market institutions to function when they are imposed by an external authority, rather than being embedded within existing social dynamics.

International economic development and the ideology of structural adjustment

International development policies may not be cast today as strictly in the image of structural adjustment as they were in the 1980s and early 1990s. However, the development process continues to be set in the shadow of adjustment ideology. The centrepiece of all Structural Adjustment Programmes is an attempt to establish a system of price-making markets in order to regulate and guide economic activity. The goal is to remove distortions from the process of resource allocation, by subjecting that process to the disciplines of a supply–demand–price mechanism. The intention is to induce permanent changes in the relative prices of tradable goods (Edwards and van Wijnbergen 1988), such that prices be set solely in accordance with economic calculations of the value of goods, rather than by political calculations of their social worth. For many in the 'Third World', Structural Adjustment Programmes signal the shift from an oikonomic to a chrematistic society.

As such, the abstracted notion of a self-generating and self-sustaining market mechanism provides the core of the intellectual justification for SAPs. In the absence of *assumptions* about the existence of such a mechanism, the economic case for SAPs rapidly falls apart. Yet, as the analysis of the preceding chapters has shown, this is all it is: an assumption. The undoubted existence of market ideology must not be understood, in and of itself, as confirmation of the existence of the social structures that market ideology reifies. The market ideology propagated in official development discourse exists independently of the ability of developing countries to incorporate market-based institutions into the social structures of everyday life.

Indeed, there are good reasons to suppose that the process of incorporation will remain incomplete whenever market-based institutions are imposed externally, by authoritative decree. It is, perhaps, the most basic point of Polanyian political economy that the market ideology of neoclassical economics privileges a conception of markets which are disembedded from the social circumstances in which exchange takes place, yet exchange systems are necessarily dysfunctional unless they reflect, and are embedded within, the prevailing norms of society. The Structural Adjustment Programmes of the World Bank and the IMF are an embodiment of the market ideology of neoclassical economics. They are devised by staff economists who are neoclassically trained, and they rely upon neoclassical growth theories to provide their intellectual frames of reference. However, even the way in which SAPs are implemented points to the existence of the Polanyian contradiction. Official development discourse may well reify the image of a self-generating and self-sustaining market mechanism, but the implementation of SAPs comes complete with the introduction of a vast array of political conditionalities. As such, the market-based institutions which SAPs attempt to establish must be seen as anything other than 'automatic' features of everyday economic life.

The increasing prominence of conditionalities is usually attributed to the rightward drift in the early 1980s in the World Bank's preferred method of policy implementation (Mehmet 1999: 127). Viewed in this way, they are a manifestation of the increasingly widespread acceptance within policy circles of the idea of moral hazard. In the standard interpretation, moral hazard can only be avoided if the costs of development aid are distributed between the donor and the receiving communities. The argument that was popularized by the World Bank in the early 1980s was that the costless receipt of development aid provided no incentive for receiving communities to effect behavioural change that would make them less reliant on external assistance in the future. Indeed, it was even argued that costless receipt of development aid created perverse incentives that served to entrap the poorest countries of the world into ever greater reliance on the help of others.

It would be a mistake, however, to turn conditionality solely into an issue of the left–right politics of policy implementation. It is more fundamental than can be accounted for solely by reference to a temporary rightward shift in the leadership of the World Bank. The whole structure of World Bank and IMF interventions has increasingly been assimilated into a framework of thinking that associates development with the introduction of market-based institutions. Moreover, in circumstances in which the social support structures for market-based institutions have been missing, the introduction of such institutions has taken the form of imposition. Within such a context, the argument that 'the market' arises naturally appears somewhat hollow.

However, the image of an autonomously constituted 'free market' is part of both the conditionalities of international institutions and the governance mindset within which conditionalities take shape (Cheru 1997: 165). As Philip McMichael observes, this represents 'a double fiction: it dissolves historically-specific political cultures, and it replaces them with an economic abstraction' (McMichael 1998: 105). It also represents a significant change in the underlying operational ethos of the institutions that oversee the process of international economic development. Countries in search of development finance have grown increasingly reliant on the World Bank and IMF guaranteeing large-scale resources in aid of structural adjustment. This takes one of two forms: either the direct supply of loans, or the provision of assurances backed by international law to persuade private investors to make credit available on a commercial basis (McLean, Quadir and Shaw 2000: 296). Either way, it leaves poor countries as potential captives of the ideological preferences of the World Bank and the IMF.

This moves the operation of the institutions away from their original remit. In the case of the IMF, this was to provide additional liquidity for economies that were experiencing temporary balance of payments disequilibria. In the case of the World Bank, it was to provide funding for projects that promised to meet officially sanctioned development targets. In neither case were the institutions to act as anything more than service providers (Harris 1999: 198), while donor countries retained the right to use that provision in a manner that they deemed most appropriate. The IMF has revised its own role such that it no longer merely acts to stabilize international bond markets in a way that eases the flow of credit into temporarily illiquid economies. Rather, it now acts outside the market environment, forcibly restructuring the governance basis of illiquid economies in an attempt to enhance their creditworthiness in the minds of bondholders. Alongside this, the World Bank now prioritizes economy-wide lending over project lending (McMurtry 1999: 95). This is another change designed to expose the governance basis of poor countries to both the policy and the ideological preferences of international institutions. Such changes represent a shift to prioritizing accumulation relative to legitimation (on which see Chapter 8). However, they have also elicited considerable controversy, setting the context for concerted political mobilization against the international institutions. It is to these challenges that I turn in the following section.

Local level politics and resistance to adjustment ideology

Resistance to the development initiatives of the World Bank and the IMF tend to take one of two forms. Both are evidence of local level resistance, in that they are not formally sponsored by governments or others working on behalf of the state. However, the locales in which such resistance takes place differ significantly. On the one hand, the forced imposition of social structures cast in the image of 'the market' meets resistance from people struggling directly against the effects of conditionality. In other words, there is political mobilization against adjustment ideology in countries where the adjustment process is an on-going aspect of everyday life. On the other hand, political mobilization against adjustment ideology also occurs in countries where there is no direct experience of the adjustment process. The local level politics of resistance to adjustment ideology brings together into a single, albeit virtual, community those whose lives are impacted upon by the policy initiatives of the World Bank and the IMF, and those who are concerned by the social effects of such impacts without ever experiencing them directly for themselves. I now take in turn these two aspects of local level resistance to adjustment ideology.

The conventional critique of World Bank and IMF conditionality is that it consistently penalizes the poor (Harris 1999). Adjustment tends to entail extensive contraction of local economic activities, in order to enforce a strict separation between the profitable (the chrematistic) and the non-profitable (the oikonomic). The costs of contraction are borne asymmetrically, in that the trigger for adjustment typically is financial instability, but international banks find that World Bank and IMF policy safeguards them from the risks associated with financial instability (Strange 1998b). Such protection is forthcoming despite the fact that investment risk is consciously accepted as part of the banks' normal business activities, and even in circumstances in which the instability that heightens risk is the result of banks' own investment practices.

The reverse is true for those who feel the effects of structural adjustment in their full immediacy. These people make no money from speculative investments, and neither do they seek insurance against exposure to the risks associated with speculative investments, yet still they bear the brunt of the impact of adjustment, as international institutions intervene on behalf of the financial community in order to impose greater stability on their country's finances (Soros 1998). These interventions tend to reduce the proportion of an adjusting country's budget that can be spent on public services, drastically undermining access to healthcare and education. In addition, they tend to set exacting targets for the amount of produce that can be consumed at home, in order to release more output for export markets, where it can be sold at a higher price and earn valuable reserves of foreign currency.

However, such developments are not uncontested. It is possible to point to a plethora of self-help practices enacted by local people which blur the boundaries of the conditionalities that the international institutions seek to impose. Such practices are evidence of conscious non-compliance. Governments of developing countries may sign up to SAPs, but this is no guarantee that local people will accept the practices that the programmes demand. Fantu Cheru provides an evocative label for such non-compliance; he calls it the 'silent revolution of the poor' (Cheru 1997). Examples of the deliberate frustration of programme implementation include underreporting of agricultural output to World Bank and IMF-appointed tax inspectors, private appropriation of public space designated for the international property market, and theft of primary products awaiting shipment to export markets (McMichael 1998). The poor, through everyday practices oriented towards the survival of their community, struggle against political decisions undertaken in the name of development, but which serve to cause them harm. As Cheru (1997: 161) suggests: 'Instead of castigating the poor and characterising their professions as "criminal" or "illegal", we should celebrate them for elevating the human spirit, for fighting to preserve their dignity, and for allowing the rest of us to find our own humanity.'

Through their actions, those who resist the socially dislocating effects of adjustment ideology are, at the same time, highlighting the fact that economic activity takes place within broader social structures, dominated by irreducibly human needs and aspirations. The neoclassical agent is deemed to operate in isolation from his or her peers, in which self-help strategies are literally that: there is no suggestion that such strategies are oriented towards the community as a whole, because the neoclassical agent lives alone, acts alone, and has no connection to others in terms of shared social circumstances. As is demonstrated, however, by the example of the poor refusing to comply with the implementation of Structural Adjustment Programmes, neoclassical theory talks of lives that are not lived. Cheru's 'silent revolution of the poor' refers to oikonomic practices that are oriented to the well-being of the community as a whole. The poor, in acting in the interests of broader social cohesion to blur the boundaries of World Bank and IMF conditionalities, refute the image of the neoclassical agent, despite it being the presumed characteristics of the neoclassical agent that are reified in World Bank and IMF ideology.

Further doubts must be cast against the idea that all economic agents act solely to maximize their own utility when it is recognized that resistance to adjustment ideology is not confined to those with direct experience of the adjustment process. Local level politics is also enacted in countries outside the developing world. Such resistance involves people whose connection to those who have a direct experience of the adjustment process is, at most, an emotional connection. A virtual community has been established between people who remain distant strangers, and who have little in common except a shared antipathy towards World Bank and IMF development strategies. Neoclassical theory can have nothing to say about the actions of those who protest on behalf of distant strangers from a position of relative affluence, but still we see concerted political activities against Structural Adjustment Programmes in the developed world.

One increasingly important way in which such activities are organized focuses on the manner in which the World Bank funds its development programmes. The World Bank receives from creditor governments only around one-fifth of the money it eventually disburses in loans. The remaining four-fifths is raised by selling bonds on private capital markets. Such bonds are the investment of choice for many pension funds, insurance houses, mortgage providers, trade unions, churches and local governments (World Bank Boycott 2003). World Bank bonds are considered an ultra-safe investment, because the Bank is able to mandate that all its loans are backed by sovereign guarantees from borrowing governments, irrespective of the success of the capital projects that the loans are used to support (Adams 1997). In other words, and contrary to almost all other bond issuing schemes, the returns to World Bank bonds are the same if the programmes they fund are failures as if they are successes.

The World Bank has an institutional mission to help people in the developing world out of poverty. However, because it has the ability to secure sovereign guarantees of loan repayments from borrowing governments, it has a financing structure that creates perverse incentives when understood in the context of its institutional mission. The developing world can be forced to pay for programmes that are established to assist its development, even if such programmes do nothing to relieve overall levels of poverty.

This has led to debates in the developed world about the need for the just treatment of the developing world. Pressure has been brought to bear on many of the organizations that routinely buy World Bank bonds in an attempt to persuade them to restructure their investment portfolios by turning their backs on such bonds (see World Bank Boycott 2003). This local level activism is not undertaken in the material self-interest of the participants. Indeed, it may threaten that interest, to the extent that the newly restructured investment portfolios are likely to be concentrated in potentially riskier assets than World Bank bonds.

Instead, it is necessary to understand political mobilization against the World Bank in advanced industrialized economies in terms of the desire of the participants to show sympathy for the living conditions of distant strangers. It is moral concerns for justice, and not material concerns for self-gain, that animate protests against the World Bank in the developed world. This involves a process that was fundamental to the way in which Adam Smith, for example, understood the position of the individual within society. Smith argued that individuals only develop a sense of themselves through their interaction with other people (Smith 1982 [1759]). This can be either direct interaction and, in particular, face-to-face contact, or it can be the imaginative reconstruction of the situation in which others find themselves. More than anything else, political mobilization against the World Bank on behalf of others invokes Smithian 'sympathy' founded upon an empathetic response. It is a response that is triggered by the feeling that the structural power of international institutions is used in an unjust manner, to further embed existing social asymmetries within the international economy.

Moreover, it is a challenge to the legitimacy of those institutions. Their legitimacy is officially conferred in and through the support for their actions that is offered by governments on behalf of the states they represent. Local level activism against the international institutions is an attempt to render the process of legitimation more complex than to treat governments as the sole arbiter of that process. It is to empower individuals to see themselves as potential guardians of the legitimacy of international institutions. At the very least, it increases the possibility that their concerns will be taken seriously. In the following section I turn to the specific nature of such concerns.

The World Bank and the re-making of individual rationality

One of the most controversial of all World Bank activities is its attempt to refashion individual rationalities through its development programmes. This activity, perhaps more than any other, has been the catalyst for increasing demands that international institutions be held to account for their conduct. Such demands tend to be voiced by those who have no direct experience of World Bank programmes, but who are willing to mobilize around the perceived injustice exacted upon those who have their rationality, along with their wider cognitive practices, forcibly recast from the 'outside'. The World Bank consequently stands accused of inflicting violence upon the individual, in the name of subjugating the broader human needs of individuals to the success of its own development initiatives.

It is a standard position within the IPE literature on development that the international institutions have long attempted to model all development strategies on the particular experiences of western industrialization (Mehmet 1999). In other words, the western model of industrialization has been promoted as a universal model of development. This involves imposing the economic conditions associated with western industrialization onto all societies, irrespective of the compatibility of those conditions with the existing institutional structure of developing economies. To adopt a Polanyian perspective, no thought is given to the possibility that the economy will prove to be a malfunctioning and even contradictory entity, in the event that its underlying modus operandi is incapable of being embedded within the existing cultural traditions of society. The World Bank has pushed ahead with its reform proposals while ignoring potential problems relating to the embeddedness of the new economic practices it is seeking to institutionalize (Pieper and Taylor 1998).

Such reforms exist at all levels of society, right down to the question of individual rationality. Western industrialization was constructed upon a particular type of cognition which, in turn, served to normalize particular character traits through the contribution that people exhibiting such traits were able to make to the economy as a whole. In attempting to recreate in its contemporary programmes the conditions that were deemed conducive to western industrialization, the World Bank has attempted to reconstitute individual rationality in the image of western industrialism.

It has concentrated its efforts in this respect on providing education programmes that teach people how to think in a manner which suggests an instinctive calculus approach to their social existence. This is less about developing a country's economy than it is about developing particular habits of thought (on which see Chapter 5), to which all individuals will eventually be expected to respond in a more or less consistent way. Such habits of thought serve to reproduce what Polanyi called the 'economistic fallacy' (see Chapter 6). By teaching people how to respond to an increasing number of life situations in the manner of a utility-maximizing economic agent, World Bank programmes render such actions ostensibly natural. At the very least, they reinforce the impression that any other form of behaviour is out of line with what the economy requires, and must therefore be corrected.

Polanyi argued that this was to conflate the empirical entity of economic relations, which could take many forms depending on the cultural traditions of the society in which they were embedded, with a single form of behaviour, that promoting utility-maximization and which Polanyi called 'economizing' behaviour (Polanyi 1957 [1944]: 33–42). World Bank programmes positively thrive on such a conflation (McMurtry 1999). The World Bank commits what Polanyi deemed to be the worst of analytical sins: to reduce all economic possibilities to those that correspond solely to the economy's market form (Polanyi 1957 [1944]: 50). Moreover, it does so with a considerable degree of self-assuredness, seeking to legitimize its own interventions by arguing that the character traits it is attempting to impose are, in any case, natural.

However, those attributes that are presented as natural are, in fact, learned. The habits of industrial work practices were ever thus, as Adam Smith outlined in great length in the final two books of the *Wealth of Nations*. Smith focused on those areas of cognition that would allow the individual to thrive – economically, at least – within an increasingly complex division of labour. He emphasized not only basic literacy and numeracy skills, but also how such skills could be deployed in activities that would benefit the overall operation of a market economy, such as bookkeeping and accountancy. More generally, this appealed to cognition that was rooted in calculus, prioritizing the ability to reduce all social decisions to a comparison of economic costs and economic benefits.

The World Bank continues to emphasize such cognition in its development programmes. Its interventions that are aimed at the individual are aimed at releasing the individual's thought processes from the constraints of existing cultural traditions. They are about enabling the individual to think anew, in a manner prescribed by the demands of the western model of development. Many of these changes are facilitated by non-governmental organization assistance (Williams 1999) and focus on credit and financial management training (McMichael 1998). Such training helps local people to become more attuned to commercial practices and, in particular, to the calculations of profit and loss that are the cornerstones of the western notion of 'commerce' (Mehmet 1999).

As a consequence, and irrespective of the extent to which this departs from local custom, the development programmes of international institutions are predicated on an attempt to turn local people into the utility-maximizing agents of neoclassical theory. They represent a conscious effort to make local people think of themselves first and foremost *as* individuals – not as people who make a contribution on behalf of society *to* the economy, but as people who act on their own behalf to take rewards *from* the economy. It is only once individuals have been reconstituted in their own minds as chrematistic agents that it is possible for them to display the character traits of utility-maximization. In other words, individuals need to be taught how to embody an instinctive response to any set of social circumstances, such that their response calculates the costs and benefits of intended action *to them as individuals*. The social costs and social benefits of action do not come into consideration as the calculations are undertaken in the absence of oikonomic concerns.

As David Williams notes, the interventions of international institutions give us just cause to question the assertion that social action is to be explained through appeal to an instinctive, even natural, pursuit of self-interest. In something of an understatement, he argues that 'there is a good case for saying that to the extent that persons are like this, they have to be made that way' (Williams 1999: 98–9). The chrematistic agent has a constructed personality, and the character traits on which utility-maximization depend are socialized into such agents.

Viewed through such a perspective, World Bank programmes that seek to inculcate such forms of behaviour must be seen as conscious political projects. Indeed, they are political in the most fundamental sense of the word, in that they seek to make of people what they otherwise would not be. The World Bank may seek to legitimize interventions designed to inculcate utility-maximizing behaviour on the grounds that it is, in any case, natural to act in such a way. Yet the very fact that interventions are necessary to inculcate such behaviour demonstrates that it is anything other than natural. This may be merely stating the obvious, but it is nonetheless a point worth highlighting. If utility-maximizing behaviour was natural, interventions would not be required to get people to act as utility-maximizers. The fact that people have to be taught how to incorporate the character traits of the chrematistic agent into their everyday lives shows that such traits have to be imposed. Moreover, a fundamental part of the process of teaching people how to act as utility-maximizers is to encourage them, using coercive means if necessary, to unlearn existing behavioural dispositions.

Conclusion

The process of international economic development currently revolves around conscious attempts to enforce a new economic rationality within developing countries. The process of institutional 'adjustment', on which World Bank and IMF development programmes are based, reaches all the way down to the level of the individual.

The politics of resistance to World Bank and IMF programmes also reaches down to the level of the individual. Much of the protest politics against adjustment ideology takes place in countries which are not directly affected by development programmes cast in the image of that ideology. As a consequence, it is conducted by people who have no immediate experience of World Bank and IMF programmes. This is political mobilization on behalf of other people, which involves the conscious establishment of emotional relations between people whose experiences of the economy are fundamentally different. Such relations cannot be explained through appeal to the utility-maximizing agent of neoclassical economics. This politics of protest is based on the imaginative reconstruction of what it must be like to have local economic customs subjugated in the interests of inculcating utility-maximizing behaviour as a universal feature of human societies.

The critique of such interventions is usually a moral critique. However, it is also possible to ground a critique of current processes of international economic development in matters of more practical concern. Put at its simplest, such programmes do not work. Indeed, if we return to a key insight from Karl Polanyi, we should not expect them to work. Polanyi argued that functioning market institutions could not simply be imposed, parachuted *onto* society from above (Polanyi 1982); they truly have to be instituted, in the literal sense of being established in an organic manner from *within* society. A fundamental complementarity must exist between the form that market institutions take in a particular society and the existing structure of traditions, customs and norms within that society. In the absence of such a complementarity, market institutions will not be successfully embedded within existing social dynamics and, in the absence of their successful incorporation within society, market institutions will not function. The causal sequence runs from society to economy, not the other way around. There is no automatic mechanism whereby the imposition by external authority of a market-oriented economic rationality will lead to a trouble-free transition to market society.

Conclusion

Re-founding International Political Economy

Appraisals of the subject field differ in terms of how they read the history of IPE, but one thing is certain: the subject matter on which IPE scholars focus their attention is here to stay, so there is no reason why IPE should do anything other than thrive in the future. The economy will always be discussed and debated, and there will always be a need to explain how economic relations are constituted and why they take a particular form at a particular moment of time. The substantive roots of the subject field are secure: IPE scholars will continue to *do* IPE for a long time to come. Given the sense of stability that surrounds the substantive foundations of the subject field, it therefore comes as something of a surprise that its analytical foundations are still such an open question.

Many, perhaps most, of the practitioners of IPE are content for their practice to remain a sub-field of International Relations. In this way, IPE represents the application of the theories and methods of IR to matters of a broadly economic nature: IPE is simply the extension of IR debates to economic issues. Beyond the IR variant of IPE, however, there continues to be a palpable sense of search surrounding the analytical foundations of the field.

One frequent appeal to be heard from those engaged in such a search is for the foundations of International Political Economy to be re-thought from first principles. If we accept such a proposition, then the current state of the field is difficult to appraise in the absence of a reconstruction of its origins. Can we truly know where we are now if we reflect neither on where we have come from nor the route that we have taken? There are important arguments from intellectual historians to suggest that the answer is 'no'. Jürgen Habermas, for instance, has argued that the first and most important step in the development of a critical social theory is knowledge of that theory's own past (Habermas 1972). It is therefore not only knowledge of economic processes that practitioners of IPE should seek to historicize. A similar standard should also be applied to the way in which we think about, debate and disagree over the truth claims that arise from such knowledge. Susan Strange confronts this issue in characteristically forthright fashion. In assuming that the current state of the field is determined solely by contemporary developments in IR, she says, IPE scholars are destined to lead themselves into conceptual 'culs-de-sac, strada senza uscita, no through roads... Sooner or later, it will be necessary to go back and start again at the beginning' (Strange 1998a: 21).

I agree and, to my mind, the sooner this step is taken the better. The only question that remains is what, exactly, is meant by 'the beginning'.

The answer is not to the beginning of IPE itself, for this would not lead to a route out of the IR variant of IPE so much as a route right back to its heart. IPE was constituted as the political economy branch of International Relations in the early 1970s and, as such, was built upon the theories and methods that dominated IR at that time. In particular, and given the prevailing circumstances of widespread economic instability, early practitioners within the field focused on questions of international order, asking how the interaction of 'states and markets' could be harnessed using public authority so as to maintain systemic stability (see Chapter 1). By re-focusing on such questions, we are not presented with a ready-made exit from Strange's culs-de-sac; this *is* the no through road for IPE to which she refers.

Fortunately, one potential exit is apparent, for political economy has a much longer history than as a sub-field of International Relations. In the search for suitable foundations for IPE, it is necessary to go back further than the beginning of IPE itself, to the origins of the broader tradition of political economy. That tradition, in turn, has its roots in moral philosophy.

The development of economic relations integrates individuals into a substantive social system that we know as 'the economy'. However, the individual does not enter into economic relations devoid of all social characteristics, which then form simply as an epiphenomenon of 'the economy'. The individual is already a moral agent before entering into economic relations. Moreover, the individual's status as a moral agent impacts upon and influences the precise form of the economic relations in which he or she is embedded. In order to understand 'the economy' we need to understand economic relations, but to understand economic relations we need to understand the individuals who constitute those relations, and this in turn requires that we see them as socially situated moral agents. In this way, it makes little sense to try to enforce a rigid separation between political economy and questions of the moral status of the individual. If IPE is to be re-founded within political economy, it is necessary for its practitioners to take such questions seriously.

It is for this reason that I advocate the classical tradition of political economy as an alternative starting point for IPE. The concern of the classical political economists was precisely for the moral status of the individual and for the effects on the individual of incorporation into particular processes of production. The relations of production provide one means of ordering human society, but this occurs at the expense of the autonomy of the individual. An ordered system of production thereby presents irreducible conflicts between system imperatives and the right of the individual to exercise self-determination and to exist as an autonomous moral agent. Classical political economy represents the study of such conflicts.

The classical political economists diverged on how such conflicts should be theorized and much more so on how they should be resolved. The incremental social reform of Mill and the radical class politics of his contemporary, Marx, serve as a potent example of the extent of these disputes (see Blaug 1996). For current purposes, however, the fact of their disagreement is less important than the manner in which they came to focus on such conflicts in the first place. That focus arises because the economic relations in which the individual is embedded are a manifestation of the way in which the individual is reconstituted as a moral agent over time. 'The economy' is more process than substantive entity, and that process is in turn shaped by dominant ideological mediations of the role of the individual within society. IPE scholars currently turn their attention more readily to the management of economic relations than to their constitution. However, it is the constitution of economic relations that introduces conflict between reproducing 'the economy' as a functioning system and preserving the status of the individual as an autonomous moral agent.

The future of International Political Economy

Tackling such an issue takes us right to the heart of many of the biggest problems within the social sciences. It may well even involve asking questions that we are not equipped to answer. However, this should not be a deterrent. It is better to ask questions that we cannot answer than to restrict ourselves to asking those questions for which we already possess a stock response. There are certainly reasons why some might choose to inhabit the comfort-zone of the latter approach, but this is not the road to progressive social enquiry – be that intellectually progressive or politically progressive social enquiry. It can tell us little about the nature of the world in which we live today, or about how the world came to be the way it is. It can tell us even less about how we might reshape the world for the future.

Yet these are exactly the sorts of concerns that we should hope that IPE could shed light on. As a society, we are unlikely to want to reproduce anything other than a functioning economy, because this is the basis of meeting the needs of social provisioning. However, 'the economy' is not a self-functioning entity and, as such, it has no fundamental underlying essence. To the extent that it functions at all, it has to be *made* to function. This involves various forms of suppressing the autonomy of the individual and of managing the conflicts that arise when individuals attempt to re-assert their autonomy. It is a political choice to determine which forms of suppression are to be tolerated and which are to be eschewed. As it can be nothing other than a political choice, the future might always be different from the present. But the future will only be different if decisive interventions are undertaken to change the conception of the individual within society to which political decisions are oriented. There is much at stake, then, when discussing how best to recast the foundations of International Political Economy so that IPE can inform such interventions.

For IPE to fulfil its potential, its practitioners must be able to show how political decisions shape the individual's subject position in relation to 'the economy' by first shaping individual subjectivities. It is only through demonstrating how economic relations are constituted that it is possible to show how particular forms of economic relations compromise the autonomy of the individual in particular ways. Moreover, it is only once this has been achieved that a normative choice can be made between alternative forms of economic relations as the basis for satisfying the provisioning needs of society.

This is a choice on which we should expect IPE scholars to want to comment. In the Introduction, I claimed that there exists a critical consensus amongst the community of IPE scholars. Given this, the idea that the world is fine as it is receives very little attention within the IPE literature. Many, if not most, of the interventions into that literature focus in some way on the structure of inequality within the international system. Roger Tooze and Craig Murphy may well be correct to suggest that the world's poor feature only infrequently as the direct referent of analysis within IPE (Tooze and Murphy 1996), yet the condition of poverty that the poor experience is much more commonly discussed. That discussion tends to take place within an analytical framework which concentrates on uneven distributions of power within the international system. From such a perspective, the poor are condemned to their poverty because they hold insufficient resources to structure economic outcomes to their material advantage. The poor are not understood directly as moral agents whose autonomy is constrained by a structure of social relations that reproduces a functioning economy. Their conditions of existence are subjected to concerted discussion, but they themselves are inadequately understood.

The future of IPE lies not so much in critiquing current conditions of existence within the international economy. This is already done to considerable effect and, as such, it represents the present of IPE. The future of IPE lies in deepening the analytical basis of that critique, which will involve reformulating the foundations of the subject field as a whole.

This requires a definitive break with the attenuated theory of action that currently dominates IPE. The individual is invisible as a conscious and reflexive agent in much of IPE, because the theory of action that seeks to explain behaviour empties such actors of conscious and reflexive characteristics. The individual acts instinctively given the prevailing context in order to satisfy his or her interests. Moreover, that context is infrequently conceptualized as the product of individual action. Instead, it tends to be understood in terms of the interaction between states and markets.

The 'states and markets' approach provides a common underpinning to the various theoretical perspectives within IPE. As I argued in Chapter 1, the subject field of International Political Economy is perhaps best characterized as the aggregation of potentially incommensurable theoretical claims, which are made in relation to a number of basic substantive issues, all set against the backdrop of the relationship between 'states and markets'. Explanations of outcomes are situated at the level of that relationship. As a consequence, adherence to the 'states and markets' approach becomes the means through which much work in IPE fails to understand the effects of economic processes in terms of individuals taking action to constitute the social relations in which they are embedded.

The classical political economy approach, which I advocate here as an alternative starting point for IPE, dispenses with the focus on 'states and markets'. It is very much a study of the constitution of the individual actor and then the study of individuals *in action*. The classical political economy approach provides IPE with an account of human agency that focuses on the conscious and reflexive aspects of individual action, set within the context of an irreducibly social environment. 'The economy' does not exist independently of its social environment, and neither is it enacted prior to the activities of conscious and reflexive human agents. If IPE is to help us understand the economic relations in which we find ourselves, let alone the economic relations of others, its practitioners must embrace a political economy approach such as the one offered here. IPE must be reconciled with a political economy tradition from which it has for too long stood apart. The name 'IPE' suggests a natural affinity with a political economy approach. At present, though, it gives a somewhat misleading impression. It is now time for practice to fall into line with the implications of the name of the subject field. The 'states and markets' approach is a conceptual dead end should we wish to explain the full human dimension of the way in which economic relations form at a particular point of time and space.

The future of IPE, as with the future of the economy, is there to be made. That future, as an explanatory social theory, is potentially bright. However, before its potential can be realized, considerably more attention must be paid to systematically thinking through the foundations of the subject field. For IPE to flourish, its practitioners must become increasingly sensitive to the broader history of political economy, which is the context in which the subject field should be situated.

References

Ackerman, Frank 2002 'Still Dead After All These Years: Interpreting the Failure of General Equilibrium Theory', *Journal of Economic Methodology*, 9 (2), 119–39.

Adams, P. 1997 'The World Bank's Finances: An International Debt Crisis', in Caroline Thomas and Peter Wilkin (eds) *Globalization and the South*, London: Macmillan.

Amadae, S. M. 2003 *Rationalizing Capitalist Democracy: The Cold War Origins of Rational Choice Liberalism*, Chicago, IL: Chicago University Press.

Amoore, Louise, Dodgson, Richard, Germain, Randall, Gills, Barry, Langley, Paul and Watson, Iain 2000 'Paths to a Historicized International Political Economy', *Review of International Political Economy*, 7 (1), 53–71.

Armstrong, Peter 2001 'Science, Enterprise and Profit: Ideology in the Knowledge-Driven Economy', *Economy and Society*, 30 (4), 524–52.

Arrow, Kenneth 1979 'The Division of Labor in the Economy, the Polity, and Society', in Gerald O'Driscoll (ed.) *Adam Smith and Modern Political Economy: Bicentennial Essays on* The Wealth of Nations, Ames, IA: Iowa State University Press.

Ashley, Richard 1983 'Three Modes of Economism', *International Studies Quarterly*, 27 (4), 465–99.

Ashley, Richard 1988 'Untying the Sovereign State: A Double Reading of the Anarchy Problematique', *Millennium*, 17 (2), 227–62.

Backhouse, Roger 2002 *The Penguin History of Economics*, Harmondsworth: Penguin.

Barber, William 1991 *A History of Economic Thought*, reprinted edition, Harmondsworth: Penguin.

Barrow, John 2001 *The Book of Nothing*, London: Vintage.

Baum, Gregory 1996 *Karl Polanyi on Ethics and Economics*, London: McGill-Queen's University Press.

Beck, Ulrich 2002 *Individualization: Institutionalized Individualism and its Social and Political Consequences*, London: Sage.

Bellofiore, Riccardo and Silva, Francesco 1994 'Introduction', in Alessandra Marzola and Francesco Silva (eds) *John Maynard Keynes: Language and Method*, Aldershot: Edward Elgar.

Bernstein, Michael 2003 'American Economists and the "Marginalist Revolution": Notes on the Intellectual and Social Contexts of Professionalization', *Journal of Historical Sociology*, 16 (1), 135–80.

Black, Collison 1970 'Introduction', in Jevons 1970 [1871].
Blake, David and Walters, Robert 1976 *The Politics of Global Economic Relations*, London: Prentice Hall.
Blaug, Mark 1992 *The Methodology of Economics: Or, How Economists Explain*, fifth edition, Cambridge: Cambridge University Press.
Blaug, Mark 1996 *Economic Theory in Retrospect*, fifth edition, Cambridge: Cambridge University Press.
Blinder, Alan 1999 *Central Banking in Theory and Practice*, paperback edition, Cambridge, MA: MIT Press.
Blyth, Mark and Varghese, Robin 1999 'The State of the Discipline in American Political Science: Be Careful What You Wish For?', *British Journal of Politics and International Relations*, 1 (3), 345–65.
Bonfil Batalla, Guillermo 1996 *México Profundo: Reclaiming a Civilization*, Austin, TX: University of Texas Press.
Boulding, Kenneth 1970 'After Samuelson, Who Needs Adam Smith?', Address to the Annual Meeting of the American Economic Association, Detroit, 30 December 1970.
Braudel, Fernand 1980 *On History*, translated by Sarah Matthews, London: Weidenfeld & Nicolson.
Bridel, Pascal and Huck, Elisabeth 2002 'Yet Another Look at Léon Walras's Theory of *Tâtonnement*', *European Journal of the History of Economic Thought*, 9 (4), 513–40.
Brockway, George 2001 *The End of Economic Man: An Introduction to Humanistic Economics*, fourth edition, London: W. W. Norton.
Brown, Vivienne 1994 *Adam Smith's Discourse: Canonicity, Commerce and Conscience*, London: Routledge.
Burch, Kurt and Denemark, Robert (eds) 1997 *Constituting International Political Economy*, London: Lynne Rienner.
Cairncross, Frances 1997 *The Death of Distance: How the Communications Revolution Will Change Our Lives*, London: Orion Business Books.
Campbell, R. H. and Skinner, Andrew 1982 *Adam Smith*, London: Croom Helm.
Caney, Simon 2005 *Justice Across Borders*, Oxford: Oxford University Press.
Cangiani, Michele 1994 'Prelude to *The Great Transformation*: Karl Polanyi's Articles for *Der Oesterreichische Volkswirt*', in Kenneth McRobbie (ed.) *Humanity, Society and Commitment: On Karl Polanyi*, London: Black Rose Books.
Caporaso, James and Levine, David 1992 *Theories of Political Economy*, Cambridge: Cambridge University Press.
Carnoy, Martin 1984 *The State and Political Theory*, Princeton, NJ: Princeton University Press.
Cerny, Philip 1995 'Globalization and the Changing Logic of Collective Action', *International Organization*, 49 (4), 595–625.

Cerny, Philip 1999 'Globalising the Political and Politicising the Global: International Political Economy as a Vocation', *New Political Economy*, 4 (1), 147–62.

Chang, Ha-Joon 2002 'Breaking the Mould: An Institutionalist Political Economy Alternative to the Neo-Liberal Theory of the Market and the State', *Cambridge Journal of Economics*, 26 (4), 539–59.

Cheru, Fantu 1997 'The Silent Revolution and the Weapons of the Weak: Transformation and Innovation From Below', in Gill and Mittelman (1997).

Clarke, Simon 1991 *The State Debate*, London: Macmillan.

Clower, Robert 1998 'Three Centuries of Demand and Supply', *Journal of the History of Economic Thought*, 20 (4), 397–409.

Coates, David 2000 *Models of Capitalism: Growth and Stagnation in the Modern Era*, Cambridge: Polity.

Coddington, Alan 1983 *Keynesian Economics: The Search for First Principles*, London: George Allen & Unwin.

Cohen, Benjamin 2002 'International Finance and International Relations Theory', in Walter Carsnaes, Thomas Risse and Beth Simmons (eds) *Handbook of International Relations*, London: Sage.

Cohen, G. A. 1978 *Karl Marx's Theory of History: A Defence*, Oxford: Clarendon Press.

Colander, David 2001 *The Lost Art of Economics: Essays on Economics and the Economics Profession*, Cheltenham: Edward Elgar.

Cole, Ken, Cameron, John and Edwards, Chris 1983 *Why Economists Disagree: The Political Economy of Economics*, London: Longman.

Cox, Robert 1981 'Social Forces, States, and World Orders: Beyond International Relations Theory', *Millennium*, 10 (2), 126–55.

Cox, Robert 1994a 'Forum: Hegemony and Social Change', *Mershon International Studies Review*, 38 (2), 361–76.

Cox, Robert 1994b 'Global Restructuring: Making Sense of the Changing International Political Economy', in Richard Stubbs and Geoffrey Underhill (eds) *Political Economy and the Changing Global Order*, London: Macmillan.

Cropsey, Joseph 1979 'The Invisible Hand: Moral and Political Implications', in Gerald O'Driscoll (ed.) *Adam Smith and Modern Political Economy: Bicentennial Essays on* The Wealth of Nations, Ames, IA: Iowa State University Press.

Dalton, George 1971 'Introduction', in George Dalton (ed.) *Archaic, Primitive and Modern Economies: Essays of Karl Polanyi*, Boston, MA: Beacon Press.

Daly, Herman and Cobb, John 1990 *For the Common Good: Redirecting the Economy Toward Community, the Environment, and a Sustainable Future*, London: Green Print.

Dash, Kishore, Cronin, Patrick and Goddard, Roe 2003 in Roe Goddard, Patrick Cronin and Kishore Dash (eds) *International Political Economy: State–Market Relations in a Changing Global Order*, second edition, Basingstoke: Palgrave Macmillan.

Davis, John 2002 'Collective Intentionality and Individual Behavior', in Edward Fullbrook (ed.) *Intersubjectivity in Economics: Agents and Structures*, London: Routledge.

Denemark, Robert and O'Brien, Robert 1997 'Contesting the Canon: International Political Economy at UK and US Universities', *Review of International Political Economy*, 4 (1), 214–38.

Dobb, Maurice 1937 *Political Economy and Capitalism: Some Essays in Economic Tradition*, London: Routledge.

Douglas, Ian 1997 'Globalisation and the End of the State?', *New Political Economy*, 2 (1), 165–79.

Dow, Alexander, Dow, Sheila and Hutton, Alan 1997 'The Scottish Political Economy Tradition and Modern Economics', *Scottish Journal of Political Economy*, 44 (4), 368–83.

Drache, Daniel 1996 'From Keynes to K-Mart: Competitiveness in a Corporate Age', in Robert Boyer and Daniel Drache (eds) *States Against Markets: The Limits of Globalization*, London: Routledge.

Dumenil, Gerard and Levy, Dominique 2001 'Costs and Benefits of Neoliberalism: A Class Analysis', *Review of International Political Economy*, 8 (4), 578–607.

Dupré, John 2003 *Human Nature and the Limits of Science*, paperback edition, Oxford: Oxford University Press.

Dyer, Alan 2000 'Thorstein Veblen and the Political Economy of the Ordinary: Hope and Despair', in Francisco Louçã and Mark Perlman (eds) *Is Economics an Evolutionary Science? The Legacy of Thorstein Veblen*, Cheltenham: Edward Elgar.

Edgeworth, Francis 1881 *Mathematical Psychics: An Essay on the Application of Mathematics to the Moral Sciences*, London: C. K. Paul.

Editors 1994 'Forum for Heterodox International Political Economy', *Review of International Political Economy*, 1 (1), 1–12.

Edwards, E. O. and van Wijnbergen, S. 1988 'Disequilibrium and Structural Adjustment', in Hollis Chenery and T. N. Srinivasan (eds) *Handbook of Development Economics*, Elsevier: New York.

Eichner, Alfred 1983 'Why Economics is Not Yet a Science', in Alfred Eichner (ed.) *Why Economics is Not Yet a Science*, London: Macmillan.

Ensminger, Jean 1996 *Making a Market: The Institutional Transformation of an African Society*, Cambridge: Cambridge University Press.

Fair Trade Federation 2003 *2003 Report on Fair Trade Trends*, Washington, DC: Fair Trade Federation.

Fay, Brian 1996 *Contemporary Philosophy of Social Science: A Multicultural Approach*, Oxford: Basil Blackwell.

Fehr, Ernst and Falk, Amin 2002 'Reciprocal Fairness, Cooperation and Limits to Competition', in Edward Fullbrook (ed.) *Intersubjectivity in Economics: Agents and Structures*, London: Routledge.

Fiori, Stefano 2001 'Visible and Invisible Order: The Theoretical Duality of Smith's Political Economy', *European Journal of the History of Economic Thought*, 8 (4), 429–48.

Fitzgibbons, Athol 1995 *Adam Smith's System of Liberty, Wealth and Virtue: The Moral and Political Foundations of the Wealth of Nations*, Oxford: Clarendon Press.

Foucault, Michel 1989 *The Order of Things: An Archaeology of the Human Sciences*, London: Routledge.

Fratianni, Michele, Savona, Paolo and Kirton, John (eds) 2003 *Sustaining Global Growth and Development: G7 and IMF Governance*, Aldershot: Ashgate.

Frieden, Jeffry and Lake, David 1995 'Introduction: International Politics and International Economics', in Jeffry Frieden and David Lake (eds) *International Political Economy: Perspectives on Global Power and Wealth*, third edition, London: Routledge.

Fusfeld, Daniel 1994 'Karl Polanyi's Lectures on General Economic History – A Student Remembers', in Kenneth McRobbie (ed.) *Humanity, Society and Commitment: On Karl Polanyi*, London: Black Rose Books.

Fusfeld, Daniel 2002 *The Age of the Economist*, ninth edition, London: Addison-Wesley.

Gamble, Andrew 1995 'New Political Economy', *Political Studies*, 43 (3), 516–30.

Gill, Stephen 1991 'Historical Materialism, Gramsci, and International Political Economy', in Craig Murphy and Roger Tooze (eds) *The New International Political Economy*, London: Lynne Rienner.

Gill, Stephen 1994 'Knowledge, Politics, and Neo-Liberal Political Economy', in Richard Stubbs and Geoffrey Underhill (eds) *Political Economy and the Changing Global Order*, London: Macmillan.

Gill, Stephen and Law, David 1988 *The Global Political Economy: Perspectives, Problems and Policies*, London: Harvester Wheatsheaf.

Gill, Stephen and Mittelman, James (eds) 1997 *Innovation and Transformation in International Studies*, Cambridge: Cambridge University Press.

Gilpin, Robert 1987 *The Political Economy of International Relations*, Princeton, NJ: Princeton University Press.

Gramsci, Antonio 1971 *Selections from Prison Notebooks*, edited and translated by Quintin Hoare and Geoffrey Nowell-Smith, London: Lawrence & Wishart.

Grieco, Joseph and Ikenberry, John 2003 *State Power and World Markets: The International Political Economy*, New York: W. W. Norton.

Grimmer-Solem, Eric and Romani, Roberto 1999 'In Search of Full Empirical Reality: Historical Political Economy, 1870–1900', *European Journal of the History of Economic Thought*, 6 (3), 333–64.

Haakonssen, Knud 1989 *The Science of a Legislator: Natural Jurisprudence of David Hume and Adam Smith*, second edition, Cambridge: Cambridge University Press.

Habermas, Jürgen 1972 *Knowledge and Human Interests*, translated by Jeremy Shapiro, London: Heinemann Educational.

Habermas, Jürgen 1976 *Legitimation Crisis*, translated by Thomas McCarthy, London: Heinemann.

Hahn, Frank 2000 'Is Economics an Evolutionary Science?', in Francisco Louçã and Mark Perlman (eds) *Is Economics an Evolutionary Science? The Legacy of Thorstein Veblen*, Cheltenham: Edward Elgar.

Hall, Peter and Taylor, Rosemary 1996 'Political Science and the Three New Institutionalisms', *Political Studies*, 44 (5), 936–57.

Harris, Laurence 1999 'Will the Real IMF Please Stand Up: What Does the Fund Do and What Should it Do?', in Jonathan Michie and John Grieve Smith (eds) *Global Instability: The Political Economy of World Economic Governance*, London: Routledge.

Harrod, Jeffrey 1997 'Social Forces and International Political Economy: Joining the Two IRs', in Gill and Mittelman (1997).

Harvey, David 1989 *The Condition of Postmodernity: An Enquiry into the Origins of Cultural Change*, Oxford: Basil Blackwell.

Hay, Colin 2004a 'Common Trajectories, Variable Paces, Divergent Outcomes? Models of European Capitalism Under Conditions of Complex Economic Interdependence', *Review of International Political Economy*, 11 (2), 231–62.

Hay, Colin 2004b 'Theory, Stylised Heuristic or Self-Fulfilling Prophecy? The Status of Rational Choice Theory in Public Administration', *Public Administration*, 82 (1), 39–62.

Hay, Colin, Watson, Matthew and Wincott, Daniel 1999 'Globalisation, European Integration and the Persistence of European Social Models', *'One Europe or Several?' Working Papers*, no. 3/99, Economic and Social Research Council: Sussex European Institute.

Hayek, Friedrich von 1944 *The Road to Serfdom*, London: Routledge.

Hechter, Michael 1981 'Karl Polanyi's Social Theory: A Critique', *Politics and Society*, 10 (4), 399–429.

Heilbroner, Robert 1986 *The Essential Adam Smith*, London: W. W. Norton.

Heilbroner, Robert 1988 *Behind the Veil of Economics: Essays in the Worldly Philosophy*, New York: W. W. Norton.

Heilbroner, Robert 2000 *The Worldly Philosophers: The Lives, Times and Ideas of the Great Economic Thinkers*, revised seventh edition, Harmondsworth: Penguin.

Held, David, McGrew, Anthony, Goldblatt, David and Perraton, Jonathan 1999 *Global Transformations: Politics, Economics and Culture*, Cambridge: Polity.

Helleiner, Eric 1996 'International Political Economy and the Greens', *New Political Economy*, 1 (1), 59–77.

Hertz, Noreena 2001 *The Silent Takeover: Global Capitalism and the Death of Democracy*, London: Heinemann.

Hicks, John 1979 *Causality in Economics*, Oxford: Basil Blackwell.

Hill, Lewis 1998 'Veblen's Contribution to the Instrumental Theory of Normative Value', in Warren Samuels (ed.) *The Founding of Institutional Economics: The Leisure Class and Sovereignty*, London: Routledge.

Hirst, Paul and Thompson, Grahame 1999 *Globalization in Question: The International Economy and the Possibilities of Governance*, second edition, Cambridge: Polity.

Hodgson, Geoffrey 2001 *How Economics Forgot History: The Problem of Historical Specificity in Social Science*, London: Routledge.

Hollander, Samuel 1987 *Classical Economics*, Oxford: Basil Blackwell.

Hollis, Martin 1994 *The Philosophy of Social Science: An Introduction*, Cambridge: Cambridge University Press.

Howard, M. C. and King, J. E. 2001 'Where Marx Was Right: Towards a More Secure Foundation for Heterodox Economics', *Cambridge Journal of Economics*, 25 (6), 785–807.

Hunter, Laurie and Muscatelli, Anton 1997 'Political Economy: Whence and Whither?', *Scottish Journal of Political Economy*, 44 (4), 353–8.

Hutchinson, Frances, Mellor, Mary and Olsen, Wendy 2002 *The Politics of Money: Towards Sustainability and Economic Democracy*, London: Pluto Press.

Hutchison, Terence 1994 *The Uses and Abuses of Economics: Contentious Essays on History and Method*, London: Routledge.

IMF 2000 'A Guide to Progress in Strengthening the Architecture of the International Financial System', www.imf.org, Washington, DC: IMF.

Inayatullah, Naeem and Blaney, David 1997 'Economic Anxiety: Reification, De-Reification, and the Politics of IPE', in Burch and Denemark (1997).

Inayatullah, Naeem and Blaney, David 1999 'Towards an Ethnological IPE: Karl Polanyi's Double Critique of Capitalism', *Millennium,* 28 (2), 311–40.

Iversen, Torben, Pontusson, Jonas and Soskice, David (eds) 2000 *Unions, Employers, and Central Banks: Macroeconomic Coordination and Institutional Changes in Social Market Economies*, Cambridge: Cambridge University Press.

Jacob, Francois 1993 *The Logic Of Life*, Princeton, NJ: Princeton University Press.

Jaffé, William 1967 'Walras' Theory of *Tâtonnement*: A Critique of Recent Interpretations', *Journal of Political Economy*, 75 (1), 1–19.

Jaffé, William 1980 'Walras's Economics As Others See It', *Journal of Economic Literature*, 18 (3), 528–49.

Jessop, Bob 1990 *State Theory: Putting the Capitalist State in its Place*, Cambridge: Polity.

Jessop, Bob 2001 'Regulationist and Autopoieticist Reflections on Polanyi's Account of Market Economies and the Market Society', *New Political Economy*, 6 (2), 213–32.

Jessop, Bob and Sum, Ngai-Ling 2001 'Pre-Disciplinary and Post-Disciplinary Perspectives', *New Political Economy*, 6 (1), 89–101.

Jevons, W. Stanley 1970 [1871] *The Theory of Political Economy*, Harmondsworth: Pelican.

Johnston, Deborah 1991 'Constructing the Periphery in Modern Global Politics', in Craig Murphy and Roger Tooze (eds) *The New International Political Economy*, London: Lynne Rienner.

Kaplan, Robert 2000 *The Nothing That Is: A Natural History of Zero*, Harmondsworth: Penguin.

Kayatekin, Serap and Ruccio, David 1998 'Global Fragments: Subjectivity and Class Politics in Discourses of Globalization', *Economy and Society*, 27 (1), 74–96.

Keen, Steve 2001 *Debunking Economics: The Naked Emperor of the Social Sciences*, London: Pluto.

Keynes, John Maynard 1937 'The General Theory of Employment', *Quarterly Journal of Economics*, 51 (2), 209–23.

Keynes, John Maynard 1997 [1936] *The General Theory of Employment, Interest, and Money*, London: Prometheus Books.

Kirman, Alan 1992 'Whom or What Does the Representative Individual Represent?', *Journal of Economic Perspectives*, 6 (2), 117–36.

Kitschelt, Herbert, Lange, Peter, Marks, Gary and Stephens, John 1999 'Convergence and Divergence in Advanced Capitalist Democracies', in Herbert Kitschelt, Peter Lange, Gary Marks and John Stephens (eds) *Continuity and Change in Contemporary Capitalism*, Cambridge: Cambridge University Press.

Klein, Lawrence 1968 *The Keynesian Revolution*, second edition, London: Macmillan.

Klein, Naomi 2000 *No Logo*, London: Flamingo.

Krasner, Stephen 1976 'State Power and the Structure of International Trade', *World Politics*, 28 (3), 317–47.

Krasner, Stephen 1994 'International Political Economy: Abiding Discord', *Review of International Political Economy*, 1 (1), 13–19.

Krugman, Paul 1994 'Competitiveness: A Dangerous Obsession', *Foreign Affairs*, March/April, 28–44.

Kuhn, Thomas 1970 *The Structure of Scientific Revolutions*, second edition, Chicago, IL: Chicago University Press.

Laclau, Ernesto and Mouffe, Chantal 1985 *Hegemony and Socialist Strategy*, London: Verso.

Lakatos, Imre 1978 *The Methodology of Scientific Research Programmes*, Cambridge: Cambridge University Press.

Landreth, Harry and Colander, David 1994 *History of Economic Thought*, third edition, Boston, MA: Houghton Mifflin.

Lange, Oskar and Taylor, Fred 1938 *On the Economic Theory of Socialism*, Minneapolis, MN: University of Minnesota Press.

Lawson, Tony 1997 *Economics and Reality*, London: Routledge.

Lawson, Tony 2003 *Reorienting Economics*, London: Routledge.

Lee, Eddy 1998 *The Asian Financial Crisis: The Challenge for Social Policy*, Geneva: International Labour Office.

Lenin, Vladimir Ilich 1988 [1902] *What is to be Done?*, Harmondsworth: Penguin.

Levine, David 1998 'The Self and Its Interests in Classical Political Economy', *European Journal of the History of Economic Thought*, 5 (1), 36–59.

Lewis, Margaret 1991 'The Age Demanded: The Rhetoric of Karl Polanyi', *Journal of Economic Issues*, 25 (2), 475–83.

Lipietz, Alain 1997 'The Post-Fordist World: Labour Relations, International Hierarchy and Global Ecology', *Review of International Political Economy*, 4 (1), 1–41.

Macfie, A. L. 1967 *The Individual in Society: Papers on Adam Smith*, London: Allen & Unwin.

Marglin, Stephen and Schor, Juliet 1990 (eds) *The Golden Age of Capitalism: Reinterpreting the Postwar Experience*, Oxford: Clarendon Press.

Marshall, Alfred 1920 *The Principles of Economics*, eighth edition, London: Macmillan.

Marx, Karl 1912 [1867] *Capital: Volume 1 – The 1867 Edition*, Chicago, IL: Charles H. Kerr.

Marx, Karl 1938 *The German Ideology*, with Friedrich Engels, edited with an introduction by R. Pascal, translated by W. Lough and C. P. Magill, London: Lawrence & Wishart.

Marx, Karl 1973 [1952] *Grundrisse: Introduction to the Critique of Political Economy*, translated by Martin Nicolaus, Harmondsworth: Penguin.

Marx, Karl and Engels, Friedrich 1998 [1848] *The Communist Manifesto – A Modern Edition*, London: Verso.

Mayer, Thomas 1993 *Truth Versus Precision in Economics*, Aldershot: Edward Elgar.

McCormick, Ken 1997 'An Essay on the Origin of the Rational Utility Maximization Hypothesis and a Suggested Modification', *Eastern Economic Journal*, 23 (1), 17–30.

McLean, Sandra, Quadir, Fahimul and Shaw, Timothy 2000 'Structural Adjustment and the Response of Civil Society in Bangladesh and Zimbabwe: A Comparative Analysis', in Barry Gills (ed.) *Globalization and the Politics of Resistance*, London: Macmillan.

McMichael, Philip 1998 'Development and Structural Adjustment', in James Carrier and Daniel Miller (eds) *Virtualism: A New Political Economy*, Oxford: Berg.

McMurtry, John 1999 *The Cancer Stage of Capitalism*, London: Pluto Press.

Mehmet, Ozay 1999 *Westernizing the Third World: The Eurocentricity of Economic Development Theories*, second edition, London: Routledge.

Menger, Carl 1950 [1871] *Principles of Economics*, translated and edited by James Dingwall and Bert Hoselitz, Glencoe, IL: Free Press.

Mészáros, István 1970 *Marx's Theory of Alienation*, London: Merlin.

Mill, James 1826 *Elements of Political Economy*, third edition, London: Baldwin, Cradock & Joy.

Mills, C. Wright 1970 'Introduction', in Thorstein Veblen 1970 [1899] *The Theory of the Leisure Class: An Economic Study of Institutions*, London: Unwin Books.

Mirowski, Philip 2002 *Machine Dreams: Economics Becomes a Cyborg Science*, Cambridge: Cambridge University Press.

Mises, Ludwig von 1949 [1940] *Human Action: A Treatise on Economics*, London: Hodge.

Mosley, Layna 2000 'Room to Move: International Financial Markets and National Welfare States', *International Organization*, 54 (4), 737–74.

Murphy, Craig and Nelson, Douglas 2001 'International Political Economy: A Tale of Two Heterodoxies', *British Journal of Politics and International Relations*, 3 (3), 393–412.

Murphy, Craig and Tooze, Roger 1991a 'Introduction', in Craig Murphy and Roger Tooze (eds) *The New International Political Economy*, London: Lynne Rienner.

Murphy, Craig and Tooze, Roger 1991b 'Getting Beyond the "Common Sense" of the IPE Orthodoxy', in Craig Murphy and Roger Tooze (eds) *The New International Political Economy*, London: Lynne Rienner.

Niehans, Jurg 1990 *A History of Economic Theory: Classic Contributions, 1720–1980*, Baltimore, MD: Johns Hopkins University Press.

Nitzan, Jonathan 1998 'Differential Accumulation: Towards a New Political Economy of Capital', *Review of International Political Economy*, 5 (2), 169–216.

North, Douglass 1977 'Markets and Other Allocation Systems in History: The Challenge of Karl Polanyi', *Journal of European Economic History*, 6 (4), 703–16.

North, Douglass 1990 *Institutions, Institutional Change and Economic Performance*, Cambridge: Cambridge University Press.

O'Brien, Richard 1992 *Global Financial Integration: The End of Geography*, London: Pinter.

O'Brien, Robert and Williams, Marc 2004 *Global Political Economy: Evolution and Dynamics*, Basingstoke: Palgrave Macmillan.

Oakley, Allen 2002 *Reconstructing Economic Theory: The Problem of Human Agency*, Cheltenham: Edward Elgar.

Offe, Claus 1985 *Contradictions of the Welfare State*, Cambridge, MA: MIT Press.

Ohmae, Kenichi 1996 *The End of the Nation State*, New York: Free Press.

Olson, Richard 1975 *Scottish Philosophy and British Physics, 1750–1880*, London: Princeton University Press.

Onuf, Nicholas 1997 'Hegemony's Hegemony in IPE', in Burch and Denemark (1997).

Paggi, Leonardo 1979 'Gramsci's General Theory of Marxism', in Chantal Mouffe (ed.) *Gramsci and Marxist Theory*, London: Routledge & Kegan Paul.

Pareto, Vilfredo 1972 [1906] *Manual of Political Economy*, translated by Ann Schwier and Alfred Page, London: Macmillan.

Paterson, Matthew 2001 *Understanding Global Environmental Politics: Domination, Accumulation, Resistance*, London: Macmillan.

Pearson, Frederic and Rochester, Martin 1998 *International Relations: The Global Condition in the Twenty-First Century*, fourth edition, New York: McGraw-Hill.

Perlman, Mark 2000 'Mind-Sets, and Why Veblen was Ineffectual', in Francisco Louçã and Mark Perlman (eds) *Is Economics an Evolutionary Science? The Legacy of Thorstein Veblen*, Cheltenham: Edward Elgar.

Pettit, Philip 1978 'Rational Man Theory', in Christopher Hookway and Philip Pettit (eds) *Action and Interpretation: Studies in the Philosophy of the Social Sciences*, Cambridge: Cambridge University Press.

Phelps-Brown, E. H. 1972 'The Underdevelopment of Economics', *Economic Journal*, 82 (1), 1–10.

Pieper, Ute and Taylor, Lance 1998 'The Revival of the Liberal Creed: the IMF, the World Bank, and Inequality in a Globalized Economy', in

Dean Baker, Gerald Epstein and Robert Pollin (eds) *Globalization and Progressive Economic Policy*, Cambridge: Cambridge University Press.

Pigou, Arthur Cecil 1920 *The Economics of Welfare*, London: Macmillan.

Poggi, Gianfranco 1990 *The State: Its Nature, Development and Prospects*, Cambridge: Polity.

Polanyi, Karl 1957 [1944] *The Great Transformation: The Social and Political Origins of Our Time*, Boston, MA: Beacon Press.

Polanyi, Karl 1968 'Aristotle Discovers the Economy', in Karl Polanyi, *Archaic, Primitive and Modern Societies: Essays of Karl Polanyi*, edited by George Dalton, Garden City, NY: Doubleday.

Polanyi, Karl 1977 *The Livelihood of Man*, edited by Harry Pearson, New York: Academic Press.

Polanyi, Karl 1982 'The Economy as Instituted Process', in Mark Granovetter and Richard Swedberg (eds) *The Sociology of Economic Life*, London: Westview Press.

Poulantzas, Nicos 1978 *State, Power, Socialism*, London: New Left Books.

Przeworski, Adam and Wallerstein, Michael 1998 'Structural Dependence of the State on Capital', *American Political Science Review*, 82 (1), 11–30.

Raphael, D. D. and Macfie, A. L. 1982 'Introduction', in Smith 1982 [1759].

Raphael, D. D. and Skinner, Andrew 1980 'General Introduction', in W. P. D. Wightman and J. C. Bryce (eds) *Adam Smith: Essays on Philosophical Subjects*, Oxford: Oxford University Press.

Ricardo, David 2002 [1821] *The Principles of Political Economy and Taxation*, third edition, London: Empiricus Books.

Rizvi, S. Abu Turab 2002 'Adam Smith's Sympathy: Towards a Normative Economics', in Edward Fullbrook (ed.) *Intersubjectivity in Economics: Agents and Structures*, London: Routledge.

Robbins, Lionel 1969 *An Essay on the Nature and Significance of Economic Science*, second edition, New York: St Martin's Press.

Robertson, Roland 1992 *Globalization: Social Theory and Global Culture*, London: Sage.

Robinson, Joan 1964 *Economic Philosophy*, second edition, Harmondsworth: Pelican.

Rosenberg, Nathan 1979 'Adam Smith and Laissez-Faire Revisited', in Gerald O'Driscoll (ed.) *Adam Smith and Modern Political Economy: Bicentennial Essays on* The Wealth of Nations, Ames, IA: Iowa State University Press.

Rothschild, Emma 2001 *Economic Sentiments: Adam Smith, Condorcet, and the Enlightenment*, Cambridge, MA: Harvard University Press.

Ruggie, John 1983 (ed.) *The Antinomies of Interdependence: National Welfare and the International Division of Labor*, New York: Columbia University Press.

Russell, Bertrand 1992 [1937] *The Principles of Mathematics*, reprinted second edition, London: Routledge.

Samuelson, Paul 1992 'The Overdue Recovery of Adam Smith's Reputation as an Economic Theorist', in Michael Fry (ed.) *Adam Smith's Legacy: His Place in the Development of Modern Economics*, London: Routledge.

Schaniel, William and Neale, Walter 2000 'Karl Polanyi's Forms of Integration as Ways of Mapping', *Journal of Economic Issues*, 34 (1), 89–104.

Schneider, Louis 1979 'Adam Smith on Human Nature and Social Circumstance', in Gerald O'Driscoll (ed.) *Adam Smith and Modern Political Economy: Bicentennial Essays on* The Wealth of Nations, Ames, IA: Iowa State University Press.

Schumpeter, Joseph 1994 [1954] *History of Economic Analysis*, New York: Oxford University Press.

Searcy, Dennis 1993 'Beyond the Self-Regulating Market in Market Society: A Critique of Polanyi's Theory of the State', *Review of Social Economy*, 51 (2), 217–31.

Sebberson, David and Lewis, Margaret 1998 'The Rhetoricality of Thorstein Veblen's Economic Theorizing: A Critical Reading of *The Theory of the Leisure Class*', in Warren Samuels (ed.) *The Founding of Institutional Economics: The Leisure Class and Sovereignty*, London: Routledge.

Seckler, David 1975 *Thorstein Veblen and the Institutionalists: A Study in the Social Philosophy of Economics*, London: Macmillan.

Sen, Amartya 1977 'Rational Fools: A Critique of the Behavioral Foundations of Economic Theory', *Philosophy and Public Affairs*, 6 (4), 317–44.

Sen, Amartya 1987 *On Ethics and Economics*, Oxford: Basil Blackwell.

Shackle, George 1969 *Decision, Order and Time in Human Affairs*, second edition, Cambridge: Cambridge University Press.

Shackle, George 1989 'What Did the *General Theory* Do?', in John Pheby (ed.) *New Directions in Post-Keynesian Economics*, Aldershot: Edward Elgar.

Silver, Morris 1983 'Karl Polanyi and Markets in the Ancient Near East: The Challenge of the Evidence', *Journal of Economic History*, 43 (4), 795–829.

Skinner, Andrew 1979 *A System of Social Science: Papers Relating to Adam Smith*, Oxford: Clarendon Press.

Smith, Adam 1970 [1776] *An Inquiry into the Nature and Causes of the Wealth of Nations*, edited and with an introduction by Andrew Skinner, Harmondsworth: Pelican.

Smith, Adam 1980 'The Principles Which Lead and Direct Philosophical Enquiries; Illustrated by the History of Astronomy', in W. P. D. Wightman and J. C. Bryce (eds) *Adam Smith: Essays on Philosophical Subjects*, Oxford: Oxford University Press.

Smith, Adam 1982 [1759] *The Theory of Moral Sentiments*, The Glasgow Edition of the Works and Correspondence of Adam Smith, edited by D. D. Raphael and A. L. Macfie, Indianapolis, IN: Liberty Fund.

Smith, Adam 1983 *Lectures on Rhetoric and Belles Lettres*, Oxford: Clarendon Press.

Smith, Adam 1998 [1776] *An Inquiry into the Nature and Causes of the Wealth of Nations: A Selected Edition*, edited by Kathryn Sutherland, Oxford: Oxford University Press.

Soros, George 1998 *The Crisis of Global Capitalism: Open Society Endangered*, London: Little, Brown.

Sowell, Thomas 1979 'Adam Smith in Theory and Practice', in Gerald O'Driscoll (ed.) *Adam Smith and Modern Political Economy: Bicentennial Essays on* The Wealth of Nations, Ames, IA: Iowa State University Press.

Spencer, David 2000 'The Demise of Radical Political Economics? An Essay on the Evolution of a Theory of Capitalist Production', *Cambridge Journal of Economics*, 24 (5), 543–64.

Spero, Joan 1977 *The Politics of International Economic Relations*, Hemel Hempstead: Allen & Unwin.

Stanfield, J. R. 1986 *The Economic Thought of Karl Polanyi: Lives and Livelihood*, London: Macmillan.

Stewart, Michael 1972 *Keynes and After*, second edition, Harmondsworth: Penguin.

Stigler, George 1969 'Does Economics Have a Useful Past?', *History of Political Economy*, 1 (2), 217–30.

Strange, Susan 1988 *States and Markets: An Introduction to International Political Economy*, London: Pinter.

Strange, Susan 1994 'Wake Up, Krasner! The World *Has* Changed', *Review of International Political Economy*, 1 (2), 209–19.

Strange, Susan 1997 'The Problem or the Solution? Capitalism and the State System', in Gill and Mittelman (1997).

Strange, Susan 1998a 'International Political Economy: Beyond Economics and International Relations', *Economies et Sociétés*, 34 (4), 3–24.

Strange, Susan 1998b *Mad Money*, Manchester: Manchester University Press.

Swank, Duane 1998 'Funding the Welfare State: Globalization and the Taxation of Business in Advanced Market Economies', *Political Studies*, 46 (4), 671–92.

Tabb, William 1999 *Reconstructing Political Economy: The Great Divide in Economic Thought*, London: Routledge.

Tooze, Roger and Murphy, Craig 1996 'The Epistemology of Poverty and the Poverty of Epistemology in IPE: Mystery, Blindness, and Invisibility', *Millennium*, 25 (3), 681–707.

Uglow, Jenny 2003 *The Lunar Men: The Friends Who Made the Future, 1730–1810*, paperback edition, London: Faber & Faber.

Underhill, Geoffrey 1994 'Introduction: Conceptualizing the Changing Global Order', in Richard Stubbs and Geoffrey Underhill (eds) *Political Economy and the Changing Global Order*, London: Macmillan.

Underhill, Geoffrey 2000 'State, Market and Global Political Economy: Genealogy of an (Inter-?) Discipline', *International Affairs*, 76 (4), 805–24.

United Nations 2003 *World Investment 2003*, New York: The United Nations.

van der Pijl, Kees 1997 'Transnational Class Formations and State Forms', in Gill and Mittelman (1997).

Veblen, Thorstein 1919a 'The Limitations of Marginal Utility', in Thorstein Veblen, *The Place of Science in Modern Civilization and Other Essays*, New York: B. W. Huebsch.

Veblen, Thorstein 1919b 'Why is Economics not an Evolutionary Science?', in Thorstein Veblen, *The Place of Science in Modern Civilization and Other Essays*, New York: B. W. Huebsch.

Veblen, Thorstein 1964 [1914] *The Instinct of Workmanship and the State of the Industrial Arts*, New York: Augustus Kelley.

Veblen, Thorstein 1965 [1904] *The Theory of Business Enterprise*, New York: Augustus Kelley.

Veblen, Thorstein 1970 [1899] *The Theory of the Leisure Class: An Economic Study of Institutions*, London: Unwin Books.

Verburg, Rudi 2000 'Adam Smith's Growing Concern on the Issue of Distributive Justice', *European Journal of the History of Economic Thought*, 7 (1), 23–44.

Wade, Robert 2002 'US Hegemony and the World Bank: The Fight Over People and Ideas', *Review of International Political Economy*, 9 (2), 201–29.

Walker, Donald 1987 'Walras's Theories of Tatonnement', *Journal of Political Economy*, 95 (4), 758–74.

Wallerstein, Immanuel 1979 *The Capitalist World Economy: Essays by Immanuel Wallerstein*, New York: Cambridge University Press.

Walras, Léon 1984 [1954] *Elements of Pure Economics: Or the Theory of Social Wealth*, translated by William Jaffé from the fourth edition of *Les Eléments d'Économie Politique Pure*, Philadelphia, PA: Orion Editions.

Watson, Matthew 1999 'Rethinking Capital Mobility, Re-regulating Financial Markets', *New Political Economy*, 4 (1), 55–75.

Watson, Matthew 2001 'International Capital Mobility in an Era of Globalisation: Adding a Political Dimension to the "Feldstein–Horioka Puzzle"', *Politics*, 21 (2), 81–92.

Watson, Matthew 2002a 'Sand in the Wheels, or Oiling the Wheels, of International Finance? New Labour's Appeal to a "New Bretton Woods"', *British Journal of Politics and International Relations*, 4 (2), 193–221.

Watson, Matthew 2002b 'The Institutional Paradoxes of Monetary Orthodoxy: Reflections on the Political Economy of Central Bank Independence', *Review of International Political Economy*, 9 (1), 183–96.

Watson, Matthew and Hay, Colin 2003 'The Discourse of Globalisation and the Logic of No Alternative: Rendering the Contingent Necessary in the Political Economy of New Labour', *Policy and Politics*, 31 (3), 289–305.

West, E. G. 1976 *Adam Smith: The Man and His Works*, Indianapolis, IN: Liberty Fund.

Whitworth, Sandra 1994 'Theory as Exclusion: Gender and International Political Economy', in Richard Stubbs and Geoffrey Underhill (eds) *Political Economy and the Changing Global Order*, London: Macmillan.

Widmaier, Wesley 2003 'The Keynesian Bases of a Constructivist Theory of the International Political Economy', *Millennium,* 32 (1), 87–107.

Wightman, W. P. D. 1980 'Introduction', in W. P. D. Wightman and J. C. Bryce (eds) *Adam Smith: Essays on Philosophical Subjects*, Oxford: Oxford University Press.

Williams, David 1999 'Constructing the Economic Space: The World Bank and the Making of Homo Oeconomicus', *Millennium,* 28 (1), 79–99.

Winch, Donald 1997 'Adam Smith's Problems and Ours', *Scottish Journal of Political Economy*, 44 (4), 384–402.

Winch, Peter 1972 *Ethics and Action*, London: Routledge & Kegan Paul.

Witzum, Amos 1997 'Distributive Considerations in Smith's Conception of Economic Justice', *Economics and Philosophy*, 12 (2), 241–59.

Wolfe, Alan 1977 *The Limits of Legitimacy*, London: Collier Macmillan.

Woods, Ngaire 2001 'International Political Economy in an Age of Globalization', in John Baylis and Steve Smith (eds) *The Globalization of World Politics: An Introduction to International Relations*, second edition, Oxford: Oxford University Press.

World Bank Boycott 2003 *World Bank Boycott: Organisers' Tool Kit*, Amsterdam: SEED Europe.

Worswick, G. D. N. 1972 'Is Progress in Economic Science Possible?', *Economic Journal*, 82 (1), 73–86.

Young, Jeffrey and Gordon, Barry 1996 'Distributive Justice as a Normative Criterion in Adam Smith's Political Economy', *History of Political Economy*, 28 (1): 1–25.

Index